ISLAM AND THE AHMADIYYA JAMA'AT

To
Naheeda
Anam Chara

CONTENTS

Glossary of terms   vii
Foreword   xiii
Preface   xv

Introduction: 'Walking in Another Man's Shoes'   1
1.   In Search of the Tomb of Jesus   11
2.   Ahmadiyyat and its Founder, Mirza Ghulam Ahmad   31
3.   The History of the Ahmadiyya Jama'at   55
4.   'Learn From the Ants': Structure and Organisation'   77
5.   'The Remembrance of Allah': Life in the Mosque   101
6.   Ahmadi Belief and Teaching   127
7.   Ahmadiyyat: Integration and the Preservation of Faith   151
8.   Women and the Family   171
9.   'The Pen is Mightier than the Sword': Ahmadiyyat and Jihad   189
10. Tabligh and Da'wa: Recruiting for Islam   211
11. The Ahmadi: A Persecuted People   227
12. 'In Allah Do We Trust': Conclusions and Comment   241

Bibliography   249
Index   255

GLOSSARY OF TERMS

Abrogation   a literary device used in *tafsir*, Islamic exegesis, where a later Quranic verse is regarded as more authoritative than an earlier verse.

Ajle Musamma   the decreed time of death for a Muslim.

Al-Baseerat   the monthly magazine published by the *Ahmadi Jama'at* in Bradford from 1976. The title means 'in-depth understanding of, and reflection on, religious beliefs'.

'Alim   [plural: *'ulema*] a learned man in Islam, especially regarding religion.

'Alima   a learned woman within Islam.

Alladhina amanu   'those who believe'.

Al wasiyya   the Will written by Mirza Ghulam Ahmad, published in 1905, containing his wish to establish the *Khalifate* to guide the movement after his death and the creation of an official graveyard, *Bahishti Maqbara*, at Rabwah.

Amila   monthly business meetings held at each *Jama'at*.

Amir   commander, leader or head, of a particular area of jurisdiction within the movement.

Ansarullah   an auxillary organisation consisting of men over the age of forty.

Arkan   the five pillars, or main religious duties, of Islam, Viz., *shahada, salat, zakat, sawm* and *hajj*.

Atfal   male member of the *Jama'at* under fifteen years of age.

Azan/adhan   the call to prayer made from the mosque.

Bai'at	oath of allegiance, the formal rite of initiation and allegiance into *Ahmadiyyat*.
Baraka	divine blessing gained from holy people or objects.
Bid'at	innovations and practices, usually regarded as undesirable, which have been introduced into Islam.
Biradari	extended clan or family system.
Bismillah	'in the name of Allah', the opening words of most of the *Surahs* [chapters] in the Quran and words uttered on leaving the house, arriving home, eating, sleeping or before performing other daily activities.
Bukhari	the most trusted of the six collections of *hadith* accepted by *Sunni* Muslims.
Chanda	'contribution', money which every *Ahmadi* is asked to give to the cause of God.
Dai ilallahs,	a 'caller to God', someone who invites others to Islam.
Darveshon-e-Qadian	the name given to the 313 men who stayed at Qadian at the time of the partition of Pakistan and India in 1947 so as to protect the holy places found there.
Da'wa	inviting someone to Islam through one's words and actions.
Dhikr	the rhythmic chanting of Quranic verses practiced by Sufis to enhance spiritual awareness.
Dhu al-hijja	the month during which Muslims perform pilgrimage to Mecca.
Dunya	the physical world in contrast to the spiritual.
Fard	that which is obligatory.
Fatwa	a legal opinion made by a person of authority within the *Ummah*.
Fidyah	compensation paid by an individual worshipper for not fasting.
Fiqh	islamic jurisprudence, the study and understanding of Divine law.
Hadhrat	honorific title meaning 'the respected one'.
Hafiz	title given to a person who has memorised the entire Quran.

Hajj	pilgrimage to Mecca.
Haram	that which is forbidden by Islamic law.
Hazoor	a term of respect used for the *Khalifa* meaning 'your honour' or 'the honoured one'.
Ijtema	gathering of the members of a *Jama'at*.
Ijtihad	personal interpretation of the Quran.
Imam	the person appointed to lead worship in a mosque.
Iman	meaning 'faith', refers to belief in God, angels, Allah's holy books, the prophets and the last day.
Insh'Allah	phrase used repeatedly by Muslims meaning 'God Willing' or 'If it is God's will'.
Islahi committee	the committee responsible for identifying moral dangers that may affect the *Jama'at*, and with prevailing ills among *Jama'at* members.
Islam	meaning 'submission', a religion that demands submission to the will of God.
Islamabad	an *Ahmadi* centre at Tilford, near Farnborough in Surrey. The centre consists of a school building, and extensive land, purchased by the movement in 1984.
Jalsa Salana	the annual international gathering of the *Ahmadi*.
Jazia'h	a tax imposed in an Islamic state on non-Muslims so as to ensure their protection.
Jihad	armed conflict against non-Muslims or the inner struggle of an individual Muslim to gain personal righteousness [see chapter nine].
Jinn	good or bad spirits, that dwell in unclean places, which influence the lives of men.
Kafir	a derogatory term referring to an unbeliever.
Kalima	literally meaning 'the word', and also known as *shahada*, is a name used for the testimony of faith uttered by every Muslim. It states 'I bear testimony that there is no God but Allah and Muhammad is the messenger of Allah'.
Khalifa	the spiritual head of the *Ahmadiyya Jama'at*.
Khalifate	the ideal of the *Khalifa*, as the ruler over all Muslims, an idea first introduced after the

death of Muhammad in 632 AD and continuing till the fall of the Ottomon Empire in 1924. It is believed by all Muslims that Allah will restore the *Khalifate* in the last days and thus unite all Muslims and restore the strength of Islam.

Khataman Nabiyeen   the belief that Muhammad is the seal, the last and the greatest, of the prophets.

Khatme Nabuvat   a small Islamic political group directly opposed to the *Ahmadi* faith, calling for its destruction and the death of its members.

Khuddam   auxillary organisation for men aged 16-40.

Khuddam-ul-Ahmadiyya   the pledge taken by members of the *Khuddam* to be loyal to the *Khalifa* and the *Jama'at*.

Lailatul Qadr   the 'night of prayer', the 27th day of the month of Ramadan, celebrating the giving of the first portion of the Quran to Muhammad.

Lajna Imaillah   the organisation for women between the age of 16-40.

Ludhiana   the place in India where the first *bai'at* took place in 1889.

Madrasah   school attached to a mosque.

Majlis Aamala   the executive committee of the *Ahmadiyya Jama'at*.

Makrooh   arabic word meaning 'disapproved of', or something which, although not *haram* and forbidden, is frowned upon.

Maroof   a decision made by the *Khalifa* which is binding on all members of the *Jama'at*.

Masjid   See mosque.

Mubahala   a pronouncement made, usually by the founder of the movement or one of the *Khalifas*, against an opponent in which it is declared that Allah should be the judge of the issue at stake, and as such God will support those who are right but will punish [usually by death] those in the wrong.

Mujaddid   a reformer believed to be sent by God at the beginning of each new century.

Murtad   an apostate from the faith.

Musleh Ma'ud Day	a festival celebrated by *Ahmadi* commemorating the birth of their second *Khalifa* on 12 January 1889, seen as fulfilment of a prophecy made by Ahmad that he would have a son who would be *Musleh Ma'ud*, the promised reformer.
Namaz	prayer performed by the Muslim five times daily. This includes *Fajr* early in the morning; *Zuhr* at midday; *Asr* at sunset; *Magrib* later in the evening and *Isha* prayers during darkness.
Nasirat	young girls belonging to the *Jama'at*.
Pir	someone recognised as a holy person and spiritual guide, also known as *murshid* or *sheikh*.
Qadian	the spiritual home of *Ahmadi* situated in N.W. India. The birth and burial place of Mirza Ghulam Ahmad and the early martyrs of the movement.
Quran	meaning 'recitation', believed to be God's final revelation to humankind, containing the revelations revealed to Muhammad over a period of twenty-two years.
Rabwah	a town in the Punjab, Pakistan, the headquarters of the *Jama'at* since 1947
Religious Founders Day	festival of the *Ahmadi* in which people of other faiths are invited to talk about their religion and its founder.
Sadaqa	offering of money made by a member of the community to the *Jama'at* to ensure a blessing on a private venture or activity.
Salat	prayer, usually performed five times daily [see *namaz*].
Sawm	fasting during the month of Ramadan.
Shahada	confession of faith.
shalwar kameez	the traditional clothes worn by both women and men in Pakistan, India, Bangladesh, and Afghanistan. Shalwar are loose baggy trousers, kameez is a long shirt or tunic.
Sharia'h	laws governing the daily lives of Muslims.
Shirk	associating someone or something to God, regarded by Muslims as blasphemy.

Sunna	customs, or the example set by Muhammad.
Tabligh	preaching.
Tadhkirah	collection of the revelations claimed to have been received by Mirza Ghulam Ahmad.
Tafsir	commentary on the Quran.
Tahajjid	pre-dawn supererogatory [non-compulsory] prayers usually performed in private by the worshipper.
Taqwa	righteousness, or the fear of God.
Tarbiyyat	'upbringing', education of members of the *Jama'at,* particularly the young.
Tawiz	lucky charms, amulets, usually containing a verse from the Quran, used to ward off *jinn* or gain *baraka.*
Tilawat	recitation of the Quran in Arabic, at the beginning of most formal meetings held by the *Jama'at,* usually followed by a translation of that passage in the vernacular.
Ummah	the Islamic community locally or internationally.
Waqf	[pl. *waqaf*] charitable endowments, trust fund, made for the establishment of a mosque, school or other purpose.
Waqfe arzi	'temporary dedication', a time of voluntary work given by a member of the *Jama'at* for the movement.
Zakat	'purification', the giving of money to charity as prescribed by Islamic law.

FOREWORD

Michael Nazir-Ali

Dr Simon Valentine is to be commended not only for writing this book but also for the approach he has taken. Scholarly accounts of the *Ahmadiyya* movement are all too rare, especially from those outside the charmed circle of the disciples of Mirza Ghulam Ahmad. For this reason alone, this book is to be welcomed.

Dr Valentine writes in an easy and accessible style but from a clearly Christian and lay perspective. He has, moreover, adopted the approach of a participant observer. That is to say he has embedded himself in the Asian, and more particularly the *Ahmadiyya*, community in Bradford and beyond with a view to developing a sympathetic but also critical perspective on the movement, its members, their beliefs and style of life.

Because the *Ahmadiyya* are regarded as 'heterodox' by many other Muslims, they have been isolated, harassed and sometimes persecuted. This has made access to them sometimes difficult and work with them can be viewed with a certain amount of suspicion. Dr Valentine is to be congratulated for his persistence and his determination to overcome all obstacles.

He has shown how the roots of the *Ahmadiyya* lie in the desire to develop a response to Christian Mission. In this respect, there has been vigorous debate and even polemic between Christians and the followers of Mirza Ghulam Ahmad of Qadian. Dr Valentine emphasises, however, that the *Ahmadiyya* have always held to the importance of a verbal *Jihad* which is committed to peaceful debate.

They have rejected the idea of an aggressive *Jihad* and have also promoted freedom of belief and, indeed, the freedom to change one's belief. They reject the traditional view that apostasy should be punishable by death and teach, rather, that there is no punishment in this life for those who may be regarded as apostates.

Ahmadiyya-Christian relations need to move from polemics to dialogue where each acknowledges the integrity of the other but also the wide areas of disagreement between them. Such disagreement need not prevent true friendships between members of the two faiths. Dr Valentine has put us all in his debt by showing how that can be so.

April 2008   Michael Nazir-Ali
                                                   Bishop of Rochester

PREFACE

The *Ahmadiyya Jama'at*, or the *Ahmadiyya* Muslim Association, has been described as 'one of the most active and controversial movements in modern Islam'.[1] Believing in prophecy after the Prophet, the *Ahmadi* have been rejected as *kafrs*, unbelievers, by mainstream Muslims who teach the Finality of Prophet-hood: the doctrine that Muhammad was the seal, the greatest and the last of the prophets. Despite being persecuted and rejected by their co-religionists, and regarded as a non-Muslim sect in Pakistan, the *Ahmadi* adamantly declare themselves to be 'Islam in its pristine purity',[2] created by Allah to bring about 'the revival and establishment of the glory of Islam'.[3] Arising in India in the nineteenth century, the *Ahmadi* have established themselves as a vibrant Islamic reform group in Britain, and throughout Europe, America, Africa and many other localities around the world. With its message of 'Love for all, hatred for none', and its presentation of *Jihad* 'through dialogue based on logical and rational arguments' [because, as one *Ahmadi* remarked 'swords can bend heads but not minds'[4]] the *Ahmadi* present a peaceful Islam, an Islam in sharp contrast to the stereotypes of war and militancy often generated by the Western media.

---

1   Yohanan Friedmann, *Prophecy Continuous: Aspects of Ahmadi Religious Thoughts and its Medieval Background*, Berkeley: University of California Press, 1989, p. 1.

2   Aziz A. Chaudhry, *The Promised Messiah and Mahdi*, Islamabad: Islam International Publications, 1996, p.5.

3   Karimullah Zirvi, *Welcome to Ahmadiyyat: The true Islam*, Ahmadiyya Movement in Islam, Silver Springs, USA: Islamic Publications Ltd, 2002, p. 11.

4   The words of Mohsin Rizvi, the President of the Ahmadiyya Muslim Association in Sheffield, England, *The Sheffield Star*, (24 July 2004), p. 1.

My main interest in writing this book was to provide an account of the history, beliefs and purpose of the *Ahmadiyya Jama'at*, a group little known by those outside of Islam. Although a scholarly work, this book is a personal appraisal containing anecdotes and vignettes, a sociological study of an Islamic reform movement that challenges us to reassess the nature and teaching of Islam. Apart from the literature published by the *Ahmadi* themselves, and scholarly works such as Spencer Lavan's, *The Ahmadiyyah Movement: history and perspective*, [1974], and Yohannan Friedmann's, *Prophecy continuous; aspects of Ahmadi religious thought and its medieval background*, [1989] very little has been written on the *Ahmadiyya Jama'at*. As such this book is an attempt to fill that gap.

I initially made contact with the *Ahmadiyya Jama'at* in September 2001 when taking a party of mature students from the University of Bradford, studying a module on Community Religions for the BA degree in Social Studies, to *see* a mosque rather than merely *read* about such places of worship in books. I was already familiar with the movement, having taught several *Ahmadi* boys in local Bradford schools. As stated in the introduction, for almost two years I chose to live in the Muslim community of Bradford, West Yorkshire, England, [where a significant *Ahmadi* group can be found] to 'observe', and learn more about Islam. By living amongst the *Ahmadi*, I gained the knowledge and insights necessary to build up a picture of their lifestyle, teachings and, most importantly, their perception of the world. My research involved, not only a study of the *Ahmadi* in the context of Bradford, a northern industrial town in multicultural Britain, but also visits to the *Ahmadi* headquarters at Rabwah, Pakistan, and at Qadian [the birthplace of their founder, Mirza Ghulam Ahmad] in India. I spoke at length with Muslims [*Ahmadi* and non-*Ahmadi*] at other localities in Britain, and further afield in Pakistan, India, Kashmir, the United Arab Emirates, Egypt, Tunisia, Morocco and the United States. As such I believe this book provides a detailed study, an informative 'window', on the *Ahmadi*; a significant, yet little known section of contemporary Islamic reformism.

Bradford, May 2008   S.R.V.

INTRODUCTION
'WALKING IN ANOTHER MAN'S SHOES'

North American Indians have a saying, that to really understand a person, metaphorically speaking, you have to get inside his moccasins, and walk as he walks. Believing the best way to study the *Ahmadiyya Jama'at*, and to gain an understanding of the beliefs and lifestyle of the individual *Ahmadi*, was 'to walk in his shoes', I undertook both qualitative and quantitative research methodology, involving a fair amount of 'participant observation'. Bradford, an industrial town in Yorkshire, northern England, still reeling from the effects of riots in '95 and 2001, and simmering racial tension, is home to a sizeable ethnic minority community, and a significant number of *Ahmadi*. For eighteen months I lived in the Leeds Road area of the city, an area with a predominantly Asian population, living with the Muslim community: shopping in the same shops, walking the same streets, observing the same holy days and festivals. I met with Muslims from various traditions—*Deobandi, Barelwi, Wahhabi, Salafi, Ahmadi*—men and women, many of whom I regard as friends. I enjoyed Asian hospitality in different homes; I accompanied Muslims [*Ahmadi* and non-*Ahmadi*] to the cinema, auctions, family and social occasions, and of course attended the meetings taking place at their respective mosques. My observations were focused on individuals and events, practices and rituals. At times I was a participant as well as an observer, especially in the lives of the *Ahmadi*: tutoring children, helping to unload and load vans for business acquaintances, travelling to Manchester airport to pick up relatives and friends flying in from abroad. As an 'outsider' on the 'inside' I tried to appreciate their

1

experiences, discover their meanings and observe people in their everyday setting. I met and discussed with *Ahmadi*, not only in Bradford and other British cities, but much further afield in various localities in Pakistan, India and North Africa. Although not a Muslim myself, I was welcomed into the Muslim world, thereby gaining a first hand perspective of the views, concerns and interests of Muslims living in a multicultural society. Living within the *Ummah* [the Muslim community] in Bradford I was ideally situated to study Islam generally, and the *Ahmadiyya Jama'at* specifically. I was placed, as certain American writers state, 'where the rubber hits the road'.

I had read of some sociologists who, to get a real insider's view of the people they were studying, had feigned conversion and lived as members of that particular group. As a Law student at Sheffield in the late seventies, a criminology course led me to a book by the famous psychologist Leon Festinger, *When Prophecy Fails*.[1] In this 'social and psychological study of a modern group that predicted the destruction of the world'[2] a team of professional researchers, pretended to be followers of Marian Keech, a woman who predicted the destruction by flood of most of North America and small parts of South America. Keech, an ordinary housewife living in Lake City, Utah, claimed that Sananda, a reincarnation of Jesus Christ, a superior being living on a planet called Clarion, had visited her in a flying saucer. She and her small group of followers, known as '*the seekers*', spent their time in prayer awaiting the arrival of the 'guardians'; beings from Venus, who would usher in the last judgement. Unbeknown to Keech and her followers, the team carried out extensive research into the activities and beliefs of the members of the group. Of course the predicted cataclysm did not occur. Understandably, Mrs Keech and her supporters raised considerable public opposition. Due to the threat of legal action, and the desire of many local people to get her committed to a mental institution, Mrs Keech went into hiding.

In my opinion, the clandestine methods used in studying Keech and her group of apocalyptic Ufologists, although effective, seemed

---

1   Leon Festinger, Riecken H. W. & S. Schachter, *When Prophecy Fails*, NY: Harper Torchbooks, 1955.

2   Subtitle, Festinger, *When Prophecy Fails*, op.cit.

immoral, unethical and dishonest. The pretence of loyalty to a leader or a group solely for research purposes implies that those being studied, although people with genuinely held views which I may not necessarily agree with, are not worthy of my honesty or integrity. I decided that openness and honesty would be the best policy, something which I believe gained the respect of the Muslims among whom I lived. From the start I told people the facts: I was a part time lecturer at the University, someone interested in Islam as an academic subject, writing a book on the *Ahmadi* as an example of a contemporary reform movement within Islam. I jokingly remarked to one Muslim that I was not a potential convert as I was happy with the faith I had, but he could pray for me if he wished. Knowingly he smiled and with a wink of his eye he replied: 'things will happen as it is written, *insh'Allah*' [God willing]. Although the people I was observing knew the reasons for my stay in the Leeds Road area, they allowed me to participate in their activities and to take part in their lives. In fact, rather than hinder my research I found that generally the *Ahmadi* I associated with were eager to tell me about their faith. I realized however that such openness on my part could create certain problems, namely the possibility that *Ahmadi*, aware that what they said or did could well end up in print, would behave differently with me. It was also possible that they could exaggerate certain things and downplay others so as to present their *Jama'at* [community] in the best possible light. Human nature being what it is I'm sure that such 'embellishing' did take place, but generally speaking I believe the over-whelming majority of Muslims I spoke to, and associated with, spoke to me genuinely and sincerely. A significant number of Muslims living in the Leeds Road area often invited me into their homes, where I enjoyed sincere hospitality, and dishes of chicken pulao, lamb curry, lamb pulao, dhal, sweet rice, halwa or my favourite meal, Chicken tikka masala, usually consumed with a plenteous supply of freshly made nan bread.

I visited most of the mosques to be found in that area. For example, I lived about 600 yards away from the *Ahmadi* mosque. With the full permission and approval of the group I regularly attended *Juma* prayers, *Eid Milan* parties, social occasions such as weddings and other family gatherings. Consequently much of my research was informal, unplanned and unstructured. By living within the Asian community itself, and being accepted as an 'adopted brother' as one *Ahmadi* called me, I had every means at my disposal to try to understand the 'universe of meaning' held by, not only the *Ahmadi*, but by the members of the *Ummah* generally.

In preparing for this study I was greatly influenced by the pioneering work carried out by other researchers. In particular Elliot Liebow, in his study of 'two dozen Negro men who share a corner in Washington's second precinct as a base of operations in 1962-3', reminded me of the importance of empathy and tolerance in field studies of this nature.[3] For two years Liebow lived amongst the down-and-outs in Washington observing their lifestyle and group dynamics. His research involved 'a record of the day-to-day routines of these men as they frequented the street-corner, the alleys, hallways, poolrooms, beer joints and private houses in the immediate neighbourhood'.[4] By building up relationships with such men, talking with them, and listening to their views, Liebow was able to think as they thought and perceive the world as they saw it. Similar inspiration was gained from Eileen Barker's celebrated work on the Moonies in which she lived amongst the members of that organisation, attending their meetings, observing their activities, openly discussing as a non-member with members about their beliefs and practices.[5] As such, by direct interviewing of members of the sect, Barker was able to consider the reasons why they had joined the Unification Church: 'choice or brainwashing?' I was also influenced by reading the study of Italian Americans in Boston, USA, by William Foote-Whyte,[6] and the Black man in 'the promised land', [to use Claude Brown's phrase[7]], the study of Black ghettos in American northern cities in

---

3   See Elliot Liebow, *Tally's Corner: A Study of Negro Street Corner Men*, Chicago: Little Brown, 1967, p. 11.

4   Liebow, op.cit., p. 208.

5   Eileen Barker, *The Making of a Moonie: Choice or brainwashing?*, London: Blackwell Publishing, 1984.

6   W. Foote-Whyte, *Street Corner Society: the social structure of an Italian slum*, Chicago: University of Chicago Press, 1955.

7   Claude Brown, *Manchild in the promised Land*, New York: New American Library, 1966.

the work of social anthropologists such as Lee Rainwater, Ulf Hannerz, Robert Blauner, Bennet Berger and others.[8] All these studies, and many other sociological enquiries far too numerous to mention, have, amongst other things, emphasised the need for objectivity and sensitivity in attempting to understand the lifestyle of others.

In August 2002 I moved from the leafy, middle-class suburb of Allerton, Bradford, West Yorkshire into a small, very basic, terraced house on Edderthorpe Street, just off Leeds Road, not far from the city centre. This was my home, my head-quarters, my 'pad' till February 2004. A typical two-up-two-down terraced house, it was the end-dwelling of a row of four, the other three unoccupied, opposite two small mills, now used for storage. The front room upstairs I used as a bedroom, and storage space. The back room, containing my collection of over a thousand books on comparative religions, philosophy, sociology, history, dictionaries, and encyclopaedias [tools for the job] neatly arranged in wall-to-wall bookcases, with an old but reliable computer, desk and armchair, served as a most suitable study. Having no central heating, no double-glazing, slight damp on the gable wall and a basement open to the elements, it was very cold and draughty. During the winter months it was often so cold at night that I sat in the study, woollen gloves on my hands, as I worked on the computer. Two convector heaters, purchased from a nearby second hand store, and the improvised use of sheets and towels as draught excluders, kept the room reasonably warm. Much of my time, when not at the University, or at friends' or acquaintances', was spent in that room, it being far cheaper to keep one room warm than the entire house. Sitting in the armchair, with Enya, Clannad, Mike Oldfield or some other music conducive to study playing in the background, I would end each day writing up a journal containing an account of the day's events. With the curtains open I could look out of the window into the inky blackness of the night. Beyond the disused yard of the dilapidated Albion Public House [now demolished] I could watch the perpetual stream of traffic making its way up Leeds Road from the city centre to Pudsey, and the headlights of cars

---

8 Lee Rainwater, ed., *Soul: Black Experience*, New Brunswick, NJ: Transaction Books, USA, 1970.

taking clubbers and cinemagoers down into Bradford. A conveyor belt of people, either unaware or indifferent to the fact they were passing through a vibrant ethnic community, a microcosm of Islam worldwide. Although my friends referred to the house as 'Ice Station Zebra', it was home for me, a satisfactory base from which I could do my research and writing.

Due mainly to the patrons of *UK Fried Chicken*, the fast food retailer situated less than twenty yards from my front door on the corner of Edderthopre Street and Leeds Road, the street was often covered with empty cans, half filled plastic cartons of discarded remains of chicken, chips, plastic bags, broken bottles and other waste characteristic of a thoughtless throwaway society. Throughout the day articulated lorries often parked on the pavement in front of the house, blocking out the daylight, the drivers leaving their engines running as they ate their takeaways, then throwing the remains out on the street. Each night, between ten and one o'clock, young courting couples, clubbers, diners, would park their cars right up to the front door of the house, with their radios blasting out the latest Indian hits from Sunrise radio. The clatter of cans and other litter thrown without care on the pavement would announce the end of their activities and their imminent departure. Most of the time the street was untidy and dirty, a regular visiting place for emaciated stray dogs rummaging for scraps of food or cats watching out for the ubiquitous mouse. Although I never saw any, some locals claimed they occasionally saw the 'long tails', rats, burrowing into the waste bins left on the pavement opposite. The council, to its credit, sent cleansing vehicles up and down the street several times each day. The staff of *UK Fried Chicken* also did their bit to brush up the ever-accumulating litter. But they were fighting a losing battle. Despite the litter and noise that characterised life on Edderthorpe Street, I had no complaints. Spending most of my time working in the makeshift study at the back of the house I was largely immune from such disturbance, simply closing the door and letting the world get on with its business while I got on with mine. With the *Ahmadi* mosque, and other mainstream mosques just a few hundred yards away from my doorstep, and several *Ahmadi* families living nearby, I was ideally situated to undertake my research. My chosen residence, not only enabled me to live within the community, to observe life within a multicultural area of a northern city in England, but most importantly it gave me the opportunity to directly engage with Muslims in their daily routines of life.

During the summer months, in the evenings, I would sit in the living room reading or watching television. Being hot and stuffy I would leave the front door open and, while continuing to read some book or other, listen to the general mêlée of activity taking place outside. Such times were invaluable learning experiences, providing me with insights into the life of the *Ummah* in Bradford. Groups of young lads [mainly Asian] would walk past, talking of Harry Kewell's move to Liverpool Football Club, the thrilling prospect of Leeds United being relegated to the first division [most Bradfordians have a deep 'hatred' for the rival football team in nearby Leeds] or the latest Bollywood film. Riaz, on his way to the *Ahmadi* mosque from his home in Girlington, or Nasir, another *Ahmadi*, who lived with his family in nearby Great Seymour Street, would often appear and share with me a cup of tea and convivial chat. Occasionally one of the men working at *UK Fried Chicken* would, on seeing the front door open, walk over and 'pop' his head in at the door. We would talk of Islam and life, of local events and world news, of nothing and everything.

People in the area knew me, probably as the harmless odd white guy who had moved to that area to write his book. They regarded me with interest and curiosity. Some, due to my beard, skin colour, my limited Urdu and Arabic and my regular habit of wearing *shalwar kameez*[9] [well, in Summer anyway] while walking round that area, mistook me for a *Pathan* [a *Pashto* speaking Afghan]. Muslims would acknowledge me with the traditional greeting: *assalaam alaikum* [peace be with you]. The affable elderly gentleman for example, usually sitting on his doorstep on Thryberg Street, always greeted me with a '*salaam*', a smile and a wave of his hand as I went by. I walked daily around the streets and ginnels of Bradford 3, hearing the tape-

---

9   Shalwar are loose baggy trousers, kameez is a long shirt or tunic, the traditional clothes worn by both women and men in Pakistan, India, Bangladesh and Afghanistan.

recorded cry of the *muezzins*[10] calling the faithful to prayer from the mosques scattered in that area: '*Allahu Akbar*! Come to prayer. God is great'. On using my limited Urdu as often as I could I would see the smile of pleasure appear on the Muslim's face, a smile which says 'thank you for taking the trouble to respect *my* culture and learn a few words of *my* language'.

Although much of my time was spent in 'observing' the *Ahmadi* in Bradford, a city with a significant Muslim population in multicultural Britain,[11] the research for this book involved the study of a world-wide community, a community which its adherents claim, is the fastest-growing Islamic reform group. As such my research took place, not only in the streets, mosques and homes of Bradford, Huddersfield, Sheffield, London and other British towns and cities but in Pakistan, India, Kashmir, North Africa, and various other countries around the world. My search for a personal understanding of the *Ahmadi* took me to their headquarters at Rabwah in Pakistan and to Qadian, the '*Ahmadiyya* Bethlehem', birth place of their founder Mirza Ghulam Ahmad, in India. At both places, Rabwah and Qadian, I met with the officials of the movement, visiting all the departments that make up the *Ahmadi* administrative structure. I attended the *Jalsa Salana* of 2003, the annual international assembly organised by the *Ahmadi*, at Islamabad, Tilford in Surrey.[12] There I sat and spoke with kings; tribal leaders from Africa who had embraced the *Ahmadi* faith. As the first chapter explains, in an attempt to understand the *Ahmadi* teaching on Jesus, particularly their teaching relating to his old age and death, I went to Srinigar, the beautiful capital of Kashmir where, according to the *Ahmadi*, Jesus was buried. In trying to understand the hatred [and in many cases it is just that] that many mainstream

---

10 The person in a mosque who declares the *adhan*, the call to prayer.

11 According to the 2001 census Muslims made up 16% of Bradford's population compared with 2.78% of the UK as a whole. Out of a population of 457, 665 there are 68,000 Pakistanis; 12,500 Indians and almost 5,000 Bangladeshis, see Simon R. Valentine, *Muslims in Bradford, background paper for COMPAS*, Oxford: University of Oxford, 2006.

12 Not to be confused with Islamabad, Pakistan. As explained in chapter four, Islamabad is the name given by the *Ahmadi* to their centre in Surrey, England.

Muslims have towards the *Ahmadi* I spoke to Muslims, [scholars and lay persons] in the souks, bazaars and mosques of Morocco, Tunisia and Egypt. Interviewing, especially with regard to the *Ahmadiyya Jama'at* in Bradford, was to be an important element of my modus operandi. Concerning the *Ahmadi*, I originally requested to use formal interviews, carefully prepared questionnaires, with structured and open-ended questions. I offered complete anonymity for those participating and promised that any information gained would not be used in any way that could lead to further persecution of the sect, but permission was not given. However, I did manage to interview over eighty Muslims, not only *Ahmadi*, but Muslims claiming allegiance to the *Deobandi, Salafi* and *Barewli* traditions within Islam, or allegiance to none. Such interviews were completely informal, often with ordinary people in ordinary settings: a meal in a local house, a walk down to Bradford city centre, or sitting on the carpet of the worship area in the mosque. In contrast, other interviews took place with ex-politicians in the salubrious settings of the finest restaurants in Lahore, Pakistan, or while floating in a *shikhara* [wooden boat] on the beautiful, placid waters of lake Dal, Kashmir. Whenever the opportunity arose I would take out my note-pad and pen [always kept in a handy pocket] and with permission, write down anything of use. I would start with set questions which would then digress into points of interest raised by each individual interviewee. Much of the material gained from such interviews is used throughout this book. In many, if not most instances, anonymity was adopted to protect those being observed and interviewed. During such interviews I was again aware of the possibility of exaggeration: whether the interviewees were telling the truth or merely conforming to what is expected of them; whether the interviewee responded in such a way believing me to be an enquiring observer, a possible convert; or merely give what they believe the interviewer wanted to hear: 'public' rather than 'private' answers. Anyone belonging to a particular faith or culture is hardly likely to reveal the problems, the faults of such a faith to an almost complete stranger, especially a stranger from another faith community. Use is made of 'life stories', particularly personal anecdotes or longer accounts of how a person became *Ahmadi*, their place

9

of origin, and a description of the persecution they faced in Pakistan, necessitating their flight to Britain.

Having interviewed certain people, or attended any event to do with the movement, I made it a regular habit to write up my journal each night while details were still fresh and clear in the mind. An obvious problem in undertaking such research was language. At times I felt quite vulnerable as members spoke amongst themselves in Urdu, but hopefully not in a hurtful way. Other problems with such participant observation is the fact that it involves, not only the giving of 'bare-facts' about the *Ahmadi*, but also interpretation of those facts. As such, there is the obvious danger that any conclusions reached could well be affected by my own personal prejudices and preconceptions. I was also aware of the problem relating to objectivity, or the lack of it. As a Methodist local Preacher, conservative in theology, yet Christian in outlook, raised in a Christian family in a country that, although secular, has been greatly influenced by the Bible and Christianity, it could be argued that it is difficult, if not impossible, for someone like myself to present an objective study of this kind. However, 'value-neutrality' and 'value-relevance', to use the sociological jargon, can be exercised to a great extent by the adoption of a tolerant, sympathetic attitude towards others. Hopefully this has been achieved in this present study. I think it would be reasonable to say that it is possible to go a long way in understanding someone else's point of view without necessarily believing it oneself. As one colleague at the University of Bradford bluntly put it: 'you don't have to go to the north-pole to know its bloody cold!'

1
IN SEARCH OF THE TOMB OF JESUS

It was my first visit to Srinigar, the summer capital of Jammu-Kashmir, a disputed territory in northern India. My hosts, members of the *Ahmadiyya Jama'at*, a missionary-minded Islamic reform group, took me to see various architectural, botanical and cultural treasures in the city. Having paid the expectant door-keeper a nominal sum of a few rupees for permission to take photographs, we walked round the Jamia Masjid, an awesome fourteenth century mosque with its 370 pillars of cedar wood, decorative facades, and roofs embellished by Chinese and Tibetan designs. One of my guides informed me the mosque was large enough for 30,000 people to offer prayers. Later, with the snow-covered peaks of the Himalayas rising majestically in the background, we found relief from the heat of the sun beneath the branches of the ubiquitous Chinar trees, as we strolled along the tranquil pathways of the world famous Shalimar gardens. After another taxi journey through a warren-like system of streets filled with vehicles that seemed to ignore every rule in the Highway Code, we came to the edge of the city and the Hazratbal mosque. Having persuaded the soldier standing guard of my honourable intentions—a European, and an unbeliever to visit a Muslim holy site—we entered the building, an impressive white-washed seventeenth century structure, the only domed mosque in Srinigar, the others having pagoda style roofs. Containing a hair reputedly from Muhammad's head, the Hazratbal mosque has become a place of pilgrimage for Muslims from all corners of the world.

Accompanied by my well-informed guides, I wandered along narrow dusty streets and crossed bridges spanning the cool mountain waters of the river Jhelum. With each turn of the street a different vista opened up before us: a mosaic of contrasting colours and shapes, buildings of wood, brick and stone, the old and the new. Impressed by what I saw I could understand how, until the recent upsurge of militancy, [mainly Muslim extremists who want to free Kashmir from Indian control,] Srinigar had been a popular tourist destination. A cultural and religious labyrinth of almost 600,000 people: Srinigar was mysterious, mystical, timeless, yet a modern city boasting its own international airport and University. I lay on the deep cushion covering the floor of a *shikhara*, one of the brightly coloured, traditional wooden boats, the gondolas of Kashmir, and enjoyed an hour floating on the placid waters of Lake Dal. My mind filled with kaleidoscopic images of mountains, minarets and mosques. The sun was hot, life was good, I had found my Shangri-la.

The journey to Srinigar had been an adventure in itself. I was making a whistle-stop tour of the Punjab, in both India and Pakistan. My friends in India had told me that although there had been a recent lull in terrorist activity, it was still very dangerous for Europeans to travel to Kashmir, but if I wanted to take the risk and go, they would provide a guide. Seeing this as an opportunity not to be missed, and ignoring Foreign Office advice to 'Brits' not to enter Kashmir, I threw caution to the wind and, began to make preparations for the journey. Instead of taking the convenient and obviously quicker route by plane from Amritsar I decided to travel by public transport, a journey taking up to fourteen hours or more, depending on the weather and the flexibility of check-point guards. This would give me the chance to learn more about the people and the region. Accompanied by Mujeeb, affable and benign, a teacher of Arabic in his late twenties, and fluent in English, we set off at 4:30 am from Qadian in North West India. It was still dark as we boarded the bus. For five hours we travelled along dusty, pot-holed roads, occasionally slowing down to allow nonchalant cows, sacred and revered creatures, to make their way across the road.

On reaching Jammu, the winter capital of Jammu-Kashmir State, and having bartered with numerous drivers, we took a taxi, a ten-seater mini-bus, to Srinigar. The journey is long and arduous. Taking the National Highway A1, our driver, a devout Hindu, stopping once at a shrine to pray to Ganesha, the elephant God, and at several small villages for food and relief, drove for almost nine hours. Our journey took us along the Banihal pass in the Pir Panjal hills, and through the Jawahar tunnel, two kilometres long, one of the longest tunnels in Asia.

To say that the landscape we passed through was spectacular would be an understatement. The road, twisting and turning, gradually ascended up into the mountains revealing panoramic views of tree-filled valleys and precipitous slopes. Once the heights had been attained we began to descend into the vale of Kashmir, a beautiful valley of clear lakes and craggy mountains. According to folk tradition, Kashyap Rishi, [one of the earliest Hindu sages, from whom Kashmir got its name], visited the region thousands of years ago. I tried to imagine how, having left the heat of India and climbed the mountains, Kashyap must have marvelled at the lush, green valley with its cool, pleasant climate. Legend has it that, on finding the valley covered by a lake filled with malevolent demons, he drained the water away and invited people from all over India to come and live there. He called it Kashyap Murh, but as time passed and the language changed, the paradise on earth became Kashmir. I was later told by one of my *Ahmadi* guides how, with summer days averaging about 25 degrees centigrade and the temperature often falling below freezing in winter, the vale of Kashmir experienced a climate similar to that of Britain. I stared out of the taxi window at the mountains, some of which reached heights of 16,000 feet. And as I stared I felt a tremendous sense of isolation from the rest of the world, a *force majeure* inviting me to escape from the troubles of lands far away, a deep sense of peace, tranquillity, even spirituality washing over my materialist, consumerist soul.

Serpents, however, dwell in the Kashmiri paradise. Five of the other travellers in the taxi were soldiers belonging to the Kashmiri army returning home for a well-deserved furlough. One, a sergeant, knowing some English, told me of the troubles the country was facing with Muslim extremists. Squeezed uncomfortably between the back door of the vehicle and one of his younger, less conversant colleagues, and nursing a large box wrapped in polythene on his knees, the sergeant described to me how Kashmir in the 16th century had been part of the Moghul Empire, then later came under Afghan, Sikh, and Hindu control. Raising his voice above the noise of the engine and the animated dialogue taking place in Kashmiri between the other soldiers on the middle seat, he told me how at Independence in 1947 'the Kashmiris had asked for agreements with both Pakistan and India, but were attacked by Pakistan and taken by India'. 'Since then', he said, with deep furrows of concern appearing on his gently tanned brow, 'the relationship between India and Pakistan has not been good. Not only do both sides claim this land as its own', he continued, 'but the Indian government is always accusing the Pakistanis of deliberately encouraging the Muslim militants to cause as much trouble as they can, and so there is tension all the time'. I asked about the nature of the militant unrest. 'It is bad, bad for the country', he said disapprovingly, 'no one wants to come here anymore'. Keeping rigidly still in his seat, despite the obvious discomfort he was in, the sergeant explained how 'most people here are Muslim, the smallest group are Hindu, yet Hindus rule us. Because of this', he concluded, 'many Muslims want to be free of Hindu rule and either become an independent nation or belong to Pakistan. It makes sense', he said knowingly, 'Pakistan is another Muslim land'.

For a considerable length of time the sergeant, his eyes, intelligent, searching, remaining focused on mine, gave me an account of bomb attacks, killings and other terrorist activity which had occurred in Kashmir during the last few years. A heavy military presence confirmed what the sergeant said. Everywhere we went we saw soldiers; government conscripts, nervously standing at checkpoints, shop doors, roadsides. We travelled cautiously along the narrow, winding road, constantly slowing down to overtake convoys of army trucks filled with fresh-faced recruits staring timorously at us as we passed.

A few miles from Srinigar we were stopped by an army blockade and told to pull to the side of the road. Within minutes two jeeps came towards us at speed. Eight soldiers jumped out, black scarves tied round their mouths, partially hiding their faces. Holding their AK47s across their chests, they advanced up the road. The conscripts moved out of the way respectfully. My sergeant friend told me that these were the Black Commandos, the elite soldiers of the Kashmiri army. We heard the sound of automatic gunfire coming from the woods a few hundred yards up the road. Five minutes later the Black Commandos emerged from the trees, unperturbed, confident, and returned to their jeeps. The road barrier was removed and we were allowed to carry on with our journey. We later learnt that the soldiers had met militant activists, members of *Hezb-ul Mujahadeen*, who had been trying to place mines on the road. It was a sobering thought what could have happened if the army had not intervened. Just two weeks after my journey along that route I read in the *Times* newspaper that a bomb attack occurred at a bridge on that road near the village of Lower Munda, killing thirty-three people, mainly army personnel and members of their families, and wounding ten.

My most frightening experience in Kashmir however, had not been at the hands of terrorists, but while in the custody of government soldiers. After a few days in that region I returned to Jammu as I had come, in a good, ten seater mini-bus. This time my companions were all civilians. We had no soldiers with us to wave and smile at their comrades, consequently we had to stop at every single road block, and there were many, for ID checks. Having just gone through the Jawahar tunnel our driver was waved down by the militia. On noticing that I was a European, a rare sight in those parts today, there was some excitement amongst the soldiers. To my consternation, and Mujeeb's watchful concern, I was ordered at gun-point by two slovenly dressed recruits to get out of the mini-bus and was led to a small corrugated hut by the side of the road. The interior was dark and dank. The stench of urine hit you as soon as you entered. Flattened tin cans, food containers and old newspapers lay discarded on the floor. One of the soldiers—a well built, unshaven Rambo figure, dressed in his tight khaki vest and army fatigues—pointed the end of his standard AK47 at my face and began shouting in what must have been Kashmiri. Mujeeb, [thank God for Mujeeb], my guardian angel and protector, remonstrated with the soldier in Kashmiri. I asked Mujeeb what was going on. He told me that they were demanding money, 5,000 Indian rupees. I didn't like what was going on, who would? I was struck by ambivalent feelings of intransigence, obstinacy, indignation and of course, fear for my life. 'Tell them I am a British citizen, and they have no right to do this', I replied. Mujeeb began to speak in Kashmiri again with a distinct tone of anxiety in his voice. The soldier responded by waving his gun violently in my face again and offering a tirade of what, in any language, appeared to be abuse. Mujeeb, looking increasingly anxious and concerned, said: 'they don't care where you come from, they want payment'. My dilemma was clear: a definite threat to my personal safety or the payment of the equivalent of about forty pounds sterling. I had images of my bullet ridden body being thrown over the nearest ravine and my name becoming another statistic in the list of European travellers killed abroad. If I had been travelling on my own I felt sure my life would have been in real danger. But with Mujeeb by my side and eight other people waiting anxiously in the minibus outside I felt more confident. 'Tell him he has no right to do this' I said, appearing far braver than I actually felt. A lengthy conversation ensued between Mujeeb, my guardian angel, and the soldier, my extortioner and potential executioner. 'He will have 400 rupees', stated Mujeeb with deep concern etched into his youthful face. Although it really went against the grain to meet the demands of a man who could only be described as a 'thug', albeit a thug with a loaded assault weapon in his hand, I considered the merits of standing my ground and possibly losing my life for what amounted to just under four pounds sterling, or paying the man. I decided on the latter course and handed over the money. We escaped quickly, making our way back to the safety of the minibus waiting outside, as the two soldiers fought over their ill-gotten gains. That is now history; a frightening scenario at the end of an otherwise fascinating but brief visit to Kashmir

Arriving safely in Srinigar I was taken by my guide to the *Ahmadiyya* mosque. Next door stood the central police station, its walls protected by sandbags, with barbed wire, and mounted machine guns at the entrance. *Maulana*[1] Ghulam Nabi Niyaz, the resident *Imam*, a man of exuberant amiability, told me how he and the worshippers at the mosque, members of a persecuted sect within the Islamic faith, thanked Allah for this military presence. 'Who is likely to trouble us',

---

1   A title [literally meaning 'Lord or master'] preceding the name of a respected Muslim leader or scholar.

he said grinning, 'when we have our own armed guard next door'. He laughed reassuringly. The mosque itself was understandably not of the grandeur of the *Ahmadi* mosque opened in London in 2003, allegedly the largest in Western Europe, with a seating capacity of 15,000 and columns of Italian marble, nor of the splendour of other mosques I had seen while on my travels in Morocco, Tunisia and other Muslim lands. But it was solid and sound, a square building with whitewashed walls, green guttering and a small but prominent minaret. On entering the mosque compound from the main-road, I left behind the noise of perpetual traffic, the palpable sense of suppressed fear of imminent terrorist activity. The shrubs, bushes, and well-manicured lawn within presented an oasis of spirituality and calm. I was greeted by happy smiling faces; men who, having *salaamed* me, shook my hand with genuine fervour. My room was basic, having a bed and very little else, but after fourteen hours travelling in crowded buses, on narrow, winding and often pot-holed roads, it was the Ritz, the best accommodation I could have wanted. As I lay on my bed that night, having enjoyed good food and genuine hospitality, I thought of Kashmir: beautiful, beguiling, intriguing. But I had not come to Kashmir as a tourist, well, not specifically anyway. I had come, at the invitation of the *Ahmadiyya Jama'at*, to see for myself what they claimed to be the tomb of Jesus, the final resting place of the prophet Isa, the Jesus of the Gospels.

Like countless other Christians, I had attended Sunday School as a child. Under the careful eye of devout, sincere, and sometimes intimidating teachers, I had been taught the Ten Commandments, love for God and love for man and the basics of Christian teaching. This Christian upbringing, reinforced by theological study at University and a considerable amount of independent reading, had introduced me to the doctrine of the Atonement. An idea contained in both the Old and the New Testaments, then developed in various forms by the Early Church Fathers, Anselm, Aquinas, Luther, Calvin and others that because of sin, [flaws in our character, things we do wrong], we, sinful and self-seeking, are separated from the sinless God. Earnest preachers, and the dog-eared paperbacks I purchased at second-hand bookshops, explained how the answer to this problem of sin was to be found in the sacrificial death of the God-man Jesus. Throughout childhood and adolescence I was regularly reminded by pulpit orators in the Brethren Assemblies, the Church of the Nazarene and later in the Methodist Church how the vicarious death of Jesus, the innocent offender dying for our wrongs, apparently provided the 'satisfaction' necessary to appease God's anger and the demands of his holiness and justice.[2] I was taught that the death of Jesus is the ultimate panacea for the human predicament: the remedy by which we cease to be alienated from God and the means by which we can, by faith, enjoy God's greatest gift to mankind, the gift of eternal life. Coupled with this idea of Substitutionary Atonement was the doctrine of the Resurrection. The same earnest preachers that filled my nascent mind with images of Jesus, 'the Suffering Servant by whose blood we are healed', spoke also of a saviour, raised from the dead after three days in the tomb. They confirmed the words of the creed: Jesus was 'crucified under Pontius Pilate, and was dead and buried... rose again the third day, alive from the dead, and ascended into heaven.'[3]

The ideas outlined above present, I suppose, the lowest common denominator of Christian thinking on the life and death of Jesus. Teaching about Jesus put forward by the *Ahmadi* however, challenges, not only the basic beliefs of Christianity, but also important doctrines of mainstream Islam. Let me explain. Muslims traditionally have taught that Jesus, although appearing to die on the cross, was taken physically alive up to heaven by God to return as a champion of Islam in the future. As the Quran states: 'And for their [the Jews] saying, "We did slay the Messiah, Jesus, son of Mary, the Messenger of Allah"; whereas they slew him not, nor did they bring about his death on the cross, but he was made to appear to them like one crucified'. The Quran affirms: 'on the contrary, Allah exalted him to

---

2   Numerous theories of the Atonement have been put forward. The author is explaining here the commonly held doctrine of Substitutionary Atonement. See R. W. Dale, *The Atonement*, London: Hodder & Stoughton, 1887; J. K. Mozley, *The Doctrine of the Atonement*, (1915) reprinted Eugene, Oregon: Wipf & Stock Publishers, 2004 and F. W. Dillistone, *The Christian Understanding of Atonement*, Welwyn: James Nisbet & Co., 1968.

3   The Apostle's Creed, an early statement of Christian belief, see the *Book of Common Prayer*, Everyman's Edition, 1999.

Himself.[4] Christian missionaries in India in the nineteenth century used this teaching to their advantage, arguing that Jesus must have been superior to Muhammad because Muhammad died a natural death, while Jesus didn't. Mirza Ghulam Ahmad, the founder of the *Ahmadi* sect, wishing to put an end to this criticism of Islam and the Holy Prophet, agreed with mainstream Muslims that 'Jesus had not died on the Cross' but, in contrast to Muslims generally, declared that Jesus passed 'through a state of swoon', was later revived, taken down from the cross and resuscitated by Joseph of Arimathaea and Nicodemus.[5] 'If Muhammad died', Ahmad asserted, 'how can Jesus escape death?'. In his opinion the Quran clearly stated that Jesus 'would die a natural death ...'. He pointed with alacrity to the Quranic statement concerning Muhammad: 'verily, all Messengers [presumably including Jesus] have passed away before him'.[6] Ahmad placed great stress on the well known saying of Muhammad: 'Had Moses and Jesus been alive they would have no choice but to follow me'. Ahmad argued that Jesus, having been resuscitated, instead of being taken up to Heaven as mainstream Muslims claim, became 'the travelling prophet', going first to Nasibus and Iran, then to the Punjab from where 'he had no difficulty in wandering through the

---

4   Quran 4:158-59. All quotes from the Quran are taken from Malik Ghulam Farid (ed.) *The Holy Quran: Arabic text with English translation and short commentary*, Islamabad, Surrey: Islam International Publications,1994. The Farid edition is based on the Urdu translation of Mirza Bashiruddin Mahmud, completed under the auspices of Mirza Nasir Ahmad, the third *Ahmadi Khalifa*. Due to its 'doctrinal slant', mainstream Muslims regard this as 'an incorrect translation of the Holy Quran written to support the blasphemous claims' of the *Ahmadi* (see Idara Dawat-o-Irshad, USA Inc., http: //www.irshad.org/qadianism.php, website, accessed 10 August 2007). The numbering of verses in the Farid, and other translations used by the *Ahmadi*, differs slightly from Qurans used by other Muslims due to the fact that in mainstream Islam the *Bismillah*, the opening phrase to *Al-Fatihah* (the first *Surah*), is not numbered but is so in *Ahmadi* translations. The other main translation used by the *Ahmadi* is that of Muhammad Ali, in 1917, later leader of the Lahori *Ahmadi*.

5   See Muhammad Zafrulla Khan, *Deliverance from the Cross*, Southfields: The London Mosque, 1978, p. 33.

6   Ahmad is referring to Surah 3:145.

important places of Hindustan before going to Kashmir or Tibet'.[7] According to Ahmad Jesus must 'have gone to Kashmir through Jammu or Rawalpindi after possibly visiting Nepal, Benares and other places' and died in Kashmir at the age of one hundred and twenty.[8]

The idea of Jesus as 'the travelling prophet' was not original to Ahmad. I had first come across this idea in various books while studying theology at Manchester University in the early 1980's. One book in particular, *The Unknown life of Christ* by Nicholas Notovitch, told of a Russian nobleman who had travelled extensively in the East during the nineteenth century researching this subject. Notovitch states how, while in Ladakh, a region lying between Tibet and Kashmir, he had been given access to certain ancient Buddhist scrolls which told of Jesus' wanderings in the East during the period when the Gospels are silent about his life, from the time of his dispute with the Elders in the Temple at Jerusalem when he was twelve to the beginning of his teaching ministry, aged about thirty. According to Notovitch these Buddhist scrolls claimed that Jesus had travelled to the East in order to study Buddhist and Hindu teaching, before returning to Palestine, where he was crucified as the Christian Gospels narrate.[9] The original scrolls, which Notovitch claimed to have read and partially copied, have proven to elude all attempts at discovery. Notovitch later published what he claimed were copies of large parts of the scrolls.[10]

---

7   M. G. Ahmad, *Jesus in India, Being an Account of Jesus' Escape From Death on the Cross and His Journey to India*, 1899, later translated, London: Islam International Publications Ltd, 1989, pp. 46, 22, 66. Khwaja Ahmad adds to these details by maintaining that Jesus went to the East when he was thirteen years of age, debating with the Buddhist and Hindu leaders of that time, and later travelled to Kashmir with his mother, Mary, and his brother, Thomas the disciple. See Khwaja N. Ahmad, *Jesus in Heaven on Earth*, Woking: Woking Muslim Mission & Literary Trust, 1952, pp. 353-58; 369, 383.

8   Ahmad, *Jesus in India*, op.cit., p. 66.

9   N. Notovitch, *The Unknown Life of Jesus Christ*, 1894, reprinted, Joshua Tree, California: Tree of life Publications, 1990.

10 Other writers have since presented a similar thesis to that of Notovitch. See Andreas Kaiser, *Jesus Died in Kashmir*, New York: Gordon and Cremonesi, 1977; Holger Kersten, *Jesus Lived in India*, London: Penguin, 1981; P.

Although finding Notovitch's arguments fascinating, I was not convinced. Years later, when meeting members of the *Ahmadi* sect in Bradford, West Yorkshire, although aware the idea that Jesus travelled extensively was not original to them, I was struck by their passion in trying to prove it as fact. In reading the relevant *Ahmadi* literature, the reason for such a passionate proclamation of the claim that Jesus travelled and died in the East became clear. Proclaiming himself as reformer of Islam, and wanting to undermine the validity of Christianity, Ahmad went for the theological jugular, the foundational teachings of the Christian faith. 'The death of Jesus Christ', explained one of Ahmad's biographers 'was to be the death-knell of the Christian onslaught against Islam'.[11] As Ahmad argued, the idea of Jesus dying in old age, rather than death on a cross, as taught by the gospel writers, 'invalidates the divinity of Jesus and the doctrine of the Atonement'.[12]

What then is the evidence used by the *Ahmadi* to support the claim that Jesus, instead of dying on the cross, travelled to Kashmir, where he died in old age? I had had several meetings with Ibrahim, a lapsed Irish Roman Catholic, who converted to the *Ahmadi* faith several years ago, at Bradford and London. Unexpectedly we bumped into each other at Rabwah, during my visit to Pakistan. Dressed in a black suit and wearing his Afghan hat, Ibrahim was a veritable bearded giant, a large, solid man, apparently a black belt in one of the martial arts, someone who used to work as a Club bouncer before his conversion to *Ahmadiyyat*. On discovering my intention to go to Srinigar he shared his thoughts with me on the life, travels and death of Jesus. 'As you go into Kashmir', he said in a soft brogue accent which belied his stature, 'and you see the mountains, you have no doubts that Jesus, and Mary, went to that place: it's in the air, you can feel it'. I found his comments stimulating, romantic, enticing but cerebrally weak. I remained silent on that point and spoke of my excitement of going to

C. Pappas, *Jesus' Tomb in India; the Debate on His Death and Resurrection*, Fremont, California: Jain publishing Co, 1991.

11 Faruqui, N.A. *Ahmadiyyat: in the service of Islam*, Lahore: *Ahmadiyya Anjuman Isha'at Islam*, 1983, p. 6.

12 Ahmad, *Jesus in India*, ibid., p. 66.

Kashmir. I was pleased that Ibrahim and others like him had found something to believe in, a goal, a star to pursue. As Nietzsche had said, in a different context: 'be free, live without regret'.[13] Ibrahim had found his star. He was living without regret. But much more was needed than a romantic inclination to convince me of Jesus' travels to the East. We both smiled. He shook my hand with a vice-like grip and wished me well in my search for truth.

Ahmad, in his book *Jesus in India*, put forward, what in his opinion was 'powerful evidence' from the gospels, the Quran and the *hadith* [reports of the words and deeds of the prophet Muhammad, regarded as authoritative by Muslims, second only to the Quran] to show that Jesus did not die on the Cross and that God directed him 'to go from one place to another'.[14] Such 'illuminating evidence', as Ahmad called it, included reference to Matthew's gospel where Jesus remarked: 'For as Jonah was three days and three nights in the belly of a huge fish, so the Son of Man will be three days and three nights in the heart of the earth'.[15] Applying a literal interpretation to every aspect of this simile, forgetting that Jesus was apparently drawing an analogy between Jonah's three days inside a fish with the time he was to spend in the grave, and ignoring other references in the gospels which directly referred to the death of the Son of Man, Ahmad reasoned that just as Jonah wasn't dead while in the fish, Jesus was not dead in the tomb.[16] 'Like the prophet Jonah', opined Ahmad, '[Jesus] would only pass through a state of swoon', and would be revived

---

13 Nietzsche described the *ubermensch*, the 'overman', who, free from the chains of religion, slave morality and the common herd, would live without regret, see F. Nietzsche, *Thus Spoke Zarathustra: A Book for Everyone and No one*, (1883-85), London: Penguin Classics, 1961, *passim*.

14 See Kanz-ul-Ummal, vol. 2., *Al-Hadith*, p. 3, a *hadith* from Abu Huraira cited by Ahmad, *Jesus in India*, ibid., p. 53. For the definition of *hadith* see J. L. Esposito, *The Oxford Dictionary of Islam*, Oxford: OUP, 2003, sv.

15 Matthew12:40, all quotations are taken from the *New International Version of the Bible*, London: Hodder & Stoughton, 1979.

16 See Matthew 26:2 which refers to the betrayal and death of the Son of Man. Other direct references to the suffering and death of Jesus can be seen in Mark 9:9, 10:32-34; Luke 9:44, 24:7; John 8:28. This theme is continued throughout the rest of the New Testament as seen in Romans 5:10, Hebrews 6:6, 1 John 4:10f.

later by the disciples.[17] On reading this argument my mind turned to other statements made by Jesus: 'I am the door', 'I am the true vine', 'it is easier for a camel to go through the eye of a needle than for a rich man to enter the kingdom of heaven', words surely meant to be taken figuratively, as symbols, picture language often exaggerated so as to convey spiritual rather than literal truth.[18] I thought of the dangers, if not absurdities, of understanding such words literally. Ahmad found further 'proof of Jesus' survival' after the crucifixion in Jesus' statement concerning his mission to 'the lost sheep of the house of Israel', and in Jesus' declaration there are 'other sheep, that are not of this fold' that must also be brought into the kingdom.[19] In studying the relevant Christian commentaries on this biblical passage, I discovered that this, and other references to the 'lost sheep of Israel' are usually understood as referring to the debate within the early Church as 'to whether the message and powers of the Kingdom of God were open to Gentiles as well as Jews',[20] while Jesus' comment about 'other sheep' is interpreted as a reference to the 'worldwide mission of Christianity' which 'will include gentiles as well as Jews within the people of God'.[21] Ahmad however, applying a different interpretation, concluded that such words can only be understood in the light of Jesus' mission to the East 'to invite to the truth the lost Jews who had come to be known as Afghans'.[22]

Similar to mainstream Muslims, Ahmad regarded the Christian belief of the Messiah, a prophet of God, who could die an accursed death, as one of the main arguments against the historical reliability of the crucifixion. Ignoring the biblical references which state that it was the divine plan to allow Jesus to die, thereby becoming a curse, so as to redeem fallen human-kind from the curse of God's law [as

17 Ahmad, *Jesus in India*, op.cit., p., 22.

18 John 10:9, John 15:1, Matthew 19:24.

19 Matthew 15:24, John 10:16.

20 H. C. Kee, section on Matthew, *Interpreter's One- volume Commentary on the Bible*, Nashville: Abingdon Press, 1971, p. 628.

21 See C. K. Barrett, *Peake's Commentary on the Bible*, London: Nelson,1981, p. 856 or any other standard biblical commentary.

22 Ahmad, *Jesus in India*, op.cit., p. 65.

traditional Christianity argues], Ahmad maintained that God would never allow a person he loved to die in such an ignominious way. I could see how Christians and others might well regard the logic of his reasoning as tantalising but flawed. Fully acknowledging that 'in the books of the New Testament words of this kind occur, [that is words which talk of Jesus' escape from death [as] a miracle]', Ahmad dismissed such words, and the claims such words contain, as 'a mistake of the writers of these books'.[23] With alacrity Ahmad referred to the *Gospel of Barnabas*, a work which although claiming to be a life of Christ written by Barnabas, a follower of Jesus mentioned in the *Acts of the Apostles,* is generally regarded as 'a medieval forgery, a mediocre parody of the gospels', which denies the death of Jesus on the cross.[24] Amongst other things this book claims, not only that Judas was changed by God 'in speech and in face to look like Jesus' and crucified in Jesus' place, but that 'God, seeing the danger of his servant, commanded Gabriel, Michael, Rafeal, and Uriel, . . . to take Jesus out of the world' rather than die at the hands of the Romans.[25] The historicity, and therefore the reliability, of the *Gospel of Barnabas* is seriously questioned by academics. As Ahmad himself readily acknowledges, 'this book is not included in the gospels and has been rejected summarily'.[26] On researching the details of the *Gospel of Barnabas* I discovered that the date and authorship of the book are unknown but due to the fact that the oldest copies are written in Italian and Spanish most scholars, even many Muslim writers, would regard it as medieval in origin.[27] As well as the obvious weakness of relying on such a dubious text, I could sympathise with those who

---

23 Ahmad, ibid., p. 25.

24 C. Glasse, *The Concise Encyclopaedia of Islam,* San Francisco: Harper Row, 1989, sv, p. 65.

25 Gospel of Barnabas, 216:2; 215:1, see R. Blackhirst, *The Medieval Gospel of Barnabas,* full text of the Italian MS in English with notes, website, http://www.latrobe.edu.au/arts/barnabas/entry.html.

26 Ahmad, *Jesus in India,* op.cit., p. 26.

27 Ata-ur-Rahim, (in his book *Jesus: A Prophet of Islam,* Karachi: Begin Aisha Bawany Waqf, 1981,) argues that the Gospel of Barnabas was accepted by the Church up till 325 AD when the Council of Nicaea condemned it and ordered its universal destruction. Although many Muslims use Rahim as an authoritative guide I can find no historical evidence to support his claims.

maintain that Ahmad's argument, either intentionally or otherwise, seemed to miss what Christians believe to be the whole point of the gospel story. Saint Paul, writing to the early Christians at Galatia put it well when he said: 'Christ redeemed us from the curse of the law by becoming a curse for us . . . so that by faith we might receive the promise of the Spirit'.[28]

So much for theology and biblical interpretation. Turning to the historical and archaeological evidence put forward by Ahmad, to my Christian and potentially biased perspective, much of it seemed similarly tenuous and strained. He referred, for example, to Marham-i-Isa, the 'ointment of Jesus', a medicine apparently prepared for, and applied with miraculous effect, to the wounds of Jesus after he had been saved from the cross. Mention of this ointment is found in a medical book written after the death of Jesus and used by physicians for hundreds of years.[29] Ignoring the possibility that the original medical book could have been spurious in its claims about the ointment, or written by those who knew they were onto a hagiographical [if not financial] winner in terms of producing something for the credulous and superstitious, Ahmad refers to the hundreds of other later medical books written by believers that refer to, and confirm the original. With this in mind he triumphantly concludes how the 'ointment of Jesus' is not only 'a very important piece of evidence', but that it is 'illuminating evidence', 'transparent proof' which 'destroys the belief about the Cross'.[30]

Other archaeological evidence presented by Ahmad includes reference to a coin found in India during his lifetime 'on which is inscribed the name of Jesus in Pali characters'.[31] Providing no evidence to support such a claim he asserts how 'this coin belongs to the time of Jesus', and on that assumption alone authoritatively states how 'this shows that Jesus came to this land and received kingly honour'.[32] Ahmad refers to a second coin showing 'the figure of an Israelite'

---

28 St Paul in Galatians 3:13, 14.
29 Ahmad, *Jesus in India*, op.cit., pp. 55-56
30 Ahmad, ibid., pp. 59, 60, 61.
31 Ibid., p. 52.
32 Ibid., p. 53.

and makes the astonishing claim: 'it seems that this too is the figure of Jesus'. Further astounding claims are made by other *Ahmadi*. For example, a statue of a man was found at Taxila, an ancient site, near Rawalpindi, Pakistan. Because this statue has a distinctive beard and garb, and resembles the image of Jesus painted by European artists, one *Ahmadi* writer asserts: 'it is hardly open to doubt that this figure is that of Jesus...'.[33] Faith is a marvellous thing, blind faith even more so. Several months prior to my visit to Srinigar I had discussed these points relating to Jesus' alleged visit to Kashmir with a friend, a Muslim, a former student at the University of Bradford. With a look of acute incredulity he remarked: 'Ahmad's argument is like saying that the Emperor Domitian came to Britain because coins bearing his image have been found at St Albans or that George Washington visited Saudi Arabia because an American dollar was found in the desert'. I think my student friend had made an astute observation.

As well as biblical, Quranic and archaeological evidence Ahmad makes reference to 'evidence from books on Buddhism' for Jesus' travels in the East.[34] Significance is seen in the fact that 'titles given to the Buddha are similar to the titles given to Jesus' and 'the events of the life of Buddha resemble those of the life of Jesus'. Nineteenth century teachers of comparative religion were amazed at the striking similarities between Christianity and Buddhism. Apart from anything else the Buddha taught the perfecting of such qualities as generosity, patience, wisdom, loving kindness and, most importantly, pacifism.[35] However, although similarities do exist between the life and teaching of Christ and that of the Buddha, there are also great differences. Buddhism for example 'does not involve belief in one omnipotent, personal God; unlike Christianity the 'Buddhist understanding of the world is non-theistic'.[36] The Buddhist beliefs in reincarnation and the transmigration of souls are but two examples of how the teaching of the two faiths differ. Ahmad, dismissing the

---

33 See K. N. Ahmad, *Jesus in Heaven on Earth*, op.cit., p. 377.

34 Ahmad, op.cit., p. 67.

35 J. R. Hinnells, ed., *Dictionary of Religion*, London: Penguin, 1995, sv., Buddha.

36 Hinnells, op.cit., sv., Buddhism.

differences, suggests that the similarities occur because Jesus, while travelling in the East, taught the Buddhists of India and Tibet thereby influencing the development of Eastern philosophy. He draws our attention to the belief held by Buddhists that another Buddha, being *Bagwa* [white] and *Metteyya* [a traveller], would appear in the East in the future. Ahmad, again dismissing the obvious problems that exist with such an idea [one of which is the fact that Jesus being Jewish and living in the Middle East, would have had a dark, not white skin] sees the alleged travels of Jesus to the Himalayan region as fulfilment of this prophecy.[37]

I was taken by Professor Mir, a lecturer in statistics at the local University, the *Amir* of the *Ahmadi* mosque and other members of the *Jama'at* by taxi through the bustling streets of Srinigar. We stopped at Khaniyar Street and on getting out of the taxi walked to the narrow alley where stands Roza bal, the building allegedly containing the body of Jesus. A large group of boys, of varying ages and sizes, played cricket in the passageway leading to the door of the tomb. They continued playing, running here and there, oblivious if not indifferent to the purpose of our visit. To our disappointment the entrance to the building was closed, padlocked and chained. The warden, apologetic yet adamant, informed us that the local magistrates had ordered the closing of the building due mainly to the resentment of other local Muslims. Despite earnest appeals he refused to unlock the door and provide us with temporary access. Peering through one of several windows on the exterior wall I could just make out the shape of the symbolic coffin lying on a pedestal almost within touching distance. With a deep sense of frustration I imagined the basement immediately beneath this structure where, allegedly the body of Jesus lay. With permission I took photographs and observed the *Ahmadi*, my escorts, perform their prayers at what they believed to be the tomb of the prophet Isa. With the game of cricket still in progress, and boys dressed in jeans and designer T-shirts shouting enthusiastically for the ball, I walked round the building deep in thought. In the pleasant warmth of a typical Kashmiri day in May the building looked bland, non-descript, uninteresting.

---

37 Ahmad, *Jesus in India*, ibid., p. 68.

It stood, box-like, pre-fabricated, measuring about thirty by twenty feet, dwarfed by the towering minaret of an adjacent mosque. Was this really the resting-place of the man who had founded one of the world's greatest religions, a man professed by millions of Christians round the world to be, not just a good man or a prophet, but the Son of God, the saviour of the world?

For several months I read everything I could get my hands on relating to this issue and objectively considered the truth or otherwise of the story. Ahmad argued in *Jesus in India*, that 'fair minded investigators' and those possessing 'honesty and love of fairness' would not be able to reject the idea that 'the blessed footprints of Jesus' walked 'on the rocky soil of Nepal, Tibet and Kashmir'.[38] However, as in my student days in Manchester, although I read his book several times, and read other books supporting his view, I was not convinced. Maybe it was because I was a Christian and I looked at life through Christian eyes, or Ahmad was merely clutching at straws to refute the Christian faith, but the evidence put forward, in my opinion, seemed flaccid to say the least. For me the story, like the legend which tells of Joseph of Arithamea taking the holy-grail to Britain, or the idea that the ten lost tribes of Israel took ship to America as the Mormons claim, will always remain a myth, albeit interesting myths. The conclusive test would be the use of radio-carbon dating, or the analysis of DNA testing on the remains of the body that lies in the tomb, but of course permission would have to be gained from the requisite authorities. Fearful of successful Christian missionary activity and the consequent decline of Islam, Ahmad wanted to discredit the opposition. If Jesus did not die on the cross, and thus did not rise again from the dead, as he knew, the entire Christian faith would simply fall like a house of cards. 'The death of Christ was, therefore', concludes one *Ahmadi*, 'rightly regarded by the Founder of the *Ahmadiyya* movement as taking away the heart out of Christianity'.[39] To argue that Jesus had died like any other man, as Ahmad maintained, 'to Christianity meant the death of its central figure,

---

38 Ibid., p. 78.
39 M. Ali, *The Ahmadiyyah Movement*, trans. S. M. Tufail, Lahore: *Ahmadiyyah Anjuman Isha'at Islam*, 1973, p. 12.

with whose death collapsed the whole structure of its dogmas'.[40] As the apostle Paul remarked to the early Christians at Corinth: 'If there is no resurrection of the dead, then not even Christ has been raised. And if Christ has not been raised, our preaching is useless and so is your faith'.[41]

40 Ahmad, *Jesus in India*, op.cit., p. 59, 78.
41 1 Corinthians. 15:13-14.

2
AHMADIYYAT AND ITS FOUNDER, MIRZA GHULAM AHMAD

In British schools today children are taught the Five Pillars of Islam: the basic duties which should be observed by all Muslims. These duties include *shahada* [confession of faith], the duty to testify that there is no God but Allah and Muhammad is the messenger of Allah; the performance of *salat* or prayers five times daily; the paying of *zakat* or a proportion of income to 'charity'; the practice of *sawm* or fasting during the holy month of *Ramadan* and going on *hajj* or pilgrimage at least once in one's lifetime. More advanced courses at Colleges of Further and Higher Education inform their students, as well as these five *ibadatim* [duties,] there is also *iman,* six articles of faith: belief in Allah, his messenger, holy books, angels, the day of judgement and destiny. Such religious teaching, although a commendable and necessary element of any education preparing youngsters to live in a multi-cultural society, tends to present Islam as one monolithic, homogenous group and the idea that all Muslims share the same beliefs and practices. Nothing could be further from the truth. Islam, like Christianity, is a highly fractured faith, embracing a multitude of differing views and outlooks. As one recent writer remarked: 'some Muslims are for royalty, some for socialism and communism, some for a military junta, some for capitalism, some for an Islamic republic; but a good proportion live in and support a multiparty system ... there are three hundred million black Muslims, six hundred million white Muslims, two hundred million yellow-skinned Muslims'. In fact it has been argued that 'no other world religion spans such a range of racial, linguistic and cultural differences as Islam'.[1] Just as in Christianity the major traditions of Roman Catholicism, the Orthodox Church and Protestantism, have numerous sub-divisions, so the Islamic faith has numerous strands and sub-groups. Most people who take an interest in world news, although not aware of the doctrinal, historical and ritualistic differences, are familiar with the two main groups of Islam, namely *Sunni* and *Shia*. The *Sunni* segment, accounting for at least 80% of the world's Muslim population, is divided into seventy-three different groups, each declaring [to a lesser or greater degree] its own interpretation of the Islamic faith. With such different groups in mind John Esposito, a leading writer on Islamic Studies, reminds us of the need to 'move beyond a monolithic worldview that sees Muslims and the Muslim world as a unity'.[2]

The *Ahmadiyya Jama'at* is one of the numerous groups making up the *Sunni* division of Islam. Although the *Ahmadi* have adopted a name, and established their own hierarchy and infrastructure, this, as they claim, does not point to the establishment of a new religious faith. 'It is not a new religion', declares one *Ahmadi* writer, 'nor is it an innovation'. Instead 'it is a fresh presentation of Islam'.[3] Founded by Mirza Ghulam Ahmad in India in the last quarter of the nineteenth century, the *Ahmadi* regard themselves as nothing less than 'the true Islam',[4] 'the most dynamic denomination of Islam in modern history', and 'Islam in its pristine purity'.[5] 'The objective of the *Ahmadiyyat* is believed to be 'the same as that of Islam, to establish the relationship of love between God and His servants and

---

1   Enes Karic, former Minister of Education, Science and Culture of Bosnia-Herzegovina, and currently Professor of Islamic Studies at the University of Sarajevo, cited by John L. Esposito, *The Islamic Threat, Myth or Reality*, Oxford: CUP, 2002, p. 18.

2   John L. Esposito, *The Islamic Threat*, op.cit., p. xiv.

3   Karimullah Zirvi, *Welcome to Ahmadiyyat: The true Islam*, Silver Springs, USA: *Ahmadiyya* Movement in Islam, 2002, p. 267.

4   Aziz A. Chaudhry, *The Promised Messiah and Mahdi*, Islamabad: Islam International Publications, 1996, p. 5; *Ahmadiyya Muslim Association, North East: 2001-2002, Annual Report*, London: *Ahmadiyya* Muslim Association, 2002, p.3.

5   Chaudhry, op.cit., p. 5.

unity between different sections of mankind'.[6] Believing itself to be the 'true Islam' *Ahmadiyyat* attempts to bring about 'the revival and establishment of the glory of Islam'.[7] The *Ahmadi* regard their movement as the sect 'with salvation', created so as to 'rejuvenate Islamic moral and spiritual values'. Tahir Selby, a former mechanic living in London, a lapsed Christian, now practicing as an *Ahmadi Imam*, similarly declared how Ahmad, the founder of the movement, came 'to reform the Muslim community; establish the supremacy of Islam over all other religions and spread the message of Islam all over the world'.[8] As the third *Khalifa* [the Head and world leader of the *Ahmadi* movement] declared to a gathering of his followers at Rabwah in 1972: 'our goal is, as you know, to make Islam prevail over the whole world'.[9] 'The work of the *Ahmadiyya* movement... in one word', suggests Muhammad Ali, the first leader of the Lahori *Ahmadi*, is 'the spiritual conquest of the west'.[10] In achieving this goal '*Ahmadiyyat* seeks to abolish all barriers set up on the basis of race and colour, so that man may unite and promote universal peace'.[11] Of course, as with all sects that believe they have a monopoly on truth, this unity will be achieved only when everyone embraces *Ahmadi* doctrine. 'Christianity and other evils' are dismissed as heresies and corruptions of true religion. Christianity for example is regarded as polytheistic, corrupted by *shirk* [associating God with other things], Christians having 'interpolated their revealed books'.[12] Ahmad went

---

6 Khuddam News, *Al-Baseerat*, Bradford: NE regional committee, (October 1996), p. 9; *Leaflet No 4, The Ahmadiyya movement in Islam*, London: *Ahmadiyya* Muslim Association UK, nd.

7 Zirvi, *Welcome to Ahmadiyyat*, op.cit., p. 11.

8 Tahir Selby, *Al-Baseerat*, Bradford: NE regional committee, (October, 1993), p.3.

9 *The Muslim Herald*, London: n.p., (December 1975/January 1976), p. 20. The term *Khalifa* and *Khalifate* will be used throughout this book instead of Caliph and Caliphate to designate the 'successors' of Muhammad.

10 Muhammad Ali, *The Ahmadiyya Movement*, trans. S. M. Tufail, *Ahmadiyyah, Anjuman Isha'at Islam*, Lahore: n.p.,1973, pp. 39-40.

11 Chaudhry, *The Promised Messiah and Mahdi*, op.cit., p. 9.

12 See Nisar Faruqui, *Ahmadiyyat: in the service of Islam*, Lahore: *Ahmadiyya Anjuman Isha'at Islam*, 1983, pp. 42, 45. The *Ahmadi* are in agreement with Muslims generally that both Christians and Jews have corrupted, and

as far as claiming that Christianity is 'the most perfect manifesta-tion of Satan'.[13] Even the teaching of mainstream Islam, especially that relating to the claims of Ahmad, are branded by the *Ahmadi* as misguided and wrong. Other Muslims are castigated because, in the opinion of the *Ahmadi*, they are 'forgetful of their duty to preach Islam to the nations of the earth', they 'are engrossed in their worldly affairs and are aspiring after political greatness'.[14] Fulminat-ing against each other like Catholics and Protestants 200 years ago in Europe, the *Ahmadi* argue, and take some satisfaction from their belief, that 'on the Day of Judgement ... Allah ... will send some of his *Ummah* to hell for making innovations in religion'.[15] Although offering a message of tolerance and respect for the views of others in the present time, the *Ahmadi* openly declare their belief in the future vindication, and ultimate triumph, of *their* claims. 'The winds are now blowing firmly in the favour of *Ahmadiyya*', declared Mirza Ta-hir Ahmad, the Fourth *Ahmadi Khalifa*, 'and they will usher in a new era of the victory of Islam'.[16] 'Just as any governmental employee is protected against adversaries by his judicial rights etc.', he continued, 'people who try to contend with those appointed and established by Allah [referring to the *Ahmadi* as those appointed by God], are [to be] destroyed'.[17]

It is important to stress at this point that the *Ahmadi*, due mainly to their founder's claim to prophet-hood and other reasons discussed elsewhere in this book, are not accepted as members of the Islamic community by mainstream Muslims. The majority of Muslims refer to the *Ahmadi* derogatively as *Qadianis* [Qadian being the birthplace of Ahmad] and *Mirzai* [a reference to the first name of the founder

---

changed, their holy books.

13 Mirza G. Ahmad, *Jesus in India*, op.cit., p. 15.

14 *Ahmadiyya Muslim Association, North East: 2001-2002, Annual Report*, Bradford: NE regional committee, p.3.

15 The words of Mirza Tahir Ahmad, the fourth *Khalifa* of the *Ahmadiyya* movement, in a *khutba* delivered on 17 May 2002, cited in *Ahmadiyya Bulletin*, London: The London mosque, (September 2002), p. 4.

16 The Fourth *Khalifa* cited by Aziz Ahmad Hafiz, 'The Latter Days', *Al-Baseerat*, (May 1996), p. 11.

17 Aziz Ahmad Hafiz, 'The Latter Days', op.cit., p. 6.

of the *Ahmadi* movement]. Perceived as being teachers of heresy, and having moved away from orthodox doctrine, they are condemned as 'apostates and *Zindique*' [heretics].[18] The *Ahmadi* are seen as a 'cult based on innumerable absurdities and profanities'.[19] Consequently they are regarded as being a 'grave threat' to the 'very existence [of the *Ummah*] as a united community',[20] a group deliberately making Muslims 'ever more confused and demoralised'.[21] 'May Allah protect Muslims', remonstrated Dr Syed Rashid Ali, 'from the fraudulent doctrine of *Ahmadiyya/Qadianiyah*'.[22] The hatred of Muslims towards the *Ahmadi* was reflected in the words of General Zia ul-Haqq, former President of Pakistan, who in 1984 declared his determination to ensure 'that the cancer of *Qadianism* is exterminated', a threat that was encapsulated in the anti-*Ahmadi* legislation he introduced later that year.[23]

'The *Qadianis*', declares one Bradford-based Muslim writer, are to be seen 'as heretics or non-Muslims according to the evidence of the Holy Quran, *hadiths* and consensus of the Muslim *Ummah* because of their denial in the finality of the prophet-hood of prophet Muhammad'.[24] In conversation with Muslim shop-keepers and traders in Britain, North Africa, Pakistan, America and elsewhere I often heard the *Ahmadi* described as *murtad* [apostates] or *kafir* [unbelievers]. Mainstream Muslims, generally speaking, will have very little to do with the *Ahmadi*. Hada, the manager of *UK Fried Chicken*, the fast food restaurant on the corner of Edderthorpe

---

18 *Fatwa* issued by the *Daily Afaq*, Lahore, (8 September 2003). A *zindiq* is an atheist or heretic, someone who presents heretical teaching as true Islam, thereby threatening the unity of the *Ummah*.

19 M. Fadil Khan, *Hadhrat Pir Meher Ali Shah of Golra Sharif*, 3rd ed., Lahore: n.p., 1989, p. 15.

20 Muhammad Iqbal, *Qaumi Digest*, Urdu Journal, special edition on *Qadianism*, Lahore: n.p., (July 1984), pp. 243-62.

21 Fadil Khan, *Hadhrat Pir Meher Ali Shah of Golra Sharif*, op.cit., p. 82.

22 *Anti-Ahmadiyya Movement in Islam*, leaflet printed by Dr Syed Rashid Ali, *Alfujairah*, United Arab Emirates: nd.

23 *The* (London) *Times*, (5 September 1984).

24 Muhammad Siddique, *Moral Spotlight on Bradford*, Bradford: M.S. Press, 1993, p. 176.

Street and Leeds Road, Bradford, West Yorkshire, in one of several lengthy conversations we had together, stated: 'there are too many mosques in Bradford. We ought to be united, be one. No matter what type of Muslim—*Barelwi, Wahhabi, Shia, Sunni*—I will go into their mosque for *namaz* [prayers], but not into an *Ahmadi* mosque'. I asked him why he disliked the *Ahmadi* so much. 'Because they are *kafir*', he replied, 'in fact they are worse than *kafir*. Another local Muslim told me '*Ahmadi* are *fakir* [not true Muslims];[25] the only way to live is to accept Muhammad, peace be upon him, as the last and greatest of the prophets. The *Ahmadi* refuse to do this'. *Pir* Marouf Hussain Shah, a Bradford-based Muslim leader having an international following, summed up the views of many Muslims when he told me that the *Ahmadi*, 'although they should not be persecuted, they are not Muslim. They should live in Pakistan like Christians and Hindus', he explained, 'but they should be open about who they are. They are *Ahmadi, Mirzai, Qadianis*. Just as followers of Mawdudi call themselves after their founder', he reasoned, 'so the *Ahmadi* should do the same'.[26]

Not surprisingly, the *Ahmadi* vehemently oppose such a viewpoint. Mirza Basheer-ud-Din Mahmood Ahmad, the second *Ahmadi Khalifa*, in a promotional leaflet published in the 1980's, declared: '*Ahmadi*s are Muslims and their religion is Islam'. He explained how the names used by the *Ahmadi* [such as *Ahmadiyyat, Ahmadiyya Jama'at, Ahmadiyya* movement etc.,] had been adopted 'merely to distinguish *Ahmadi* Muslims from other Muslims and *Ahmadi* interpretations from other interpretations of Islam'. As such *Ahmadi* are caught between two worlds: desperate to be acknowledged by other Muslims as Muslim, and eager to convince a non-Muslim world of the veracity of its claims. However, irrespective of the truth or otherwise of its message, the *Ahmadiyyat* forms a vibrant movement within contemporary Islamic reformism.

---

25 *Fakir* literally refers to a Sufi holy man who performs feats of endurance or magic, or to street beggars.

26 Information gained from a private interview with *Pir* Maroof at his house at Southfield Square, Bradford, November 2003. Mawdudi was an Indo-Pakistani reformist thinker, d. 1979, the founder of the *Jama'at-i-Islami*.

Concerning the size of the sect it is difficult to get beyond the *Ahmadi* propaganda. When I asked to see the official statistics I was told they do not exist, a comment I found difficult to reconcile with the movement's regional annual accounts of converts and their request for, and meticulous recording of, *chanda* [financial contributions] from each of its members. Even their own sources provide differing accounts of conversions and membership. One leaflet printed by the movement states how 'its estimated fifteen million followers constitute a positive element of Islam', while a Centenary celebration booklet applauded how, 'from one person, our founder, the *Jama'at* has now reached over 12,000,000 people'.[27] Other promotional literature produced by the *Ahmadi* claim a membership of up to 180 million worldwide or boast how over forty-one million people in the year 2000 alone became *Ahmadi*.[28] 'Just last year', declared Karimullah Zirvi in 2002, 'more than 81 million men, women and children all over the world have joined *Ahmadiyyat*'.[29] Even allowing for apparently large numbers of *Ahmadi* in certain areas, particularly in Nigeria and Pakistan, the movement constitutes only a small proportion of practicing Muslims worldwide.[30] Like most sects however, the *Ahmadi* believe in the ultimate triumph of their message and, as Ahmad himself predicted, their 'community will increase all over the world and will be the true inheritors of the Holy Quran, Islam and the Holy Prophets'.[31]

---

27 Mirza Basheer-ud-Din, *Invitation to Ahmadiyya*, London: London mosque, 1980, p. 3. There are an estimated 286,000 *Ahmadi* in Pakistan, see census, USSD International Freedom Report, 1998.

28 *Ahmadiyyat: The true Islam*, Leaflet printed by the *Ahmadiyya* Muslim Association UK, Millennium Gift series no. 8, and *Invitation to Islam*, Millennium Gift series no. 10.

29 Karimullah Zirvi, *Welcome to Ahmadiyyat: The true Islam*, Ahmadiyya Movement in Islam, Silver Springs, USA: Islamic Publications Ltd, 2002, p. 12.

30 Official statistics for the membership of the Lahori group could not be obtained. A figure of 30,000 members worldwide was given to me by various persons within the movement.

31 *Hadhrat* Mirza Ghulam Ahmad, *Malfoozat*, vol. 3, pp. 237-47, cited in 'How Allah deals with those who accuse the Divine Appointee of falsehood', in *Review of Religions*, vol. 96., no. 5, (May 2001), p. 23.

Prophets proclaiming a divine calling to redeem the world are nothing new in the history of religions. Christian history is replete with such names as Montanus, the second century charismatic, who accompanied by two prophetesses, Prisca and Maximilla, gathered his followers at Pepuza in Phrygia [modern day Turkey] to await the descent of the heavenly Jerusalem.[32] During the Reformation period legions of self appointed prophets, encouraged by Luther's criticisms of the Roman Catholic Church and the consequent breakdown of the accepted world order, proclaimed the approaching apocalypse and the imminence of Christ's return.[33] The modern era has similarly seen the rise of numerous religious leaders claiming to be the messengers of God, and different groups offering their own unique path to salvation. Charles Russell and the Jehovah's Witnesses, Joseph Smith and the Mormons, the Reverend Moon and the Unification Church are well known examples of such new religious movements. The more extreme element of such religious fervour is seen in the teachings of preachers such as David Quresh, the charismatic leader of the Branch Davidian sect at Waco, Texas. His claims to divine revelations, and the apparent stockpiling of weapons in preparation for the apocalypse and the end of the world, led to the massacre of the sect by US government soldiers in April 1993. The emergence of cults, sects and reform movements has been a global phenomenon. Believing their actions would hasten the occurrence of doomsday, the Japanese Aum Supreme Truth Cult, founded by the mystic Shako Asahara, was responsible for poisoning the Tokyo subway with sarin gas in 1995.

Islam has also had its fair share of men, even women, who have claimed divine approval for their mission. Mirza Ghulam Ahmad, the founder of the *Ahmadiyya Jama'at*, although preaching a message of peaceful proselytism, in contrast to the views held by the more extreme religious groups, was one such teacher declaring his credentials as a messenger of God. Who was this man? According to the *Ahmadi*

---

32 F. L. Cross (ed.) *The Oxford Dictionary of the Christian Church*, Oxford: Oxford University Press, 1974, sv Montanism.

33 Thomas Münzer (c1490-1525), Hans Hut (d. 1527) and various Anabaptist preachers represent this radical movement. See R. Tudur Jones, *The Great Reformation*, Leicester: IVP, 1985.

their founder was 'a champion of Islam', the *Mujaddid*, the 'expected reformer of the age' who brought about 'the renaissance of Islam in the latter days'.[34] They proudly proclaim him to be 'the lone warrior of Islam' who conducted 'a lone defence of [the Islamic faith] with all his strength, his pen, his tongue, his wealth, and all he could give in this unequal war'.[35] He is accepted as 'the Promised Reformer whose advent was awaited under different names and titles by the adherents of various religions'.[36] Like the eschatological expectations of all Messianic faiths the *Ahmadi* proclaim that the coming of Ahmad 'would finally usher in a golden era of one universal religion which for ages man had dreamt of and yearned'.[37] The establishment of this 'golden era', an age when the peoples of the world would embrace one faith [namely the *Ahmadi* interpretation of Islam,] has become the raison d'être of the *Ahmadi* movement. However, the majority of mainstream Muslims, as mentioned above, reject Mirza Ghulam Ahmad as 'a hypochondriac who was subject to fits of melancholia, a self-deluded person professing communion with God, an impostor who fabricated revelations from on high'.[38] Seeing Ahmad as 'a liar' who undertook 'the manipulation of the Quran and the *hadith* for his own ends',[39] the *ulema*, the Islamic scholars in India at the time, pronounced a *fatwa of Kufr* [declaration of heresy] against him. This *fatwa* has not been revoked.

Qadian, in North-West India, is the *Ahmadi* Bethlehem. It was here that their founder, Mirza Ghulam Ahmad, was born. It is also his final resting place. Until the partition of India in 1947 Qadian was the headquarters of the *Ahmadi* movement before it moved to a new centre at Rabwah in Pakistan. 313 members of the community, the *Darveshan-i-Qadian* ['among the Darveshes'] were left to protect

34 *North East: Annual Report 2001-2002*: Bradford: *Ahmadiyya* Muslim Association, 2002, p. 4.

35 Faruqui, *Ahmadiyyat: in the Service of Islam*, op.cit., p. 8.

36 *Jihad: the True Islamic Concept*, leaflet, London: *Ahmadiyya* Muslim Association, n.d.

37 Leaflet, *Jihad: the True Islamic Concept*, op.cit.

38 S. P.Tayo, *Facts About the Ahmadiyya Movement*, Trinidad; n.p.,1979.

39 M. Fadil Khan, *Hadrat Pir Meher Ali Shah of Golra Sharif*, op.cit., p. 102.

the sacred sites in the town, particularly Ahmad's tomb. The number of such guardians was significant. According to tradition, Muhammad, with a force of 313 men, had defeated a much larger Meccan army sent out to destroy him at the battle of Badr in 624 AD. The battle was seen as 'a symbol of the victory of Islam over polytheism and unbelief and a demonstration of divine guidance and intervention on behalf of Muslims, even when outnumbered'.[40] On my visit to the town I met with Bashir Kalaphana, one of the few remaining members of that original group of 313 *darveshes*. Tall, erect, strong, looking younger than his seventy five years, he stood before me in the heat of the Aqsa mosque. His face leathery, his eyes warm and wise, he told me through an interpreter of his pride in safeguarding this holy site. 'It has been the purpose of my life', he said, 'my task for Allah to honour *Hadhrat*[41] Ahmad, peace be upon him'. Driving into the town on the main highway from the Wagah border crossing and Amritsar, one of the first things I saw was the white minaret of the promised Messiah, the *Minaratul Masih*, situated in the precinct of the Aqsa Mosque. It was getting dark as we approached the town and the illuminated *Minaratul Masih*, 105 feet high, built in three stages, and mounted by ninety-two steps, could be seen for miles across the flat terrain of the Indian Punjab. I learnt later that this mosque, with its white minaret, had been built specifically by the *Ahmadi* as fulfillment of a prediction made by the Prophet Muhammad that the promised Messiah will arise near a white minaret East of Damascus. The foundation stone was laid in 1903 and it was completed thirteen years later.

At Qadian there is also the *Khalifat* library containing important documents and original books relating to the *Ahmadiyya* movement. The *Bahishti Maqbara*, the 'heavenly graveyard', containing not only Ahmad's grave, but also the grave of *Hadhrat* Noor-ud-Din [the first *Ahmadi Khalifa*] and other companions and relatives of Ahmad, lies on the edge of the town. I was allowed to visit the site during my brief visit to Qadian. It is a beautiful, peaceful place, the air filled with the

---

40 John L. Esposito, *The Oxford Dictionary of Islam*, Oxford: OUP, 2003, sv., Badr, battle of.

41 *Hadhrat*, an honorific title meaning 'the respected one'.

scent of roses, bouganvillea, marigolds, poinsettia bushes and other flowers and shrubs. The graveyard, extremely well kept and maintained, is a place of sanctity for the *Ahmadi*. Established by Ahmad in his will after he had seen an angel showing him the place of his burial, it has now become the burial place reserved for those *Ahmadi* who contribute at least 10% of their possessions to the movement. There is a marked site in the graveyard where Ahmad's funeral took place and where the first *Khalifa* was elected, both events occurring on the same day, 27 May 1908. Nearby is Mubarak House, Ahmad's residence where, in a room called *Baitul Fikr* he meditated and wrote many of his works. At *Baitul Dua* it is said that Ahmad used to pray. In a room known as *Hujrah* it is claimed that Ahmad saw a vision in which he, having written down some decrees about the future, placed them before God for his signature. God, who looked like a judge or ruler, firstly flicked the pen in the direction of Ahmad thus removing the excess ink, before putting his signatures on the documents. The dream ended there and Ahmad, on waking, saw numerous fresh red spots on his clothes. An eyewitness, Abdullah, later begged for the shirt. It is now in Abdullah's grave in the graveyard at Qadian.

The facts of Ahmad's life are as follows. Although Ahmad himself tells us that he was born in 'the last days of Sikh rule in 1839 or 1840',[42] it is generally assumed that his birth occurred in the mid 1830's, probably 1835.[43] The details of his family background and upbringing are better-known. Ahmad, the second son of Mirza Ghulam Murtaza, a chieftain of the Punjab region, was raised in a noble Moghul family of Qadian His privileged family position secured a good education, providing a grounding in the Quran, some Persian books, Arabic and logic. He received his primary education in his own village of Qadian and then in the town of Batala, about

---

42 Mirza G. Ahmad, *A brief Sketch of my life*, Lahore: *Ahmadiyya Anjuman Isha'at* Islam, 1996, p. 10.

43 Muhammad Ali, *The Ahmadiyyah Movement*, Lahore: *Ahmdiyyah Anjuman Isha'at Islam*, 1973, p. 1; A. R. Dard, *Life of Ahmad: Founder of the Ahmadiyya Movement*; Lahore: A Tabshir Publication, 1948; Mirza Nasir Ahmad, the *Review of Religions*, vol. 61 [1967]; Spencer Lavan, *The Ahmadiyya Movement, A History and Perspective*, Delhi: Manohar Bookservice, 1974, pp. 22.

ten miles away from the family home.[44] His father, wishing Ahmad
to enter the legal profession or the civil service [partly in an attempt
to get him to act as a legal representative to regain forfeited family es-
tates], secured for him a job as a court clerk in the civil administration
of the district of Sialkot, about 150 miles from Qadian, a position he
held from 1864-68.[45] Ahmad hated the work, mainly because he saw
his working colleagues as immoral and worldly. As he stated: 'I found
many of them to be the devil's brethren in arrogance, waywardness,
neglect of the religion and all kinds of other low morals'.[46] Apparently
a quiet, serious, scholarly young man, Ahmad, to the disappointment
of his father, retired to private quarters, spending much of his time
praying, reading the Quran and other holy books. As his son, Mirzaan
Ahmad, who was about twenty-five years of age at the time, states:
'He [Ahmad] had a copy of the Holy Quran which he was continually
reading and marking. I can say without exaggeration that he might
have read it ten thousand times'.[47] Troubled with constant ill health
[his biographers mention that he suffered from certain ailments: syn-
cope, polyuria, diabetes][48] Ahmad spent the rest of his life studying,
writing and debating. Concerning family life, at the age of seventeen
he married his cousin Hurmat Bibi and had two sons but the marriage
was not successful, ending in separation and divorce. In 1884 Ahmad
married again and had four sons and two daughters.

Following the death of his father in 1876 Ahmad claimed to receive visions and revelations. 'In short', he declared, 'about forty years
of my life were spent under the care of my revered father. Just as he
was taken from the world, I started receiving Divine revelations with
great intensity'.[49] Having commenced receiving revelations at roughly
the same age as the prophet Muhammad himself, Ahmad described

44 Muhammad Ali, *The Ahmadiyyah Movement* , op.cit., p. 1.

45 Ali, ibid., p. 1.

46 Mirza G. Ahmad, *A brief Sketch of my life*, op.cit., p. 13.

47 Cited by Muhammad Ali, *The Founder of the Ahmadiyya Movement*, Lahore: *Ahmadiyyah Anjuman Isha'at Islam*, (1937), 3rd edition 1984, p. 9.

48 Ali, ibid., p. 45.

49 Mirza, G. Ahmad, *A Brief Sketch of my Life*, op.cit., p. 17. 208 of these revelations were recorded in his book *Haqeeqatul Wahi*.

his experiences in similar terms to the revelations received by the Prophet. In these 'fine visions', as Ahmad calls them, he claimed to meet 'some of the prophets of the past and saints of high ranks who have passed in this *Ummah*'.[50] In one such vision, Ahmad claimed he was told to fast, which he did do for six months, taking only one meal after sunset. 'As a result of fasting', he stated, 'the wonders that were disclosed to me, were various forms and types of visions'.[51] He wrote in his biographical sketch how 'once, while fully awake, I saw the holy Prophet Muhammad ... along with Hasan, Hussain, [Muhammad's grandsons] and Ali [Muhammad's cousin and son-in-law]. God be pleased with him, and Fatima [the Prophet's daughter], God be pleased with her. This was not a dream', he declared, 'but a state of wakefulness. In short, in this manner', claimed Ahmad, 'I met many sanctified personages, an account of which would be lengthy'.[52] On one occasion, in words strikingly similar to words spoken by Jesus in the gospels, Ahmad declared: 'I am the light of this dark world, he who follows me will be saved from falling into the pit prepared by the Devil for those who walk in darkness'.[53] 'I have seen Jesus many a time in *Kashf* [vision in the waking state]', he asserted on another occasion, 'and I have met some of the prophets while fully awake. I have also seen our Chief, master and leader, the Prophet Muhammad many a time in the waking state, and I have talked to him – in such a clear state of waking that sleep or drowsiness had nothing to do with it. I have also met some of the dead at their graves or other places ... and have talked to them'. As well as the visions, Ahmad stated that 'spiritual illuminations appeared symbolically in the form of green and red pillars, so beautiful and captivating that it is impossible to describe them in words'.[54]

In order to understand Ahmad [his beliefs, teachings and claims] he must be seen within his historical context. India throughout the nineteenth century was subjected to aggressive, and successful,

---

50 Ahmad, *A Brief Sketch of my Life*, ibid., p. 18.

51 Ibid., p. 19.

52 Ali, *Founder of the Ahmadiyya Movement*, op.cit., p, 12.

53 Mirza G. Ahmad, *Jesus in India*, op.cit., p.19.

54 Mirza G. Ahmad, *A Brief Sketch of my Life*, op.cit., p. 19.

Christian missionary activity. The American Presbyterian Mission, for example, had established its headquarters at Ludhiana, near to Qadian, in 1834. By introducing new forms of religious organisations, printing of religious tracts, translating of Scriptures, grammars and dictionaries in Punjabi, Urdu, Persian, Hindi and Kashmiri, and the adoption of belligerent methods of evangelism, Christian missions quickly expanded throughout the Punjab and the North West Frontier.[55] Islam was also being attacked by Hinduism, particularly the *Arya Samaj* movement,[56] which carried out a vociferous preaching and printing campaign against the basic teachings of the Islamic faith. With large numbers of Muslims converting to Christianity, and many Muslim countries colonised by Western powers, it appeared as though Islam was in decline. It was of paramount importance for Muslim leaders generally, including Ahmad, to reject the claims of Christianity. Ahmad was particularly keen to refute the idea of the physical existence of Jesus in heaven. As explained in chapter one, Christian missionaries were using this doctrine to great effect in winning converts from Islam to Christianity. With cogent logic Christians argued that Jesus must have been divine, and superior to Muhammad, as Muhammad died a natural death, Jesus did not. According to traditional Islamic teaching, Jesus, after he had been taken up to heaven by Allah, possessed the same body he had had on earth, a body which did not need food, neither did it change. On the basis that Jesus' body had not undergone any change during the past two thousand years Christian missionaries argued with gusto that Jesus must have been different from all other human beings [even Muhammad] and a participant in the divine attributes. As one *Ahmadi* remarked 'to spread the light of Islam in Europe it was essential therefore to eradicate such false notions with regard to Jesus Christ; without this, Islam could not flourish in Christendom'.[57]

55 K. W. Jones, *Socio-religious Reform Movements in British India*, Cambridge: Cambridge University Press, 1989, p. 87.

56 *Arya Samaj* 'the noble society', Hindu reform movement emphasizing the infallibility of the Vedas; the ideals of chastity and renunciation, founded in India in 1875 by Swami Dayanda, see L. Rai *History of the Arya Samaj*, New Delhi: Munshiram Manohavid Publishers Ltd, 1993.

57 Muhammad Ali, *Founder of the Ahmadiyya Movement*, op.cit., p. 13.

Ahmad was one of many Muslim teachers at that time who wanted to see a revival of Islam. This had been the purpose of his life since his youth. He had spent years studying the Quran, and the books of other world faiths, particularly Christianity, so as 'to realise the great dream of his life—to establish the superiority of Islam over all other religions'.[58] One writer remarks that Ahmad, in reading comparative religions, had 'come to the conclusion that, while other religions contained only partial truth, Islam contained the whole truth, and was, on account of this superiority, destined to be the future religion of the world'.[59]

In order to show the superiority of Islam over all other faiths Ahmad published his *Barahin-i-Ahmadiyyah* ['the *Ahmadiyya* proofs'] over a four year period from 1880-1884. The culmination of years of study and analysis of the main arguments used by Christians and Hindus against Islam, the *Barahin-i* represented a major apologetic work, critically acclaimed by many Muslim scholars at the time. As one of Ahmad's biographers remarked: 'in this work the truth of the teachings of Islam was established by forceful arguments, and the objections against Islam by *Arya Samaj, Brahmo Samaj*[60] and Christians... were thoroughly dealt with and their basically wrong principles were powerfully refuted'.[61] However, although useful as a defence of Islamic doctrine, other aspects of the work caused a storm of controversy within the Muslim community. According to Muslim tradition, God would send a *Mujaddid,* or reformer, at the end of each century to bring the faithful back onto the right path. The Fourteenth *Mahdi* [the divinely guided one] was expected around the last decade of the nineteenth century. Other strands of Islamic eschatology talk of the appearance of the *Mahdi,* the *Messiah* and Jesus at the end of the age. Ahmad, to the anger of many Muslims, began to claim that such prophecies were fulfilled *in him.* Claiming to be

---

58 Ali, op.cit., p. 16.

59 Ibid., p. 2.

60 A religious movement founded by Raja Ram Mohan Roy in Calcutta in 1828. It taught the belief in one omniscient and omnipresent God, rejected idol worship and the caste system. See S. Parmananda, *The Brahmo Samaj Movement and its Leaders,* Delhi: Anmol Publications, 1989.

61 Ibid., p. 2.

the promised reformer for that age, he wrote: 'then, when the thir-teenth century came to a close and the fourteenth century was about to dawn, God the most high, informed me by revelation: you are the *Mujaddid* of this century'.[62] From that time Ahmad openly declared that he had been appointed as a reformer 'so that you may warn of bad consequences a people who fell in errors because of generations of neglect and lack of admonition, and so that manifest becomes the path of those culprits who do not want to accept the true path even after receiving the guidance'.[63] Shortly after the publication of *Barahin-i-Ahmadiyyah* Ahmad published a leaflet in which he an-nounced that 'the author has been given the knowledge that he is the *Mujaddid* of this time and that spiritually his excellences resemble those of the Messiah, the son of Mary, and one of them bears a very strong resemblance and a close affinity to the other'.[64] In 1890 Ahmad announced that it was disclosed to him that Jesus Christ was dead and the Messiah, whose return was promised to Muslims, would be a *Mujaddid* of India. In the following year Ahmad claimed that he was that promised Indian Messiah, and that 'he had come in the power and spirit of Jesus, and that his personality and character bore close resemblance to Jesus'.[65] In another pamphlet, *Fatahi Is-lam*, Ahmad, denouncing Christianity and Judaism as error, wrote: 'I have been sent in the name of the Messiah, so that the doctrine of the cross may be shattered to pieces. Therefore, I have been sent to break the cross and to kill the swine [reference to the Jews]'.[66] 'I have no hesitation', he stated, 'in affirming that I am the *Imam* of the age', the one 'who must, under Divine command, be obeyed by all'. He claimed to be *Masih-I mawud*, 'the promised messiah' and 'the *muhaddath* of God', a person who has the qualities of a prophet but

---

62 The Islamic 14th century began in 1883 AD. Ali, *The Ahmadiyya Movement*, op.cit., p. 21.

63 Ali, *The Ahmadiyya Movement*, ibid., p. 21.

64 *Ishtihar*, published in 1885, cited by M. Ali, ibid., p. 3.

65 Karimullah Zirvi, *Welcome to Ahmadiyyat: The true Islam*, op.cit., pp. 49-50.

66 Cited by M. Ali, *Founder*, op.cit., p. 33. Ahmad wrote several other books at that time in support of his claims. As well as *Fatahi-Islam* [victory of Islam] he wrote *Tauzihi-Maram* [explanation of objectives] and *Izalai-A`uham* [removal of suspicions].

is not necessarily appointed as one. Professing to be 'the light of this dark age',[67] Ahmad claimed to have received *ilham* [personal divine inspiration] and *wahy* [a message from God for all mankind]. In November 1904 Ahmad declared, not only was he *Mahdi* for Muslims, and *Messiah* for Christians, but that he was raised for Hindus as a manifestation of Krishna.[68] In 1894 lunar and solar eclipses occurred over the Punjab during the month of *Ramadan*, and in *Ramadan* in the following year, but in the West. Although such eclipses have occurred many times during *Ramadan*, the *Ahmadi*, in reference to a prediction in the *hadith* that such would occur as signs of the appearance of the promised *Messiah* and *Mahdi*, saw these as vindication of Ahmad's claims.

From the 1880's onwards, 'Ahmad blazed forth into an unprecedented whirl of public activity and wider publicity'.[69] With the publication of his numerous works, particularly the *Barahin-i-Ahmadiyyah*, and the public declaration of his divine calling, Ahmad, the recluse and ascetic, became a public speaker, entering debates with members of the *Arya Samaj*, Christian missionaries and members of the *ulema* [learned scholars within Islam]. In 1883 he offered to have a *mubahalah*, [a public debate], with Swami Dayananda, founder of the *Arya Samaj* and one of his most vocal critics. The *mubahalah* was a prayer and debating 'challenge' instituted by the prophet Muhammad in 632 AD, where each party would call immediate destruction upon themselves if they were proved to be liars. Muhammad had called the Christians of Najran to travel to Medina and debate the personality of Jesus. A place was fixed outside the city but, according to tradition, when the leader of the Christian delegation saw the prophet arrive with the members of his family, and with a portentous storm build-

---

67 M. Ali, *The Ahmadiyya Movement*, op.cit., p. 22. As discussed in detail in chapter six of this book the *Ahmadi*, eager to mollify other Muslims, stress that Ahmad was not *mustaqill*, an independent prophet bringing new law, but he was *zilli*, or a 'shadow', someone attaining prophet-hood by faithfully following one of their predecessors in the prophetic office. As such he is regarded as *ummati*, a prophet but a lesser prophet.

68 K. S. Mian Rahim Bakhsh, *The Debt Forgotten*, Columbus, Ohio, USA: *Ahmadiyya Anjuman Isha'at Islam*, 1993, p. 16.

69 Bakhsh, *The Debt Forgotten*, op.cit., p. 16.

ing up on the horizon, he called out to his followers 'to enter into full agreement with Muhammad', pay the *jazia'h* tax[70] and live under the protection of Islam.[71] Dayananda declined to accept the challenge. Ahmad, possibly piqued by the snub, predicted Dayananda's death. In a vision Ahmad claimed to see his critic dying in the near future, a prediction that was fulfilled later that year. Similar treatment was meted out in 1897 to Pandit Lekh Ram, another opponent of the *Ahmadi* and member of the *Arya Samaj*, who wrote numerous leaflets criticising the Islamic faith. As well as accusing Muhammad of immorality, Lekh Ram argued that Islam was discredited as a religion due to the aggressive *Jihad* manifested by that faith throughout its history. As with Dayananda, Ahmad predicted that Ram, refusing to enter into debate, would shortly die. As one *Ahmadi* writer informs us: 'the prophecy was proclaimed in a poster published on 20th February 1893, and it was couched in words of clear import to the effect that the said Lekh Ram would pay the penalty of his wickedness and would suffer a severe chastisement which would take place in a most extraordinary manner indicative of a bloody death within six years of the date of the issue of the poster'.[72] In March 1897 Lekh Ram was assassinated. Ahmad's biographer describes with an obvious sense of satisfaction how Lekh Ram:

had started the day muttering his prayers in the usual Hindi mode in a squatting posture with his body uncovered except for a loin-cloth. When he had finished his [prayers], he straightened himself in his position, thus exhibiting his bare abdomen to full view. It is related that just at that moment, a dagger flashed out from the hands of the would-be convert who was lying huddled up next to the *Pandit*. Like lightning, the knife plunged in the soft folds of the bulging belly up to the hilt, throwing out, instantaneously, the intestines, and the *Pandit* collapsed with a big yell resembling the bellow of a bull; he expired shortly afterwards in hospital under a surgical operation.[73]

---

70 poll tax paid by conquered peoples under Islam whereby they gained protection and escaped military service.

71 Al Tabari, commentary on Quran 2:192-193.

72 Bakhsh, *The Debt Forgotten*, op.cit., p. 52.

73 A. R. Dard, *Life of Ahmad: Founder of the Ahmadiyya Movement*, op.cit.

AHMADIYYAT AND ITS FOUNDER

Waheed Ahmad in his *Book of religious knowledge for Ahmadi Muslims*, declares triumphantly: 'the fulfilment of this prophecy was a great sign of the truth of the Promised Messiah'.[74] Although some suspected Ahmad's hand in the death of this pamphleteer, nothing could be proved.

Another incident of *mubahalah*, and predictions of an opponent's death, occurred in the case of John Alexander Dowie. Born in Edinburgh, Scotland, Dowie had been ordained in South Australia as a Congregational minister, before going to America where he established the 'Christian Catholic Apostolic Church' near Chicago in 1896. The *Ahmadi*, in their literature like to describe Dowie as 'an outstanding Christian missionary'.[75] The image is portrayed of a leading Christian preacher and thinker, 'a great theologian', refuted by the arguments of the *Ahmadi* founder. When talking with officials at the *Ahmadi* headquarters at Rabwah, Pakistan, they quoted with alacrity the example of Dowie, 'a very great Christian man'. Crest-fallen and deflated they expressed surprise when I genuinely told them: 'I've never heard of the man, who was he?'. Later research revealed to me that Dowie, an obscure, little-known eccentric, as well as being hostile to Islam, claimed to be a prophet, 'Elijah the restorer'. In 1902 Ahmad, on reading the criticisms of Islam published by Dowie in his newspaper *Leaves of Healing*, invited him to meet for *mubahalah*. Many American newspapers at the time, getting wind of an apparently sensational story, advertised the forthcoming contest between a little-known maverick Nonconformist and the founder of a Muslim sect, both men being presented as eccentrics. Ahmad predicted that Dowie would be 'consumed with the wrath of God, and die in the life-time of the promised Messiah'. He added, 'if Dowie should slink away from this spiritual strife, even then a calamity shall crush upon him'.[76] Dowie, treating his antagonist with contempt, wrote in his paper:

74 W. Ahmad, *A Book of Religious Knowledge for Ahmadi Muslims*, Athens, Ohio, USA: Fazl-i-Umar Press, 1988, p. 208.

75 Bakhsh, *The Debt Forgotten*, op.cit., p. 51.

76 *Barahin-i-Ahmadiyyah*, vol. V, cited by Bakhshs,. op.cit, p. 59.

There is in India a stupid Muslim Messiah who writes to me oft and oft again that the tomb of Jesus the Christ is in Kashmir. People inquire of me why I do not send him a reply. But do you think I should answer these gnats and flies on whom if I were to stamp my foot I would crush them to death and destruction!

The following year Ahmad reissued the challenge, but Dowie ignored it. Ahmad claimed to receive further revelations about this affair in which God told him 'thou shalt predominate and prevail'. He was told: 'unto thee should be given another happy sign by means whereof a glorious triumph shall be thine'. With much satisfaction the *Ahmadi* inform us how Dowie's followers turned against him and how 'he was struck with a dire disease and lost all movement of his limbs'. Stricken by palsy 'his senses too left him and he ultimately became stark mad'.[77] We are told how Dowie, rising to speak to a congregation 'was struck with paralysis, and except for some idiotic and incoherent mutterings from his transformed being, nothing could be heard'. Following this so-called 'great sign from God', Dowie died in 1907, an event seen by the *Ahmadi* as further vindication of the founder of their movement. However, some of Ahmad's opponents, despite predictions being made about their deaths, did not die as he had announced. In a debate in May 1893 Ahmad had said that Abd Allah Atham, a Muslim convert to Christianity, 'would be thrown into Hell within 15 months'. Atham eventually died in July 1896. Ahmad, obviously embarrassed by the failure of the prediction wrote several pamphlets trying to re-interpret his prediction in such a way to fit the circumstances of Atham's death.

Ahmad was credited with making other predictions of a less sinister nature. His followers claim that in 1905 he fore-told the occurrence of the First World War nine years later. 'God's wrath will manifest itself in the form of a calamity over mankind', Ahmad declared, 'in a moment, the entire world will be turned upside down, and streams of blood shall flow as profusely as the water of the rivers... the running waters of the mountains shall turn red with the blood of the corpses like the red wine. All the *jinn* and men will be shaken with the terror

---

77 Muhammad Ali, *The Ahmadiyya Movement*, op.cit., p. 4.

of it'.[78] Ahmad, in another prophecy, stated that the people of Bengal 'shall be conciliated', words taken by the *Ahmadi* as a prediction of the unification of Bengal in 1911 following the partition of that area into three provinces six years earlier. In 1905 Ahmad claimed a further revelation in which he received the phrase 'Oh! Where is Nadir Shah gone!', words understood as a reference to a future ruler of Afghanistan, who would assume that name. Similarly the statement 'the Turks shall be defeated in the land near by, but after their defeat they shall defeat their foes', was seen as a prediction concerning the collapse of the Turkish Empire while the words 'the Most High God shall manifest His glory unto the mountain and crush it to pieces; all this He shall do for the sake of his slave', was perceived as a prediction of the Great Kangra Earthquake of 1905.

With the contemporary *ulema* rejecting his claims, issuing a *fatwa* denouncing him as *kafir*, and with only a small group of followers, Ahmad experienced periods of doubt and depression. In 1894, in his book *Noorul Haq* [light of truth], Ahmad revealed something of the frustration and disappointment he felt at that time. 'Oh God! Am I not from thee?' he pleaded. 'Curse and denial have now become excessive. Judge between us and our people with justice for thou art the best of those who judge'. In earnest he cried out: 'O God! Please send thy succour for me from the heaven and help thy servant in the time of diversity'. 'I have become like the weak and disgraced', he lamented, 'and people have rejected me and reproached me'.

Despite such occasional feelings of self doubt, Ahmad was convinced that he had been called of God to revive Islam. In 1886, after having spent forty days in *'Chilla'* [spiritual retreat] at the town of Hoshiarpur, he claimed to receive further revelations which led to the announcement of his divine mission three years later. In December 1888 Ahmad announced that God had commanded him to form a *Jama'at*, an organisation, 'to defend and extend the cause of Islam and to place the service of Islam above all considerations'.[79] On 23 March 1889 at Ludhiana the *Ahmadiyya Jama'at* was officially formed when forty-one followers took *bai'at*, a pledge of allegiance

---

78 Bakhsh, *The Debt Forgotten*, op.cit., p. 55-6.
79 Cited by Bakhsh, ibid., p. 57.

to Ahmad. The first official gathering of *Ahmadis* took place almost three years later, at Qadian, on 27 December 1891. It was at this assembly that Ahmad announced that there would be a Conference at Qadian every year. At the second Conference, attended by 500 followers, the foundations of the world-wide *Ahmadiyya* movement were established. The movement's first missionary, Sayyed Muhammad Ahsan, was financed and the decision was made to establish a printing press at Qadian where a school was also later founded. The movement established its weekly newspaper, *Al Hakam* in Urdu in 1897, followed by *al-Badr* three years later. In 1902, in an attempt to share and propagate ideas with people all over the world, Ahmad started a new magazine, *The Review of Religions*, 'to draw the world to truth - to teach true morals, to inculcate true beliefs, to disseminate true beliefs and, last though not least, to make men act upon the principles of truth ordained'.[80] This periodical has remained the literary standard bearer of the movement to this day.

Aware of a contest of leadership that could arise after his death, Ahmad, in 1906, organised the *Sadr Anjuman-i-Ahmadiyyah* [Central *Ahmadiyya* Association] to serve as an executive body until his death, when it would choose his successor. In April 1908 Ahmad fell ill with an attack of diarrhoea while visiting Lahore. He died on 26 May 1908 and was buried at Qadian. While some saw him as a false prophet, others regarded him as an exceptional teacher, manifesting unique qualities and gifts. The London *Times*, for example, in an obituary, noted his piety, stating that he was 'venerable in appearance, magnetic in personality and active in intellect'.[81] Certain mainstream Muslim writers, in an attempt to malign him have suggested that Ahmad 'died in the toilet in 1326 AH', or died of cholera, an ailment inflicted upon him by God due to the falsehood of his claims.[82] *Ahmadi*, obviously rejecting such an idea as 'totally false', maintain their founder died of neurasthenia, mental fatigue

---

80 Editorial, first edition of *The Review of Religions*, (July 1902).
81 Obituary cited by Iain Adamson, *Ahmad the Guided One: A Life of the Holy Founder of the Movement to Unite All Religions*, Islamabad: Islamic International Publications Ltd, 1996, p. 339.
82 S. P.Tayo, *Facts About the Ahmadiyya Movement*, op.cit., 1979, p. 43.

and diarrhoea, brought about by overwork.[83] By the time of his death Ahmad had an estimated 400,000 followers in India.

---

83 Hafiz S. Muhammad, *True Facts About the Ahmadiyya Movement*, Lahore: n.d., p. 49.

3
THE HISTORY OF THE
AHMADIYYA JAMA'AT

All religious groups inevitably face internal dissension, giving rise to denominational blood-letting and schism. Such was the case in Christianity with the initial divisions between the followers of Peter, Paul or James and then the later splits: the controversy of 1054 and the split between the Roman Catholic and the Orthodox Church; the Reformation of the 16th century and the formation of Protestantism; the Clarendon Code of 1662-1665, a series of harsh anti-Puritan laws enacted during the reign of Charles II demanding conformity to the Established Church which, instead of stamping out religious Dissent in England, encouraged the different strands of Nonconformity to grow, giving rise to the numerous sub-divisions that characterize the Christian faith today. Mention has already been made of the numerous traditions which make up contemporary Islam, the division of *Sunni* and *Shia* and the seventy-three different groups that regard themselves as *Sunni*. With regard to such internal disputes the *Ahmadiyya Jama'at* has been no exception. Although not manifesting the internecine hatred shown by rival groups in the different world faiths, from its earliest days the *Ahmadiyya Jama'at* experienced internal conflicts, resulting in the division of two groups: the Lahori *Ahmadi* and those associated with Qadian.

As indicated earlier, Mirza Ghulam Ahmad, shortly before his death in 1908, suggested the idea of an *Anjuman* [a collective body of the senior members of the movement] under the name of *Sadr Anjuman-i-Ahmadiyyah,* to administer the newly formed *Ahmadi* movement.[1] As Ahmad stated: 'the decision of this *Anjuman* in all matters shall be final'.[2] The *Anjuman* was therefore established 'with the fullest powers in all affairs relating to the movement'. It was to be, as Ahmad remarked, 'the successor of the divinely appointed *Khalifa*'.[3] On the death of Ahmad, Noor-ud-Din, recognised by the *Ahmadi* as Ahmad's 'most favourite companion' and 'the first to enter into *bai'at*[4] to him' became *Khalifat al-masih-I anwal*, 'the first successor of the Messiah' and leader of the movement.[5] When Noor-ud-Din died in 1914, after only six short years in office, Mirza Basheer-ud-Din Mahmood Ahmad, Ahmad's son, was chosen as the second *Khalifa* and later declared to be *Hadhrat Musleh Ma'ud* [the promised reformer]. However, not all *Ahmadi* were happy with Basheer-ud-Din's appointment, title or authority. The group that later became known as the Lahori *Ahmadi*, argued that the *Anjuman* and not an individual person, was to be Ahmad's successor, and opposed the idea of appointing a *Khalifa*. They accused the Qadiani *Ahmadi* of *gaddi*, the succession of the sons and posterity of a saint succeeding him on a hereditary basis. Critics within and without the movement argued that a dynasty was being created, a claim apparently supported by later appointments to the *Khalifate*. The third *Khalifa*, *Hadhrat* Mirza Nasr Ahmad [*Khalifa* from 1965-1982] for example, was Ahmad's grandson; the fourth *Khalifa*, *Hadrat* Mirza Tahir Ahmad [*Khalifa* from 1982-2003] was also a grandson of Ahmad while the present *Khalifa*, Mirza Masroor Ahmad, is Ahmad's great grandson.

Emphasising how Ahmad, in *Al-wasiyyah* [his official will], had appointed the *Anjuman* to be his successor, and wanting to do away

1   Nisar A. Faruqui, *Ahmadiyyat: In the Service of Islam*, Lahore: *Ahmadiyya Anjuman Isha'at Islam*, 1983, p. 29.
2   *Al-Wasiyyah*, 'The Will', cited by Muhammad Ali, *The Ahmadiyya Movement*, trans. S. M. Tufail, Lahore: *Ahmadiyyah Anjuman Isha'at Islam*, 1973, p. 30.
3   Al-Wasiyyah, in Ali, *The Ahmadiyya Movement*, op.cit., p. 32.
4   Oath of allegiance, the formal rite of initiation and allegiance into *Ahmadiyyat*.
5   Karimullah Zirvi, *Welcome to Ahmadiyyat: The True Islam*, Silver Springs, USA: *Ahmadiyya Movement in Islam*, 2002, p. 305.

with the idea of a *Khalifate* that demanded total obedience from its members, a section of the *Ahmadiyya* movement, led by *Maulvi* Muhammad Ali and Khawaja Kamal ul-Din, [two companions of Mirza Ghulam Ahmad] broke away, forming the *Ahmadiyya Anjuman Isha'at-i-Islam Lahore*, or the Lahore *Ahmadiyya Association for the Propagation of Islam*.[6] With its motto: 'Allah is with us', [words of comfort uttered by Muhammad to Abu Bakr, the companion of the prophet who became the leader of the Islamic community in 632 AD], this group is also known as the Lahori *Ahmadi* because it left Qadian and established its headquarters at Lahore in Pakistan.

As well as the issue of succession, there were two other main reasons for this split within the *Ahmadi* movement. One of these issues concerned the status of Ahmad. The Lahori *Ahmadi* agree with the Qadiani group that the founder of the movement was a *Mujaddid* [reformer], and the promised *Messiah* and *Mahdi*, but reject the idea that he was a prophet. They regard Ahmad as *muhaddath*, someone who, although having the qualities of a prophet, is not actually appointed to prophet-hood.[7] He is, in the opinion of the Lahori group, a great *wali* [saint] who made prophesies, and to whom Allah speaks. In contrast to what they see as an error of the Qadiani, the Lahori are adamant that Ahmad never claimed to be a prophet and that he 'never changed his claim, views or definition of prophet-hood'. As such the Lahori group, similar to mainstream Muslims, emphasise their belief in Muhammad as 'the greatest and the last of all prophets', and how 'no prophet, whether new or old, shall come after' the prophet of Mecca.[8] It is maintained that *wahy-e-risalat* [the revelation given to a messenger of Allah] began with Adam and ended with Muhammad.[9] The Lahoris believe that *wahi-e-nabuwwat* [prophetic revelation] has ended, but *wahi-e-walayat* [saintly revelation] as experienced by Ahmad continues. As discussed in chapter six, the

---

6   See Faruqui, *Ahmadiyyat: In the Service of Islam*, op.cit., p. 29.

7   Karimullah Zirvi, *Welcome to Ahmadiyyat*, ibid., p. 308.

8   Hafiz S. Muhammad, *True Facts about the Ahmadiyya Movement*, Lahore: *Ahmadiyya Anjuman Ishaat-i-Islam*, nd, inside front cover.

9   Statement made by Ahmad on 2 October 1892, in the Jamia Masjid, Delhi, cited by Nisar A. Faruqui, *Ahmadiyyat: In the Service of Islam*, op.cit., p. viii.

Qadiani *Ahmadi* argue that Muhammad, although the greatest, was not the last of the prophets, and Ahmad was another prophet, albeit a lesser one.

The third main point of division between the two *Ahmadi* groups relates to the way other Muslims, who refuse to accept the claims of Ahmad, should be viewed. Mirza Basheer-ud-Din Mahmaud Ahmad, the second *Khalifa*, stated that *Ahmadis* should regard Muslims who are outside the *Ahmadiyya* Movement as being non-Muslim, and outside the fold of Islam.[10] The Lahori *Ahmadi*, strongly objecting to this view, believe that anyone who recites the *kalmia shahada* [profession of faith] must be regarded as a Muslim. They regard as fundamental 'that every professor of the *kalimah* [there is but one God, Muhammad is His Messenger] was a Muslim though he might belong to any sect of Islam, and nobody went outside the pale of Islam unless he denied himself the Messengership of Muhammad'. Ahmad's views on this matter were contradictory giving rise to confusion amongst his followers. In one passage he states how 'it has been my belief since the beginning that nobody can become an infidel or *dajjal* [the deceiver, the anti-Messiah] by denying my claim', while in another context Ahmad wrote 'he who denies this mission will be declared infidel'.[11]

Despite official protestations to the contrary, as indicated above, there is little love lost between the two groups. As Muhammad Ali stated in 1931, 'the *Ahmadiyya Anjuman Ishaat-i-Islam*, Lahore, have kept on fighting with the Qadianis for over twenty years about [the] doctrine of the continuance of prophet-hood and its unavoidable result that all those Muslims who do not believe in the new revelation are *kafirs*'.[12] A constant struggle for legitimacy has existed between the two *Ahmadi* factions. Keen to distance themselves from the main Qadian group, and escape the persecution facing *Ahmadi* in Pakistan, the Lahori *Ahmadi* emphatically declare on their official

---

10 Hafiz S. Muhammad, *True Facts*, op.cit. Also Ali, *Anjuman Isha'at Islam*, Lahore, 1973, p. 25.

11 Yohanan Friedmann, *Prophecy Continuous: Aspects of Ahmadi Religious Thought and its Medieval Background*, Berkeley: University of California Press, 1989, p. 156.

12 Muhammad Ali, *The Ahmadiyya Movement*, op.cit., p. 349.

website: 'This is not a Qadiani website: we believe that no prophet can come after [the] Holy Prophet Muhammad'.[13]

The rivalry between the two groups is clearly seen in the publication by both Lahori and Qadiani of various apologetic works. For instance the Lahori *Ahmadi* published a book, *Truth Triumphs* by Al-Hajj Mumtaz Ahmad Faruqi which, in the opinion of the Qadiani *Ahmadi* made 'dirty personal attacks on *Hadhrat* Khalifatul Masih II, Muslih Maud, which embody a shocking violation of the Islamic sense of decency and morals'.[14] In response to what they perceived to be the 'foul mouth, and shameless, abusive language' of the Lahori, the Qadiani published a work of their own, *Truth Prevails*, putting forward a defence of the *Khalifate* and other beliefs.[15] When I was leaving Qadian to journey to the Wagah border to spend my last few days with the Lahori *Ahmadi* at Lahore my companions handed me several pieces of literature, including *Truth Prevails*, and was told to study it and ask my hosts for answers to the queries raised. A similar attitude of combative defiance was evident with the Lahori *Ahmadi*, some of the elderly members in particular, lachrymose and agitated, talking with me before my departure to Qadian, priming me with objections to raise about Ahmad and prophet-hood.

In 1984 the Government in Pakistan enacted the anti-*Ahmadiyya* legislation which made the *Ahmadi* a non-Muslim group. The Lahori *Ahmadi* had to change its name from *Isha'at-i-Islam Lahore [Ahmadiyya Association for the propagation of Islam]* to *Ahmadiyya Anjuman Lahore*. Elsewhere in the world they continue to use the original name. Like the Qadiani group the Lahori are well organised, having an efficient administrative hierarchical structure. Rejecting the idea of *Khalifate* in terms of absolute authority the Lahori *Ahmadi* appoint an *Amir* or President, elected for life, as their spiritual and administrative head. Ultimate authority however rests with the *Ma-*

---

13 See www.muslim.org. I am indebted to Dr Zahid Aziz of the Lahori *Ahmadi*, England, for his constructive advice in writing up this section.

14 The words of the manager of Nazarat Ishaat-i-literature-wa-tasnif, frontispage of Qazi M. Nazir, *Truth Prevails*, Rabwah: *Nazir Isha'at Literature–wa-Tasnif*, 1966.

15 Qazi, M. Nazir, *Truth Prevails*, Rabwah: *Nazarat Isha'at Literature–wa-Tasnif*, 1966.

jlis-i-Moatemideen, the 'General Council of Trustees', a body elected by members in Pakistan, consisting of fifty members, forty of whom are elected by the subordinate *Anjumans* and ten nominated by another council. The members of the *Majlis-i-Moatemideen* can sit on the council for three years. Routine daily activities are organised by the *Majlis-i-Muntazimma* or Managing Committee. This committee, set up by the General Council, is made up of twenty members including the President, General Secretary and the Financial Secretary. All issues and proposals are routed to the *Majlis-i-Moatemideen* through the *Majlis-i-Muntazimma*. Two other Committees have been formed to help the General Council with specific tasks; the Foreign Missions Committee and the Finance Committee. The entire *Jama'at* forms the *Ahmadiyya Majlis-i-Aamah* or *Ahmadiyya* Conference. This is normally convened during the Annual *Dua-iyya* [gathering for prayers] to consider any matter that may be placed before it by the *Majlis-i-Moatemideen*. Any decision to appoint or remove an *Amir* has to be ratified by the *Majlis-i-Aamah*.[16] The Chairman of the *Jama'at*, who resides for life, is always the *Amir*.

The Lahori group has always remained a very small community, possibly only 30,000 members worldwide.[17] 'Thirty seven years have passed since the day we started our work here in Lahore', remarked a leading Lahori *Ahmadi* in 1952, 'but it is discouraging to note that, so far, we have failed to emerge out of the four walls, hemming us in'.[18] The same sentiment is expressed by the Lahori *Ahmadi* today. It was suggested in 1952 that the reasons for such lack of growth by the group 'lies in the fact that our centre does not hold any attraction. We have before us a number of young men whose fathers or grandfathers were ardent members of the movement: but that spirit and ardour seems to have flown out of their own hearts'.[19] The General Secretary of the movement in 1968 expressed similar disappointment when

16 Information mainly gained from leaflets provided by the movement.
17 It has proven difficult to obtain official membership figures for the movement. The figure of 30,000 members was given to me unofficially by several members.
18 Address by Al-Hajj Sheikh Mian Muhammad, published in *Paigham-i-Sulha*, (6 February, 1952), p. 7.
19 *Paigham-i-Sulha*, op.cit, p. 7.

he stated how 'the great expectations we had fondly entertained in regard to our own peoples ... [that] they would gladly come forward, eager to join hands with us, in these great works, have all proved to be the merest moonshine'.[20]

The Lahori *Ahmadi*, although much smaller than the Qadiani group, and gaining few converts to its cause, had missions around the world from the earliest days of its formation. By 1922 groups had been established in London, Berlin and Trinidad. Two years later the Java Muslim Mission was established, with a similar group in Thailand in 1930. A significant Lahori presence has been established in Nigeria since 1962.[21] As Muhammad Ali, head of the *Ahmadiyya Anjuman Isha'at Islam* during its early days and internationally respected writer, remarked: 'similarly independent and semi-independent Islamic missions run by members of the Lahore section of the *Ahmadiyya* movement are working in Indonesia, Guyana, Surinam, Holland, and the United States of America, Burma, Formosa and Ghana'.[22]

In May 2004 I spent several days visiting the Lahori *Ahmadi* community, Darus Salaam, New Garden Town, Lahore. My flight with Emirates Airlines had gone to Lahore via the United Arab Emirates with a fifteen hour delay at Dubai. I had booked into a hotel and slept for several hours before walking round the streets, viewing the splendour of a modern city, high rise buildings, all concrete, steel and glass. The flight from Dubai to Lahore arrived at 3 am. My hosts had done everything possible to meet my every need. In organising the trip I had liaised with Dr Zahid Aziz, one of the leaders of the Lahori movement in the UK. I had emailed him asking: 'concerning the Lahori *Ahmadi, insh'Allah,* my flight arrives at Lahore at 2 a.m. on... Please could you give me directions how to get to your headquarters? It would be a real blessing to immediately get a few hours

---

20 *Report of the 52ⁿᵈ Annual Meeting of the Ahmadiyyah Anjuman Isha'at-i-Islam,* Lahore: *Ahmadsiyyah Anjuman Isha'at-i-Islam,* p. 5.

21 See Muhammad Ali, *The Ahmadiyya Movement,* op.cit., pp. 318ff.

22 M. Ali, ibid., p. 325. For a concise discussion of the work of the *Ahmadi* in America see Yvonne Haddad (et.al), 'Mission to America: Five Islamic Sectarian Communities in North America', *International Journal of Middle East Studies,* vol., 27, (February 1995), pp. 93-7.

sleep on arrival as I will have missed out on a lot of sleep due to a delay at Dubai. With your permission I would then like to stay with your people, meeting with your leaders on that Monday, all the next day [possibly with some time to see some of the sites in Lahore] then travel to Rabwah on the...'. In another email I made other requests to Dr Aziz, stating: 'For the past two years in Bradford I have been an "observer" at many of the activities at the *Ahmadi* mosque, even the *khutba* and Friday prayers, quietly sitting at the back of the hall. Would it be possible to join you in such activities at Lahore and meet yourself and the other leaders of the group?' Dr Aziz had previously supplied me with several publications relating to the *Ahmadi* movement. He had invited me on several occasions to visit his home in Nottingham to talk about religion, an invitation I had to decline due to personal circumstances. When I arrived in Lahore I was grateful for the meticulous and conscientious way he had organised my trip fulfilling every detail of my requests. Despite the flight from Dubai arriving so early in the morning, I was met at the airport by Professor Aziz Ahmad, the General Secretary of the *Ahmadiyya Anjuman Lahore*. We travelled from the airport into Lahore through empty, ghost-like streets. Although night, the heat was oppressive. We arrived at the main gate to the settlement. A uniformed, armed guard, checked us out and opened the gate. I was taken to Brigadier Sayyid's house and, after receiving the warmest of welcomes and refreshments, led to a first floor bedroom; spacious, clean with a large ceiling fan stirring the murky air. I unpacked quickly, undressed, lay on the bed and fell into a deep restful sleep.

A few hours later, and after enjoying the hospitality of Brigadier Mohammad Sayyid and his family over breakfast, the day's itinerary began. I met with the *Amir*—the present Head of the Lahori group, Professor Abdul Karim Saeed—and officials of the Central *Anjuman*. I was given a briefing about the Lahori *Ahmadi* and taken on a walk around the settlement. Darus Salaam is situated on sixteen and a half acres of land, 60% of which is covered by residential blocks, 20% used for offices, a library, mosque and graveyard while a further 20% is used as roads and parks. I was told that about sixty families lived on the site of which 95% are *Ahmadi*. Previously the headquarters had been situated on Brandreth Road, a site near to the old historical centre of

Lahore. In the early '60s the *Anjuman* purchased twenty four acres of land, the present site at New Garden Town, outside the limits of the Municipal Corporation of Lahore which was taken over by the Lahore Development Authority at that time. The Lahori are a peaceful people, genuinely hospitable and welcoming, people who simply want to live at peace with God and their neighbours. Oppressed and anxious, they live as strangers in their own country, a minority sect, surrounded by apathy, indifference, and often, open hostility. Little known, marginalized and persecuted, the Lahori [like the Qadiani *Ahmadi*] are desperate to be recognised by the international community. During that visit I saw eyes searching for acceptance. Hands reaching out in genuine friendship. Believing themselves to be the guardians of truth, they try to live in such a way that others will be attracted to *that* truth. They live so that the shunned prose of their lives may be seen as significant, transcendent poetry.

That afternoon, the official schedule fulfilled, I was taken by two of the young men of the settlement, Usman, an Accountant, and his friend Mudassar, for a drive around Lahore. 'Where would you like to go?', asked Usman. I will never forget his genuine air of amiability and helpfulness. At my suggestion we visited the seventeenth century Badshahi Mosque, allegedly one of the largest mosques in the world capable of accommodating over 60,000 worshippers, the last great flowering of Mughal architecture, and the less grand, yet equally fascinating Wazir Khan Mosque. In the evening, on our return to Darus Salaam, I met with the men in the mosque to observe *Maghrib* prayers; prayers performed just after sunset. The hospitality, endless and genuine, was fully appreciated. After a lengthy time of *salaaming*, talking and sharing, I was taken to the celebrated Punjab Club where I was fed and entertained. The next day I experienced the same warmth and generosity. I met with anyone who was anybody in the movement in the Library Conference room. For almost two hours, I explained why I had come all the way from England to observe the *Ahmadi*. I spoke of the book, the need to present 'real Islam', the need to move away from media stereotypes and, the need to let the world know of the persecution faced by the *Ahmadi* at the hands of their co-religionists. I asked about the *Jama'at*, about persecution, about the differences between the Lahori and the Qadiani. My questions were answered honestly and fully.

Following the Conference with the leaders, and having eaten, I was invited to meet privately with Professor Abdul Karim Saeed, the *Amir,* a man of genuine humility, and piety. We spoke for sometime, he, the leader of a worldwide Islamic reform group and I, a Christian, a lecturer and writer, two men from different worlds and cultures, yet both *talib,* seekers after truth. It was hot outside [I was told it was over 40% Celsius] yet his office, blessed by an effective overhead fan, was cool and pleasant. We spoke together, relaxed and informal, as though we had been friends for many years. I felt an instant rapport with him, not only because of our mutual interest in religion, but he was a consultant in the treatment of diabetes and I was a type 1 insulin dependent diabetic. He told me about *Ahmadi* belief and teaching, the differences between Lahori and 'our brothers at Rabwah'. We looked at photographs of his preaching tours in different parts of Africa and Asia. He shared with me his concerns for the world, for Pakistan and for Islam. We read some of his poetry, verses composed in the furnace of affliction, words expressing something of the loneliness and frustration felt by the *Ahmadi.* 'This sleeping Nation' of Pakistan, he wrote,

Why have you forgotten the glory of yester-years?
Why this slumber? When will you open your eyes?

In another poem, he expressed his sorrow, and anger, at those [apparently the religious leaders] who 'declare the day to be night, they insist on it with all their might, till everyone agrees they are right'. In a poem entitled 'Precious stones', he describes the pain of persecution of *Ahmadi* by fellow Muslims: 'My heart is filled with sorrow, but I will try not to weep'. 'I hold my tears in a heavy heart' he writes, 'of a *kalmia* that once graced a mosque. These precious stones are a part'.[23] Elsewhere, he wrote of the pleasure to see 'a dew drop at dawn', to 'touch the drops of rain', to see 'the breeze tease

---

23 'Precious stones', unpublished poem written on 2 May 1989 by Abdul Karim Saeed describing the destruction of the *Ahmadi mosque* at Abbottabad by a Muslim mob.

the dancing crop as they sway in the nearby field'.[24] But as the poem progresses his 'poetic thoughts suddenly stop' as he realises:

I see so much, why not GOD,
Who says, 'He is so very *near*'.
As I ponder in my thoughts,
A voice from within I *hear*.

And in a series of exclamations he declares that God can be seen, that those who seek him will ...

See Him in the stars and the moon,
See Him in a sea wave and a desert dune,
See Him in the cool breeze, the raging storm,
See Him in the rainbow and butterfly wings,
See Him in a child's laughter and mother's love,
See Him in the lion's roar bird [sic] when it sings,
See Him in the eagle that is soaring high,
See Him in the blueness of the morning sky.

Almost intoxicated with the realisation that the sovereign God is revealed in the world around us he concludes:

I suddenly see Him all around me,
He is everywhere, He's in every nook,
He is far, yet near; He's out, yet within,
He's not only in heaven, but wherever I look.

On reading these lines my mind recollected the words of the psalmist: 'the heavens declare the glory of God, the skies proclaim the work of his hands'.[25] The *Amir* and the lecturer, a Muslim and a Christian, united by shared values, by a struggle to understand something of the transcendence and immanence of God, a desire to find truth and a willingness to respect the view of the other.

That afternoon Usman and Mudassar again took me to the places that I wanted to see in Lahore. We visited the Lahore Fort, and the *Moti Masjid*, the 'pearl mosque' with its numerous gardens and pavilions, built by Jahangir the famous Moghul emperor in the seventeenth century. That evening, having met with the men for *Isha*

---

24 'I Suddenly See Him', unpublished poem by Abdul Karim Saeed, 1 November 1999, at Lahore.
25 See Psalm 19:1.

prayers, [those performed during the hours of darkness] a special dinner had been arranged outdoors in my honour, during which speeches were made and [to my great surprise and delight] I was presented with an Afghan carpet.

On the third day of my tour, representatives of the Qadiani group arrived at the settlement to drive me the hundred miles or so down through the Punjab to their headquarters at Rabwah. It was interesting to see how the Qadiani and Lahori *Ahmadi* reacted towards each other. Although not *salaaming*, they were civil and courteous, but reserved. After a week at Rabwah, Qadian and Srinigar, enjoying the hospitality of the Qadiani *Ahmadi*, I returned to Pakistan via the Wagah border. I expected some delay and questioning at the border, particularly on the Pakistani side as I was carrying some *Ahmadi* literature in my case. To my surprise, and some exasperation, I found that I was delayed by the Indian officials not those of Pakistan. I was asked if I had anything to declare. Just in case I was asked to empty my luggage, and the literature was found, I thought honesty to be the best policy. I stated that I carried a number of books on religion. A middle aged Hindu woman, officious and proud, asked me what kind of books I had. I said I had several leaflets and pamphlets on Islam. With the air of an administrator who knows full well she held all the cards in her hand, she asked to see the books. Perspiring in the heat, and not looking forward to the possible bureaucratic furore that could arise over *Ahmadi* literature, I slowly began to carefully unpack my luggage until I reached the pile of papers lying at the bottom of my bag. With a smile I passed the items over to the official. She looked at one of the booklets and, on seeing the word '*Ahmadiyya*' in the title of the book, expressed some concern. I was kept waiting for over an hour. By this time I had had enough. I was tired, it was very hot, and I felt uncomfortable about the fact that someone [one of the Lahori *Ahmadi*] was waiting patiently for me just a hundred yards away on the Pakistan side of the border. Raising my voice I asked what the problem was. The woman, apparently enjoying her moment of absolute control and authority, told me all the literature had to be read. With a tone of suppressed anger I reminded her that this would take many hours and the idea was totally unreasonable. I demanded to see a superior officer. Her face dropped. Reluctantly she went into a room on the other side of the hall reappearing a few minutes later with a man, who, by his uniform, was a high ranking official. He asked me what the problem was and, on being told, turned to the woman, spoke to her in Gujurati, Hindi or some other Indian tongue in what seemed to be a disapproving manner, and waved me on my way. Following this inconvenience at the border crossing I spent two more days with the Lahori *Ahmadi* before my flight back to the United Kingdom. During those last two nights I again enjoyed the genuine hospitality of the Lahori *Ahmadi*, staying in the house of Mian Fazl-e-Ahmad, a retired business man, a producer of textiles. His house, large, palatial, resonating with success, was perpetually guarded by paid security men armed with automatic weapons. In our conversations, during my last few precious hours with the Lahori *Ahmadi*, he told me of the threats that had been made on his life because of his faith. Like so many *Ahmadi* he was a target for any individual encouraged by hostile local *Mullahs* to persecute the alleged apostates.

Among the many traditions of Islam there is a saying ascribed to Muhammad in which he announced: 'the [last] hour shall not come till the sun rises from the places of its setting [the west]'.[26] Ahmad saw this *hadith* as a prediction of the ultimate triumph of Islam in the West. 'It has been disclosed in a vision to me', he declared, 'that what is meant by the Sun shall rise from the West is that the countries in the West, which in the past have suffered from the dark ages of disbelief and misguidance, shall be illumined with the Sun of Truth and shall be granted a share of the Faith'.[27]

In the vision, [declared Ahmad,] I saw myself standing on a pulpit in the city of London and delivering in the English language a well-reasoned discourse revealing religious truths. Then I caught many birds sitting on small trees. They were white in colour and their bodies were somewhat similar to those of partridges. From this I interpreted that although not me personally

---

26 Muslim, *Kitab ul Imam*, n.d.

27 Mirza G. Ahmad, *Izala Aoham, Roohani Khazain*, vol. 3, pp. 376-77, cited by Aziz A. Chaudhry, *The Promised Messiah and Mahdi*, Islamabad: Islam International Publications, 1996, p 178.

but my writings will spread among them and many sincere Englishmen will join the true religion.[28]

Believing that he had been entrusted 'to bring about the triumph of Islam and to lead it on to a world-conquest', for Ahmad 'Europe or the Western world became his special objective'.[29] As such, missionary activity has always been a major concern of the *Ahmadi*.

Although never large movements, both the Qadiani and Lahori *Ahmadi*, within a few years of Ahmad's death, had groups of converts in a number of countries around the world. As I saw in the homes of *Ahmadi* in Britain, India and Pakistan, every member of the movement [man, woman, and child] is a missionary for the faith. By word and action the *Ahmadi*'s life is an open invitation for the non-believer to accept the claims of Ahmad. Fully trained missionaries, intoxicated with their vision of a world which they believed would soon adhere to the truth of *Ahmadiyyat*, would travel under the directions of the *Khalifa*, often alone, to a particular country and, having rented or purchased suitable lodgings, would form a cell of like-minded people, gaining converts mainly from other Muslim groups. As referred to earlier such missionary activity in the *Ahmadiyya Jama'at* was greatly aided by the commencement of the movement's first newspaper, *Al-Hakam*, first published in 1897 at Amritsar. This was followed in 1902 by the publication of another newspaper, *Al-Badr* at Qadian. Both papers were important conduits for making known the speeches, addresses, and essays of Ahmad. Today *Al-Fadl*, a weekly newspaper printed at Rabwah, and the *Al-Fadl International Weekly* printed in London, [with the *Review of Religions*, first published in 1902] provide the *Ahmadi* with useful tools of propaganda and proselytism.

During the *Khalifate* of Noor-ud-Din, the first *Khalifa*, the Qadiani *Ahmadi* carried out missionary activity in Southern India, Bengal, and Afghanistan. In 1915 *Ahmadi* missions were established in Ceylon [now Sri Lanka] and Mauritius while five years later the first mission was established in the United States. The 1920s and '30s witnessed further missionary activity with groups started in West

---

28 Mirza G. Ahmad, *Izala Aoham, Roohani Khazain*, op.cit.

29 Muhammad Ali, *Founder of the Ahmadiyya Movement*, op.cit. , p. 33.

Africa in 1921, Germany in 1923, and Russia in 1924.[30] In the 1920s *Ahmadi* centres were established in Egypt and Baghdad but little is heard of them later on. More successful was the mission to Haifa, now in Israel, where a strong *Ahmadi* presence can be found to this day. Centres were established in America, chiefly at Michigan and Chicago, during the 1920s. As Friedmann remarks '*Ahmadi* centres have since been established in Athens [Ohio], Dayton, New York, Pittsburgh, Washington, and elsewhere'.[31] The opening of the *Jamia Ahmadiyya* [missionary training centre] at Qadian in 1928 furthered missionary activity leading to the establishment of the first *Ahmadi* mosque in Palestine in 1933; a mission in Nigeria in 1934; in Burma, Hong Kong, Japan, and Singapore in 1935; Hungary, Yugoslavia and Argentina in 1936; Sierra Leone in 1937; and the foundation of a mosque at Srinigar, Kashmir, in 1940. In the post-war period missionary work continued with *Ahmadi* centres established in various countries including France, South Africa, Spain and Switzerland. A mission had been started in Syria but, as in many Arab lands, the *Ahmadi* faced considerable opposition in that country, leading to the confiscation of their property in 1958. By the 1960s missions had been founded in Jordan, at Hamburg in Germany, Muscat, Lebanon, Malta, the Hague, Copenhagen in Denmark, Fiji, Guyana and Canada.[32] During this time the *Ahmadi* translated the Quran into numerous different languages, an activity traditionally frowned upon by mainstream Muslims.

The story of the martyrdom of the first *Ahmadi* missionaries in Afghanistan has become an integral element of the movement's folklore and hagiography. Ahmad had made a prediction how 'two goats will be slaughtered, and everyone who lives here will meet this end'.[33] Although vague and inexplicit, and no country is named, the

---

30 See Humphrey J. Fisher, *Ahmadiyya: A Study in Contemporary Islam on the West African Coast*, London: Oxford University Press, 1963, passim.

31 See Y. Friedmann, *Prophecy Continuous*, op.cit., p. 24.

32 Friedmann, ibid., p. 31. Details of the expansion of the *Ahmadiyya Jama'at* can be found in Mirza Bashir-ud-Din Ahmad, *Invitation to Ahmadiyyat*, Lahore: Islam International Publications, UK, 1997; A.A. Chaudhry, *The Promised Messiah and Mahdi*, op.cit., pp. 194-198.

33 See Tadkiratush Shahasdatain 'The narrative of two martyrs' by Mirza. G.

ISLAM AND THE AHMADIYYA JAMA'AT

Ahmadi later took these words of their founder to be a prophecy about Afghanistan. Syed Abdul Latif of the city of Khost was revered throughout Afghanistan for his piety and righteousness. However, in about 1901, on reading some of the works of Ahmad he became an *Ahmadi*. Interested in learning more about Ahmad and the movement he had founded, Latif sent one of his most trusted followers, Abdur Rahman, to go to Qadian. Rahman went as requested and he also, on talking with Ahmad, was converted to *Ahmadiyyat*. Ignoring the obvious dangers to his safety, but keen to tell others about his new-found faith, instead of returning to Latif, Rahman travelled to Kabul to talk with the ruler of the country. The religious leaders, regarding *Ahmadiyyat* as heresy, persuaded the ruler to sign a *fatwa* of death against Rahman. Having been arrested, a mantle was tied round his neck, and he was strangled to death. Two years later, while on his way to Mecca to perform *hajj*, Abdul Latif also visited Qadian and spoke at length with Ahmad. He also travelled to Kabul to talk with the ruler on his return but met a similar fate as his former disciple. The religious leaders in Kabul again persuaded the ruler of the errors of the new movement. Latif was taken outside the city walls, placed in the ground up to the waist, and stoned to death. According to the *Ahmadi* the first part of Ahmad's prophecy had come true, 'two goats' had been slaughtered. The second part of the prophecy was believed to have been fulfilled two months after Latif's execution when Kabul was caught in the grip of a cholera epidemic resulting in the loss of many lives.

As described in chapter eleven, the *Ahmadi* in Pakistan have been subjected to fierce and prolonged persecution. With the partition of India and Pakistan in 1947 the majority of *Ahmadis* were to be found in the latter of the two countries. Two years later the *Ahmadi Khalifa*, *Hadhrat* Mirza Basheer-ud-Din Mahmood Ahmad, made the town of Rabwah, on the west bank of the Chenab river in the Punjab, the world headquarters of the movement. Mainly due to pressure from the *Ulema*, and continuing opposition from all strands of mainstream Islam, on 7 September 1974 the National Assembly of Pakistan passed

Ahmad, and the Ahmadiyya Muslim Community Website, www.alislam. org/books/tadkiratush.html, article entitled 'Argument 10: prophecies'.

a resolution which declared that all *Ahmadi* in that country were to be regarded as a non-Muslim minority. Later legislation passed by General Zia-ul-Haq in 1984 punished *Ahmadi* with imprisonment for practising their faith. Many *Ahmadi* mosques were burned to the ground or desecrated in other ways. *Ahmadi* all over Pakistan were harassed, persecuted, or murdered. When faced with such persecution many *Ahmadi* left Pakistan and settled in other countries particularly Britain, America, Canada, Germany, France, Holland, and Sweden. In 1984 *Hadhrat* Mirza Tahir Ahmad, the fourth *Khalifa*, took up residence in London and established the movement's temporary international headquarters at the mosque in Southfields.

An *Ahmadi* group had been established in England as early as 1912, when Khwaja Kamal-ud-Din formed a centre for the Lahori group at Woking, Surrey. In 1913 a notable convert to Islam had been gained in the person of Lord Headley.[34] A Qadiani *Ahmadi* missionary, Chaudhry Fateh Muhammad Syaal, arrived in England in July 1913. In the following year, with the establishment of a small group of *Ahmadi* in London, *Khalifa* Mirza Basheer-ud-Din Mahmood Ahmad instructed Mr Syaal to purchase a house with land where a mosque could be built. Six years later in August 1920, with an appeal for funds being raised in Qadian, and most of the money coming from *Ahmadi* women, Mr Syaal acquired a one acre site at 63 Melrose Road, Putney [now 16 Greenhall Rd, Southfield]. Within a few years plans for the construction of a mosque were finalised, the foundation stone being laid by the second *Khalifa* on 19 October 1924. Construction began in September 1925 and ten months later the work was completed. Named the *Fazal* Mosque [*Fazal* meaning 'grace'] it was formally opened in October 1926. Having established a mosque in London during the 1920s the *Ahmadi*, continuing in their work of missionary activity, established centres in Glasgow in 1949 and missions at other places, including Western Ireland. During the 1960s a worship centre was set up in a house in Fartown, Huddersfield, West Yorkshire, culminating in the opening of a mosque in

---

34 Lord Headley, (1855-1935), Irish Peer, statesman and writer, accepted Islam in 1913 adopting the name Al-Haj El-Farooq.

1980, establishing this town as the centre of *Ahmadiyya* activity in the north of England.

The *Ahmadi* presence in Bradford, West Yorkshire, presents a paradigm of *Ahmadi* missionary activity and settlement in other places throughout the Western world. Abdul Haque, a textile worker, after first visiting Glasgow in 1961, went to Bradford, setting up a shop called 'Noor Hosiery Works'. Having gained the necessary visas, his family joined him in 1965. Setting up home in the Leeds Road area of Bradford, his family living upstairs, a drapery shop and a knitting machine in the cellar, he epitomized the industrious work ethic of the early Asian immigrants who came to Britain seeking employment and a better standard of life.[35] In 1962 Chaudhry Rehmat Khan, the *Imam* of the London Mosque, visited the city and, using Haque and his circle of friends, established the *Jama'at* in that region.

Since that date, like Muslim groups generally, meetings have been held at various houses and other places in Bradford. The earliest of such meetings were held in the home of the first Bradford President, Chaudhry Mansoor Ahmad, on Little Horton Lane and later at 76 Downay Road. In 1963 the Bradford *Jama'at* held *Eid* prayers for the first time in congregation at 82 Little Horton Lane. During the 1970s meetings were also held at 45 and 51 Cecil Avenue until other premises were gained at Stirton Street, before hiring the YMCA on Little Horton Lane.[36] 1975 was an important year for the *Ahmadi* of Bradford with the arrival of Ameen Ullah Khan Salik as the first Missionary to that locality while in the following year the local *Jama'at* began producing its own newspaper, *Al-Baseerat*.

In 1980 the *Ahmadiyya* community in Bradford numbered over a hundred members. A mosque was established when a building, previously the baths and laundry on Leeds Road, was purchased from the Metropolitan Council for £31,000. This building, due to vandals, lead thieves and general decay, was in a sorry state of disrepair. The *Ahmadi*, believing in *Waqar-i-amal*, 'dignity of labour', [the idea

---

35 *Al-Baseerat*, Monthly Magazine of the Bradford *Ahmadiyya Jama'at*, 1976-1996, (July 1996).

36 *Al-Baseerat*, (July 1996), op.cit. See also Report by Bilal Atkinson, regional Amir, *Ahmadiyya Muslim Association, North East, 2001-2003 Annual Report*, London: n.p., 2003, p. 6.

that every member, no matter what their profession or status in life should give time to manual labour], and with the benefit of a £25,000 City Challenge grant, carried out the necessary renovation work. A worship area was constructed, and the former swimming pool was converted into a sports hall. The mosque was officially opened on 10 October 1980 by the third *Khalifa*, who, when carrying out this function, suggested *Baitul Hamd* [praiseworthy place] as a suitable name for the building.

As with settlement patterns elsewhere, Bradford is typical of many European cities in illustrating the opposition the *Ahmadi* face, not from non-Muslims but from members of the *Ummah*. As is to be expected, most Muslims in Bradford, many of whom come from rural Pakistan where anti-*Ahmadi* sentiment is strong, regard *Ahmadiyyat* 'to be outside the pale of Islam'.[37] To the shame of Islam generally, the mid 1980s witnessed anti-*Ahmadi* riots in Bradford which received national press coverage. Refusing to recognise the movement as an Islamic group the Bradford Council of Mosques in 1985 organised an opposition campaign against the *Ahmadi*. Individual Muslims, influenced by relatives and leaders arriving from Pakistan, made threats against those who should have been regarded as fellow Muslims. Events came to a head when the *Ahmadiyyat* organised a Religious Founder's day in Bradford Central Library. A large mob, led by local *Mullah*s, marched through the city centre, intent on disrupting the meeting. Stones were thrown, threats made and at least one window was broken. The police, fearing an escalation of violence, instead of arresting the trouble-makers, brought the meeting to an end and led those attending the meeting to safety through a back door of the Library. Opposition to *Ahmadi* was also seen in the protest of mainstream Muslims over the *Global Village* Book. In 1996 the local Council, and the Council for Voluntary Services, decided to publish a Directory, entitled '*Global Village Guide to Bradford*', listing black and other minority community groups in the Bradford Metropolitan District. Due to pressure from Muslim leaders, and the local Council fearing ethnic disturbances, the *Ahmadiyya Jama'at* was listed in the

---

37 M. Z. Khan, *Ahmadiyyat: The Renaissance of Islam*, Lahore: Tabshir Publications 1978, p. 133.

section entitled 'other' faith groups, rather than in the section for 'Muslim groups'. Due to justified objections raised by the *Ahmadi* the Directory was withdrawn although copies had already been sent to over 200 organisations in the city.[38]

A moment of great joy for the *Ahmadiyya Jama'at* in Britain was the opening of the *Baitul Futuh* Mosque, ['House of victories'], in Morden, London in October 2003, one of the largest mosques in Western Europe. 'It has cost 15 million pounds to build, every penny coming from voluntary contributions', declared Dr Muhammad Iqbal, an *Ahmadi* living in Bradford, while taking me down in his car for the inauguration weekend. With undisguised alacrity he told me how the 'mosque stands on a five acre site, and can hold 10,000 worshippers, and has almost 40,000 square feet of carpet'. On arrival at the mosque I found that the descriptions given by Iqbal and others were not exaggerations. I was taken on a tour of the site by Naseem Bajwa, my friend of several years and *Imam* of the Bradford mosque. The mosque, a blend of the traditional and the modern, constructed on the site of an old dairy mill, offers many facilities such as various Conference halls and auditoriums, administrative buildings, a library and dining facilities. I read with interest the official press releases issued by the *Ahmadi* that 'the dome of the mosque, situated in the main worship hall, measures sixteen metres in diameter and fifty-one feet high and has seven miles of timber and 450 square yards of steel'. I read elsewhere that 'the mosque is decorated throughout with Italian marble'. *Imam* Bajwa explained to me how 'everything is state-of-the-art. The rooms have a special ventilation system, and an automatic sensor operated heating and cooling system is installed under the floors. A broadcast suite allows prayers to be beamed live worldwide'.

The tour ended, and after being interviewed on the *Ahmadi* satellite station about my opinion of the mosque and the movement generally, we joined about 500 other invited guests, 'leader members of the wider public such as MPs, Mayors, Ambassadors, Councillors and others' to sit in the dining hall.[39] We sat at a table with other

38 Khuddam News, *Al-Baseerat*, (October 1996), p. 9.
39 Official report of the inauguration event, *Ahmadiyya Bulletin*, (October/

Ahmadi worthies, officials from *Jama'ats* in Germany and Denmark. We listened with interest to the *Khalifa, Mirza Masroor Ahmad,* speak about the aims of the *Ahmadi* to unite all religions and faiths with its central message: 'Love for all, hatred for none'. Speeches of welcome and congratulation were given by the Mayor of Merton, the *Ahmadiyya Amir,* and Jim Karygiannis a Canadian MP, who, amongst other things, encouraged his hosts by telling them: 'No matter what others say of you, YOU ARE MUSLIM!'.

With the assistance of *Imam* Bajwa I managed to have a brief conversation with the *Khalifa.* I waited patiently in a queue of well-wishers and admirers. My turn came and having shook the *Khalifa's* hand I thanked him for the invitation to attend the inauguration. He nodded his head and smiled. I expressed admiration for the mosque, and congratulated him on its completion. He smiled again, remaining solemn and silent. Trying to think of something of common interest I told him how earlier that year I had visited the Agricultural University at Faisalabad, Pakistan, where he had earned a masters degree in 1976. Again he smiled but had little to say. The interview ended, I returned to my seat and enjoyed the conversation of friend Bajwa and a splendid meal of Indian cuisine.

There have been several influential and famous *Ahmadis.* Sir Chaudrey Muhammad Zafrulla Khan, the first Foreign Minister for Pakistan, was, in 1958, appointed Vice-President of the International Court of Justice, in 1962 became president of the 17th Session of General Assembly of the United Nations, and two years later served as a judge at the International Court of Justice. As one statesman has said, Zafrulla Khan 'is looked upon as a top-most statesman, in the Middle East in general and in Egypt and other Arab countries in particular'.[40] Another famous *Ahmadi* was Professor Abdus Salam, theoretical physicist who in 1955 served as Scientific Secretary to the Geneva Conference on the Peaceful Uses of Atomic Energy, and became the first Pakistani to win the Nobel Prize, when he was awarded the prize for Physics in 1979. Other well known *Ahmadi*

November 2003), p. 14.

40 Al-Sayed Mustafa Momin, interview to A.P.P., published in various newspapers, (24 May 1955), see www.alislam.org/library/zafar2.html.

include Yusef Lateef, the American Jazz musician and Malik Ram, the famous Urdu scholar and expert on Mirza Ghalib.

The *Ahmadi* today are proud of the fact that their organisation has its own satellite TV channel, *Muslim TV Ahmadiyya International*, which, as I am constantly reminded by my *Ahmadi* friends, 'can be found on Sky Channel 675'. However, despite the fact that there have been some *Ahmadi* of note, that the sect has missions around the world and mosques of splendour in London and elsewhere, the *Ahmadi*, both the Qadiani and Lahori groups, remain a small minority group, marginalised by mainstream Muslims. When I talk to fellow academics, Church people, or friends about the *Ahmadi*, the name is usually unknown to them. When talking to Muslims '*Ahmadi*' is usually a term of derision and opprobrium. Writing just after the Second World War, H.A.R. Gibb remarked; 'on the whole, the *Ahmadiyya* are an unimportant element in Indian Islam and only slightly more important as carriers of the liberal interpretation of Islam into the more backward parts of Muslim Africa'.[41] The situation is still the same today.

---

41 Hamilton A. R. Gibb, *Modern Trends in Islam*, Illinois: University of Chicago Press, 1947, p. 62.

4

'LEARN FROM THE ANTS'
STRUCTURE AND ORGANISATION

It may come as a surprise to most people to learn that there is a small part of the English County of Surrey named Islamabad. A former school, and a considerable amount of land just outside the village of Tilford, was purchased in the 1970s by the *Ahmadiyya Jama'at*. With their *Khalifa* taking up permanent residence in the United Kingdom in 1984, the *Ahmadi* have held their *Jalsa Salana* [International Assembly], usually in the last week of July, each year, at this location.[1] During the *Jalsa* thousands of *Ahmadi* [an estimated 25,000 attended in 2003] arrive from all over the world to meet with their co-religionists: to discuss, learn, share, and to renew old friendships and acquaintances. The first *Jalsa Salana* was held at Qadian in December 1891 when Mirza Ghulam Ahmad met with his followers for a three day Conference to discern what they believed was God's plan for the newly formed movement. The purpose of the *Jalsa* today is the propagation of Islam, [or the *Ahmadi* version of it] and the welfare of new converts world-wide.[2] As Ahmad opined: 'the major aim of the gathering' is that the sincere members of the *Jama'at* should be able to derive religious benefits', 'acquire more knowledge' and 'advance

---

1   The *Jalsa Salana* has been held at Islamabad, Surrey, every year since 1985 with the exception of 2001 when, due to the outbreak of the foot and mouth disease, it was held in Germany.

2   Karimullah Zirvi, *Welcome to Ahmadiyyat, the True Islam*, Silver Springs, USA: *Ahmadiyyat* Movement in Islam, 2002, p. 401.

in their God realisation'.[3] Ahmad clearly saw the advantage of individual *Ahmadi* 'meeting their friends', and by doing so 'broaden their circle of brotherhood' and 'strengthen the mutual ties'. Up to 1947 the *Jalsa* was held in India, and then at Rabwah, Pakistan, until 1983 when, due to persecution, it was expedient to move the headquarters and the Conference to London. The *Ahmadi* see the *Jalsa Salana* as a showcase to the world: a platform from which, by MTA [the *Ahmadi* satellite TV station,] newspaper, and radio reports, the *Jama'at* can present the movement and its message to the world.

In late July 2003, having been invited to attend the *Jalsa Salana* of that year, I made my way to London. Taking the National Express bus to Victoria Coach Station, then the underground train to Southfields, I walked to the *Ahmadiyya* mosque on Gressenhall Road. I was warmly received, and being offered a lift by minibus, I arrived a few hours later at Islamabad. Arriving at midnight of the first day of the Conference, and seeing muddy fields and a city of tents, I thought I had inadvertently stumbled on a rock concert or a weekend retreat for Scouts. The organising of such an event is formidable, a task the *Ahmadi* accomplish with almost military precision. All regional *Jama'ats* contribute, not only financially, but also in terms of labour, to the planning of this annual event. All work is carried out voluntarily under the system of *waqar-i-amal*, or 'dignity of labour', a system which literally pulls all hands, irrespective of social, financial or educational standing, to the proverbial pumps. As I made my way to my sleeping area, and during the next few days, I saw clear evidence of the preparatory work undertaken: the printing of relevant handbooks and literature, identity cards, press releases for the media, the purchasing of food for thousands of visitors, the provision of bedding and camping equipment, the erection of marquees and tents, the setting up of broadcasting equipment for radio and television, and a plethora of other tasks incumbent on a sect desperate to please their God, and their *Khalifa*.

The schedule for the three day *Jalsa* follows a well planned routine of sleep, meals, prayer meetings, lectures and other sessions. I awoke

3 Asmani Faisla, cited by *Information booklet: Jalsa Salana 2003, Ahmadiyya* Muslim Association UK, London Mosque, p. 2.

at 3 o'clock on the Saturday morning with hundreds of tired but ardent worshippers, yawning, stretching and rubbing their eyes before washing for *Tahajjud* prayers, the non-obligatory early morning prayer-time. Later that day, still suffering from sleep deprivation, I dined with kings and tribal leaders from various parts of Africa. Many *Ahmadi* reminded me how Ahmad had been told in one of his revelations how kings and rulers would seek a blessing from him. The *Ahmadi* see the attendance of such leaders as fulfilment of this prediction. Dressed in brightly coloured traditional garb, and attended by their keepers, they discussed with me religion, politics, and the economic hardships faced by their countries. At other meals I joined the general mêlée, an organised free-for-all, at the *langar* [the *Jalsa* kitchen] where thousands of people 'queued' for the free provision of food. I witnessed vast numbers of people [of every colour and race] assembled together from numerous countries around the world. A sea of humanity bound together as sisters and bothers, sharing meagre resources, united in humility, worshipping their God.

The highlight of the Conference for the *Ahmadi* is the arrival of their leader, the *Khalifa*, presently Mirza Masroor Ahmad, the supreme Head of the Worldwide *Ahmadiyya* Muslim Community. He arrives, the *Ahmadi* Pope, in a special car with body guards, crowds lining the way, and red carpet to boot. Once in the main marquee he spoke to his people: thousands of submissive acolytes sitting expectantly, while thousands more sat outside watching screens around the site depicting the *Khalifa's* lecture. Despite a general request for silence and order the *Khalifa* was regularly interrupted by individual *Ahmadi* who, standing up and overtaken with enthusiasm, cry out: '*Nara' takbeer Allah Akbar*', ['all people say that Allah is great']; or in reference to the *Khalifa*, '*Hadhrat Khaliftul Massih al khalias, zin da ba'id*' ['He is the fifth successor to the promised Messiah, may he live long'] or, '*Sallallah-ho Allah hai, rassalam*' ['Peace and blessings of Allah be upon him']. The entire assembly would then join together in making the same declaration of loyalty to God and their leader. I sat in the area reserved for guests, with a headset, through which the voice of a translator enabled me to understand the different speakers who delivered messages in Urdu, Gujarati, Arabic and other languages. Other occasions of solemnity include the hoisting of the *lawa-e-Ahmadiyyat* [the *Ahmadi* flag] by the *Khalifa*, and the international *bai'at* ceremony on the Sunday when, by satellite link, it is said that thousands did *bai'at* [initiation] simultaneously all around the world. New converts pledging their allegiance to the *Khalifa*, placed their hand on his, were led away in lines, each person putting their hand on the person in front to ensure a link is maintained with their spiritual leader. The *Khalifa*, prostrating himself before Allah, then leads the faithful in prayer. Throughout the various sessions guests, including MPs, Local Councillors and other dignitaries, are seated in the VIP marquee. International question and answer sessions are held on the Sunday, transmitted live throughout the world by means of MTA. The *Jalsa Salana* provides the *Ahmadiyya Jama'at*, not only with an annual occasion for theological and administrative reflection, but with a much needed exercise in public relations.

The *Ahmadiyya Jama'at*, regarded as heretical and non-Muslim by mainstream Islam, is arguably the best-organised of any Muslim reform movements. A relatively small group, [about 10,000 members in Britain], the *Ahmadiyya Jama'at* has a well organised hierarchical structure providing an ideological framework with a message that is relevant to every aspect of a member's life. Strong internal discipline and coherence is maintained, thereby preserving and passing on religious norms and practices. Organised, and disciplined, the *Ahmadi* live within their own socially and ideologically defined parameters, yet interact in a selective way with the majority host society. Like other ethnic groups they have established a range of institutions within the *Jama'at* which structure and preserve the life-style of the community. This provides the members with a world-view, and the strength, support and ideology needed, to live within a confrontational Islamic society and an indifferent wider, secular society. 'Learn from the ants', stated one *Ahmadi* in conversation with me at the *Jalsa*. 'We are like an army, a work force of ants. Each person having his part to play in the service of truth'. By such means the *Ahmadiyya Jama'at* appears strong and centralised. At each centre, such as Bradford, England, there is a President, and a working committee or *Aamala*. The local branch is divided into groups, which provide religious education, social functions and sports activities for its members. The *Imam* leads prayers and provides commentary on the Quran and *hadith*, visits people, teaches classes and runs discussion groups. Although the movement accepts grants and other financial support, [as seen in the money given by the local Council to construct a sports hall at the Leeds Road mosque, Bradford,] 'the Ahmadiyya Muslim Association', as the editor of *Al-Baseerat*, the magazine published by the Bradford *Jama'at* states, 'is self-supporting and completely independent apart from some income from hospitals and schools run by the community'.[4]

It is argued that Mirza Ghulam Ahmad, aware of the need to ensure the continuance of the movement in the future, directed that 'the institution of *Khalifat* should be established after his death', and that 'the members should elect a successor who will carry on his work and be the spiritual and worldly head of the community'.[5] As such the *Ahmadi Khalifate* was established. The *Khalifa*, who presides over the movement for life, is regarded by the *Ahmadi* as nothing less than the successor of the Prophet, 'the true *Khalifa* for the Muslim world'. Therefore all Muslims are called upon to 'accept him and become united'. As well as being seen as 'the worldly and spiritual head of the [*Ahmadi*] community',[6] who provides 'unity, security and progress for the *Jama'at-I-Ahmadiyya*',[7] the *Khalifa* is considered to be 'the patron and guardian of the true *Khilafat* [*sic*]'[8] originating from the 'rightly guided Caliphs' of the seventh century. As one *Ahmadi* writes, the *Khalifa* 'has the allegiance of the community for the cause of Islam', and *Ahmadi* 'promise to follow him in all that is good and … Islamic'.[9]

Approximately 600-700 members of the Electoral College, comprising *Amirs*, missionaries and the heads of central organisations have the right to vote for the *Khalifa*. They must attend a special meeting at Rabwah. Operating something like the College of Car-

---

4   *Al-Baseerat*, (July 1985), p, 2.

5   Tahir Selby, *Al-Baseerat*, (October 1993), p. 4.

6   Tahir Selby, *Al-Baseerat*, op.cit., p. 8.

7   Zirvi, *Welcome to Ahmadiyyat*, op.cit., p. 302.

8   Chaudhry Hadi Ali, 'Establishment of *Khilafat*', *Review of Religions*, Vol. 96, no. 5, (May 2001), p. 38.

9   *Al-Baseerat*, (June 1995), p. 2.

dinals and Bishops in the Vatican, and the election of a Pope within the Roman Catholic Church, names are proposed, seconded, then accepted or rejected by raising of hands. The *Khalifa* within the *Ahmadiyya Jama'at* is seen as God's representative on earth: leading, guiding, teaching, and preserving the faith. When a *Khalifa* has been elected 'every man, woman and child of the community must render complete and utter obedience to him, and reaffirm their *bai'at* to him'.[10] As the *Khalifa* asserted: 'the *bai'at* is made on the principle of "we hear and we obey" '.[11] Although not democratic in a western sense, and criticised by some for his apparent absolutism, the power of the *Khalifa* must be wielded according to 'the limits prescribed by *Sharia'h*, Islamic Law'.[12] Critics of the *Ahmadi* see the *Khalifa* as despotic and undemocratic for, although the *Khalifa* is obligated to consult 'the group of pious people' in 'all important matters', he 'is not obligated to do so as they suggest'.[13]

The idea of *Khalifate* is not new to the *Ahmadiyya Jama'at*. The Quran mentions how Muhammad, just before his death, predicted that *Khalifas* would be raised to continue the work he had begun.[14] Following the death of Muhammad the Muslim community elected Abu Bakr as the first successor or *Khalifa*. This began the period of *Khalifat-I-Rashida*, or 'rightly guided *Khalifas*', a period of about thirty years covering the *Khalifate* of Abu Bakr, Umar, Uthman, and Ali. Regarded by Muslims as a golden period in Islamic history, it is generally believed that, although these *Khalifas* were elected through the people, they were divinely appointed and ordained so as to proclaim the teachings of Allah and Muhammad. Abu Bakr and his successors were seen as restorers of the unity of Islam and establishers of

---

10 Karimullah Zirvi, *Welcome to Ahmadiyyat*, op.cit., p. 304.

11 'Friday Sermon of the *Khalifa*', delivered on 12 September 2003 at the London Mosque, *Ahmadiyya Bulletin*, (January 2004), p. 7.

12 Karimullah Zirvi, *Welcome to Ahmadiyyat*, op.cit., p. 299.

13 Zirvi, ibid., p. 299.

14 In the Quranic verse known as *Ayat-e-Istikhlaf*, Surah Al-Nur (24:56), Allah pronounces 'we will establish *Khilafat* amongst you'. Muhammad explained how 'ultimately *Khilafat* will be established among you on the path and pattern of prophet-hood', see Mishkat-Bab Al Anzar Wal Tahzir.

the faith.[15] 'At that time', remarks the editor of *Review of Religions*, 'Muslims accomplished much as they were united under one banner'.[16] However, with the death of Ali in 660 AD it is believed that *Khalifat-I-Rashida* came to an end and a new age, characterised by divisions, the rise of sects and internal fighting, began. Most Muslims assume that a link exists between the establishment and flourishing of the *Khalifate* and the prosperity and success of Islam. 'As soon as the bright light of *Khilafat* [sic] began to wane', remarked one writer, 'the Islamic influence and world domination began to diminish'.[17] *Ahmadi*, accepting this view, believe that God removed the *Khalifate* as a punishment because of the disobedience and unfaithfulness of Muslims generally. 'The followers of Islam', it is argued, 'due to their idleness and indifference, were overpowered by the enemies of Islam and became helpless and were enslaved'.[18] *Khalifas* were still appointed after the death of Ali, the *Khalifate* becoming a hereditary position. According to the *Ahmadi*, these *Khalifas* 'were only worldly leaders, not divinely inspired'.[19] This *Khalifate* came to an end in 1924 with the fall of the Ottoman Empire.

Today many Muslims lament the fact that 'Islam is torn with strife and with internal and external intrigues and conspiracies and is in dire need of a leader, a man of integrity ... [who would] lead the Muslim nation'.[20] In the light of the decline of Islamic nations, especially under European colonialism, 'the establishment of *Khilifat* [sic]' is regarded 'as the only cure' for such malaise.[21] As one writer remarks: 'There can be no doubt that according to the Quran and the practice of the Holy Prophet there can be only one Head of State of

15 Much of the information for this section was taken from an article on 'Khalifat in Islam', *Al-Baseerat*, (May 1994), p. 2.

16 Editorial, *Review of Religions*, vol. 96, no. 5, (May 2001), p. 2.

17 Hadi Ali, *Review of Religions*, vol. 96, op.cit., p. 36.

18 See *Al-Baseerat*, (May, 1994), p. 3.

19 *Al-Baseerat*, ibid., p. 3.

20 Hadi Ali, *Review of Religions*, op.cit., p. 33.

21 Chaudhry Rehmat Ali, *Sabaq Phir Parh*, vol., 2, no. 8, (August 1992), p. 12.

the whole Islamic world who is, in fact, the *Khalifa*'.[22] Consequently the aim of many Muslims world-wide, including extremist groups such as *Hizbut Tahrir* and *Al-Muhajiroun*, is to re-establish the *Khalifate* thus giving their faith the unity, leadership and strength needed to bring about the promised 'victory of Islam'.[23] Some see such leadership in figures such as Colonel Gaddafi of Libya or Saddam Hussein, before his downfall at the hands of American and British forces in the last Gulf war. The *Ahmadi* however believe the *Khalifate* is a spiritual, not a political, institution. 'It is certainly not an ideological *Khilafat* [sic] based on secular rule', declared one writer, 'it is the best concept of the true *Khalifate* which the prophet-hood has saturated with the holy water of faith and good deeds and enlightened with the divine light of prophet-hood'.[24] Therefore the mere declaring 'a political ruler or king a "*Khalifa*" ', according to the *Ahmadi*, 'does not constitute his rule as *Khalifate* since such a political system cannot fulfil the conditions of *Khalifate*, nor can it establish faith in the hearts of people or turn them into true believers set on the path of righteousness and good deeds'.[25] According to the *Ahmadi* the crucial element of any true *Khalifate* is that it is always introduced by a prophet. The *Ahmadi* believe Ahmad was *that* prophet, and the *Khalifate* introduced by him fulfils this role of the true and righteous leadership needed to unite Islam. As another *Ahmadi* writer declared: 'Allah – appointed *Hadhrat* Mirza Ghulam Ahmad to be the promised Messiah and *Mahdi*, who would, through his advent, bring about the true teachings of Islam'.[26]

---

22 Rehmat Ali, *Sabaq Phir Parh*, op.cit., p. 12.

23 *Hizbut Tahrir*, '*The Party of Liberation*', was founded by Taqiuddin al-Nabhani in 1953. It has three main aims: the re-establishment of the *Khalifa* state; Pan-Arabism and the liberating of '*the Muslim lands usurped by the Kuffar from the Muslims*'. Al-Muhajiroun holds similar views. See Suha Taji-Farouki, *A Fundamental Quest: Hizb al-Tahrir and the search for the Islamic Caliphate*, London: Grey seal, 1996; Simon R. Valentine. *A Guide to Islam*, Sheffield; S. Yorkshire Police Authority, 2007.

24 Hadi Ali, *Review of Religions*, op.cit., p. 35.

25 Hadi Ali, ibid., p. 38.

26 *Al-Baseerat*, (May, 1994), ibid., p. 3.

The international headquarters of the *Ahmadiyya Jama'at* are presently based at Rabwah and London. Situated on flat featureless land, [apart from the remains of a ridge, now mostly quarried away], on the banks of the River Chenab, ninety miles South West of Lahore, Rabwah, Pakistan, is a new town and a thriving religious community. In 1948 large numbers of *Ahmadi* migrated from their headquarters at Qadian, India, to settle in the new Muslim State of Pakistan, established in the previous year. They were given this land because it was considered useless: 'a waste, desert land with no vegetation and frequent dust storms'.[27] To the chagrin of Muslims in the Punjab the *Ahmadi* created on this wasteland an independent centre, a Vatican style State, with its own government, complete with finance and information bureaus. It now stands, a town of about 49,000 residents, 95% of which is *Ahmadi*. The original name of the place was *Chak Digiyaan*, roughly translated as the 'small, uninhabited place'. The *Ahmadi* renamed it Rabwah, the 'elevated place', in remembrance of the elevated place where it is believed Jesus and Mary migrated to. 'And we made the son of Mary and his mother a sign', declares the Quran, 'and gave them shelter on an elevated land of green valleys and springs of running water'.[28] For the *Ahmadi* the choice of name was significant. They saw a parallel between the flight and claims of Jesus and the claims of their founder, and their own flight from India. For them it is indeed a city set on a hill, a place of refuge, a light to the world. For mainstream Muslims however the choice of this name was both insensitive and offensive. After many years of protest and petitioning, the Punjab Authorities changed the name to *Chenab Naghar*, meaning 'small town on the river Chenab'.

On a warm, sunny afternoon in May I walked for a couple of hours around the town of Rabwah, wandering down broad, potholed streets, looking at the rows of modern houses, each house surrounded by a wall enclosing well-maintained gardens. Some of the streets were lined with trees and beautiful, flowering bougainvillea, jasmine and other shrubs. Rabwah, like all other towns, had its libraries, police stations, schools and [as my hosts later stated with

27 Zirvi, *Welcome to Ahmadiyyat*, op.cit., p 329.
28 Quran 23:51.

unconcealed joy] even its own outdoor Olympic size swimming pool. The *Ahmadi* are justifiably proud of the newly constructed *Fazl-e-Umar* Hospital, a state-of-the-art facility, dispensing free medicine and treatment to those who cannot pay. There was also the modern, fully equipped, *Talim-ul-Islam* College, providing all modern facilities in the training of the young. Although isolated, a train line runs through the town, linking Rabwah with Karachi. At Rabwah the two main administrative departments of the *Ahmadi* administration are to be found: *Sadr-Anjumen Ahmadiyya*, responsible for organising the movement's activities in India, Pakistan and Bangladesh and *Tahrik-Jadid Ahmadiyya* responsible for all other foreign countries. The *Sadr Anjuman Ahmadiyya*, otherwise known as the Central Ahmadiyya Association, created by Ahmad in 1906, is subdivided into numerous other offices dealing with appointments, promotions, financial bookkeeping, preaching, discipline, *tarbiyyari* [moral training], *tablighi* [preaching] and numerous other matters essential in proclaiming 'truth' around the globe.[29]

The *Ahmadi* had invited me to spend a few days in Rabwah. I was made to feel very welcome, being given excellent accommodation, food and even a personal chauffeur, Ayyub, and chaperone to take me to all the sites of note in the town. Basharat, the assistant, a gentle giant of a man, always smiling, resonating humility, had been assigned to take care of my daily needs in the accommodation building, a task he performed with alacrity. My appointed escort, Naimat Ullah Basharat, [not to be confused with the assistant] an *Ahmadi* missionary who had spent many years in Denmark and England, but who now filled an administrative role in Rabwah, was a gentle, unassuming and peaceful man. Although quiet by nature, when his confidence had been gained, he would talk freely, proving to be a helpful and informative guide. During the few days I had him as a companion I raised questions on many areas of *Ahmadi* life, particularly the personal and family life of an *Ahmadi*. 'Do you have any hobbies or interests?', I asked. 'Oh yes', he replied with gusto, 'I train converts, I undertake *tabligh*'. Thinking that he had not understood my question [although his English was first rate] I replied: 'no, do

---

29 Zirvi, *Welcome to Ahmadiyyat*, op.cit., p. 329.

you like sport or have interests outside of the *Jama'at*?' He smiled and looked at me as though I had asked something really absurd. 'We are dedicated to the *Jama'at*', he replied gently. Unperturbed, I continued with my interrogation. 'Do you like television' I asked, wondering if he watched cricket, or the equivalent Pakistani soaps to Coronation Street or EastEnders. His face lighted up. 'Oh yes', he exclaimed, 'we have many channels here. We watch the news'. 'Do you like reading?', I inquired in an attempt to get an impression of the lifestyle of a sect member. 'Oh yes', he replied again with enthusiasm. 'I read the Quran, the works of the Prophet, peace be upon him'.

No sooner had I stated my intention to visit the main places of worship in Rabwah, than I was taken by Basharat, my escort, to the Mubarak mosque, one of the two main worship centres, an impressive structure built in 1947 and enlarged in the 1990s. It was a warm, still night, the air buzzing with the sound of crickets. Inside it was relatively cool with several large electric fans rotating overhead. Four or five large entrances, with opened doors, were situated on the wall behind me, allowing the sound of the *Imam*'s prayers to escape into the darkness of the night. The high ceiling, supported by numerous solid pillars, gave the hall a sense of space, airiness, a sense of 'the other'. About 100 worshippers, standing in rows on one side of the extensive carpeted interior, had gathered for *Isha* prayers. A motley assortment of *topi'd* men and boys dressed in all manner of Western and Asian clothes. Several boys, curious as to who I was, saluted me as they made their way to the front of the hall. Some, not lacking in confidence, came over to me, shook my hand and *salaamed*. I sat for some time, a few feet behind the main worshippers: watching, observing, respecting.

The quietness and serenity of the Mubarak mosque stood in sharp contrast to the Al-Aqsa mosque where I went for *Juma* prayers on the Friday. We arrived late. Several of the attendants at the doors carried weapons, firearms, outdated Enfield rifles, relics of the Second, or even the First World War. Like many others I was stopped and searched. Basharat showed the guard my official pass, a certificate signed by the highest *Ahmadi* authority, and with a wave of the hand I was allowed to pass. The hall, the main worship area, was already filled to over-flowing. I was told afterwards there had been over 20,000 worshippers present. Even allowing for expected exaggeration there must have been a congregation of about 15,000. I removed my sandals and tried to fight my way into the hall so as to be able to see the *Imam*, but to no avail. I was unceremoniously trapped in the hall-way, nimbly stepping from one foot to the other, trying to be as inconspicuous as possible, as thousands of men performed *raka*, the prostrations in prayer. Finding a place to stand, I listened to fifteen thousand male voices uttering prayer in unison. It was a moving experience. The *Imam*, out of sight, hidden amidst a sea of attentive humanity, delivered a *khutba* [sermon] in Urdu. As he preached I looked around the hall, viewing faces concentrating on the words spoken, faces seeking meaning for their lives, searching for an explanation for the constant threat of opposition that surrounded their town. I was later told the *Imam* had spoken on the theme of extension, the need to build more mosques throughout Pakistan and [as is the case in any growing religious group, whether it be Christian, Muslim or any other religion] had requested the faithful to give more money.

To the surprise [and consternation] of Basharat, my security conscious minder, I decided I would like to walk the short distance from the Al-Aqsa mosque to my residence. This would give me the chance to see a small part of Rabwah for myself rather than visit the places carefully selected for me by the powers that be. Basharat, after running over to the driver who had been appointed to taxi me round the town, telling him of the unexpected change of plan, skipped his way over the puddles and potholes to my side. As we made our way towards the town centre I stopped and spoke to street sellers and to individuals arranging the multi-coloured displays on their roadside carts. I watched the children playing a game [which Basharat informed me was called *Sabat Qudmi*, 'to hold fast',] that involved hopping on one leg in a circle while you attempt to push others out by using the shoulder. Most of those I met could speak English and speak it well. Despite Basharat regularly looking anxiously at his wristwatch, I entered conversations with these people on various themes: life in Rabwah, Pakistani politics, cricket and football. Whatever I spoke about they had an opinion. Farouk, a street vender, perpetually smiling, waxed lyrical on Bush, Blair and what he perceived to be Western interference in the Muslim world. Uthman, a tall, sinewy lad of about fourteen, shared with me his passion for Liverpool Football Club and asked about Michael Owen. An old man, sitting on a wall, his face chiselled deep with years and hard work, praised the British for providing Pakistan with an efficient railway network. It was clear that such people, in a material sense, had nothing, yet in another sense they had everything. They seemed content with their lot in life. They smiled the smile of those who were not living under the daily need to gain more and more wealth. They seemed to know what was really of value: family love, friendship and a belief in a larger plan that provided an anchor for life.

We continued our walk back to the residence. On the main highway on the outskirts of the town a constant flow of brightly coloured lorries rolled by, incessantly sounding their horns as they passed. Each truck was ornately decorated and painted. It was art-work on wheels: gaudy, loud, bright. I was told later that every family business would decorate their truck with pride. There was acute rivalry between families. Having spoken to one truck owner and his son, much to the concern of my guide, and wanting to see more of 'real' Rabwah, I took a left turn down a narrow pot-holed side street. In contrast to the main road [which incidentally was also pot-holed] this street was relatively free of traffic, with only the occasional rickshaw or cyclist going by. Nonchalant cows, and the occasional dog, emaciated and twitchy, would make their way along the gutter rummaging for food.

At the end of the street, to my surprise, I saw a small mud-built building with a wooden cross on its roof. Despite Basharat's reluctance I made my way to the door of the building where a man, tall, gaunt, silent, stood holding a stick in his hand. I asked him was it a Church and could I go in. Without saying a word he smiled revealing a row of broken and well used teeth, and disappeared round the side of the building. Within a few minutes I was surrounded by shouting, playful children, some reaching out to hold the SLR Pentax camera which I had hanging round my neck, others wanting to hold my hand. A stocky, bearded man appeared, seemingly from nowhere. In perfect English he asked me was I Christian, and being told that I was, shook my hand with the freneticism of a long lost friend. The

door of the Church was unlocked and I was soon enjoying the shade
of the small but ordered interior. The room, carpeted from wall to
wall, was empty of furniture. A carved wooden rail and a low lectern
had been placed at one end. There was also a table with copies of the
Old and New Testaments in Urdu placed on top. A picture of a Victorian gentleman with a large white beard hung on the wall with the
name William Booth placed beneath it. 'Are you Salvation Army?',
I asked with interest. With a smile stretching from one side to the
other of his amiable face he answered 'Yes'. He told me of the freedom they had to worship as Christians, how they were unmolested
and got on very well with the local Muslims. I was pleased to hear of
the tolerance of the local *Ahmadi*. However, aware of the opposition
towards minority groups in other Muslim lands, I pondered the significance of this small enclave of Christian believers. Is the presence
of this Church mere tokenism, I thought? What would happen if
converts were gained, congregations grew and the Christians built a
Church on the scale and grandeur of some of the mosques nearby?

During the remainder of my stay at Rabwah I was taken to other
places of interest around the town. The so-called 'heavenly graveyard', much larger in size than its equivalent at Qadian, is a place of
sanctity for the *Ahmadi*. Guarded round the clock for fear of des-
ecration by other Muslims, this burial place contains the bodies of
the second and third *Khalifas*, the wife and several companions of
Ahmad himself, and the body of Dr Abdus Salam, the first Muslim
and *Ahmadi* to be awarded the Nobel peace prize. With Basharat
again constantly checking his wrist-watch, aware of a tight schedule
to keep, I was taken on an itinerary including visits to the various
administrative departments of the movement: the *talim-i-tarbiyyat*,
the department for education; *hayt al-mal*, the section of the movement which dealt with financial matters; *taliif-i-isha'at* the department responsible for missionary literature and *umur-i-kharija*, the
department for foreign affairs. I was taken to the office of the *Ahmadi*
daily newspaper, *Al Faz*, regarded as the *Jama'at's* 'special educational
and religious paper'. As the *Ahmadi* understandably are proud to declare, established in June 1913, 'It is the oldest daily newspaper of the
sub-continent which has been in print till today except for the times

when its publication [was] banned by the government of Pakistan'.[30] I met all the staff, and spoke at length with the editor, Abdul Sami Khan, fifteen times imprisoned for his faith. He informed me that the 9,000 copies of the newspaper printed daily are read mainly by people in Pakistan. I was told how, since the anti-*Ahmadi* legislation of 1984, many words cannot be printed in the newspaper. For example he explained that *Sahabi* [followers of a prophet]; *masjid* [mosque]; Muslim, Islam, *tabligh* [preaching Islam] and *Muballigh* [a preacher] are just some of the many religious words that cannot be used by the *Ahmadi* in reference to their own organisation. With a stoical, resigned smile, the editor told me that the newspaper and its staff are constantly facing prosecution. He shrugged his shoulders and held both hands in the air. 'Right now', he said, 'there are about fifty cases being heard in the court at nearby Chiniot against myself, the manager and printer'.

A visit was made to a *madrassah*[31]: clinically clean, each dormitory spotless and tidy, marred only by a distinct lack of personal items on the desks or walls. You'd find no posters of Manchester United or Kylie Minogue here. I was taken to a classroom where twenty young boys were learning the Quran by rote. As soon as the door opened all the children stood up in silence. I asked one boy his name and inquired what passage he was learning. The boy, with a confidence that belied his youth, answered the questions in perfect English and began to recite verses from *Al-Baqarah* [the second chapter in the Quran] in what I presumed was perfect Arabic. The regime in the school was Spartan. The pupils would rise each day at 4:15 am and undertake *Fajr*, early morning prayers. Between 5-5:30 the time would be spent reciting the Quran before rooms tidied and further ablutions. At 6:20 breakfast would be served. Following breakfast the rooms would be inspected. From seven till almost one o'clock the pupils would be in class with two breaks for milk and biscuits. Following *Zuhr*, midday prayers, the boys would either sleep, wash their clothes or sit and talk in the common room. At 4:45 pm prayers again, this time *Asr* prayers

30 Information gained from a leaflet entitled '*A brief introduction of the Daily Alfazl Rabwah*', nd., a copy of which was given to me during this visit.
31 A school for religious education usually associated with a mosque.

followed by a time for sport, when the boys played cricket or football, between 5-6 pm. Seven was time for *Maghrib*, evening prayers, and half an hour of religious training. At about 7:40 dinner would be served, followed by *Isha*, the last prayer session of the day. From 8:15 the boys would study books about the *Ahmadi* faith and belief for two hours. At 10:15 another inspection and lights out at 10:30. This was their routine for six days of the week, the other day they were allowed to read or play games. The same discipline, regulation and order prevailed in a senior boy's school, where I was taken later. As we walked down the corridor the bell went for a change of lesson. Having had almost twenty years experience in British education as a teacher, some of which was spent teaching in inner-city comprehensive schools, I instinctively felt the urge to throw myself against the wall anticipating a swarm of overactive, vocal teenagers fighting their way along the corridor. It was refreshing to see two columns of immaculately dressed students, walking quietly and orderly in opposite directions to their next lesson.

That afternoon I had the pleasure of accidentally meeting Mirza Abdul Haq, a man for whom I had the deepest respect. I had met Mirza Sahib at the Bradford mosque in August 2002 when *Imam* Bajwa organised a special meeting with him. He was coming out of one of the main administration buildings in Rabwah, wearing a splendid *paggri* head-dress and supported by a stick. Despite his age—he was 102 years old—he looked extremely fit and healthy. What impressed me at Rabwah, was that he recognised me straight away from our earlier meeting at Bradford. A former public prosecutor, a solicitor, who had met Gandhi Mirza Sahib, he now lives at Sargodha near Lahore. He told me how he still walks several miles every day. 'I get up at 2 a.m. every day to offer prayers which is very important for health', he said. With obvious pleasure he spoke of his eighty-five children, grandchildren, great grandchildren and great, great grandchildren. Amazed by the agility of both his mind and body I asked him the secret to a long and happy life. 'To live simply, be useful to humanity and take a lot of exercise but not much food' he replied.

The hierarchical structure of the *Ahmadiyya Jama'at*, of which the *Khalifa* is the head, is a well organised and efficient administrative system. The annual *Majlis-I-Shura*, also known as the *Majlis-I-Mushawarat*, is an important consultative body, created in 1922 to advise the *Khalifa* and the national *Amirs* on matters relating to financial and educational issues, and missionary projects.[32] As the UK *Amir* stated 'the blessed institution of *Majlis-I-Shura* ranks second in importance to *Khilafat* [sic]'.[33] Consisting of the *Khalifa* and representatives from all over the world, the *Majlis-I-Shura*, held in every country where *Ahmadi* are present, discusses matters relevant to that particular country. Each local *Jama'at* will send its President and one, two or three delegates [members chosen by the *Jama'at* as representatives, depending on the size of the *Jama'at*] to the national *Shura*. The procedure for discussion within the movement, from grass-roots to the top of the organisation is, in principle at least, quite democratic. Any member can send a proposal to the local *Jama'at*. The *Majlis Aamala*, or management committee, of that local *Jama'at* will then meet and discuss any proposals handed to them. It is up to the *Majlis Aamala* to decide if any action is to be taken or matters pursued. Taking Britain as an example of *Ahmadi* organisation the various *Jama'ats* scattered around the country will send their suggestions to the national UK *Majlis Aamala* and the UK *Amir*, regarded by the *Ahmadi* as 'its brain and its heart'.[34] Having met, and discussed, recommendations are sent by the *Shura* to the *Khalifa* for approval. However, although usually following the advice given, the *Khalifa* has the power to reject any proposal if he believes it to contravene some overriding principal.

Concerning the UK *Ahmadiyya Jama'at*, as with other national *Ahmadiyya* organisations, below the *Majlis Aamala* and the *Amir* is the *Naib Amir*, or vice-president, who 'looks after the position of the *Amir* in the *Amir's* absence, and advises and helps the *Amir*'.[35] A missionary in charge looks after all the missionaries working in the UK

---

32 Zirvi, *Welcome to Ahmadiyyat*, op.cit., p. 319.

33 Report of a speech by Dr Iftikhar Ahmad Ayaz at the 20th *Majlis-I-Shura*, *Ahmadiyya Bulletin*, (July August, 1999), p. 9.

34 *Khutba* on *tabligh*, delivered on 6 June 1997, reported in *Al-Baseerat*, (June, 1997), pp. 3-4.

35 In this section I have relied heavily on Tahir Selby, *Al-Baseerat*, (October 1993), p. 5.

and advises on spiritual issues. The *Naib Amir II*, or general secretary, helps the *Amir* and supervises a long list of other, subordinate secretaries. For example the *Mal* secretary deals with the financial matters of the movement, collecting the different *chandas* [funds] and produces the budget. The *Amoora 'Amma* Secretary [General Affairs Secretary] looks after problems with members, particularly problems between married couples and any financial disputes. The *Tabligh* Secretary 'encourages members to call people to Allah'. The *Tarbiyyat* Secretary is concerned with religious education of the members of the *Jama'at* and 'ensures members get religious training etc'.[36] The *Taleem* Secretary [education] 'sets up classes, seminars, meetings etc'. The *Rishta Naata* Secretary [Matrimonial Affairs] 'helps arrange marriages, advises, removes un-Islamic customs'. The *Wassiyat* Secretary 'looks after those special members who have made a will under the terms of the *Jama'at* and have become a *Musi*' [one who has made a will].[37] The *Jaidad* Secretary deals with properties and, 'where there is a mosque this secretary will look after the property, repairs etc'. The *Tahrik-e-Jadid* Secretary deals with new schemes and 'will encourage members to contribute to the fund, a special fund set up by the second *Khalifa*'. Other Secretaries include the *Waqfe Jadid* Secretary who deals with 'new schemes for dedication', a scheme set up by the second *Khalifa* 'to help the work of those people who have temporarily or permanently dedicated their lives to the *Jama'at*'.[38] The *Waqfe Nau* Secretary deals with the scheme set up by the fourth *Khalifa* 'for members to dedicate their children to the *Jama'at*', the Secretary 'will help the parents and the children etc.' The *Ziafaat* Secretary deals with hospitality and has the duty to 'look after guests, arrange the food etc., for meetings'. 'All the publications, books etc.,' are dealt with by the *Ishaat* Secretary while the *Sami Basri* Secretary 'looks after recording functions [audio/video]'.[39]

Each of the separate organisations within the local *Jama'at* has its own President. For example, the President of the *Ansarullah* 'looks

---

36 Tahir Selby, *Al-Baseerat*, op.cit.

37 Ibid.

38 Ibid.

39 Ibid.

STRUCTURE AND ORGANISATION

after male members above the age of forty' while the *Sadr Khud-damul Ahmadiyya*, the President of the *Khuddam*, 'looks after male members up to the age of forty'. Other officials include the audi-tor, who 'checks the financial books, expenditure etc'; 'the *Amoora Kharijiyyah* deals with external affairs and looks after relations with outside groups' and the *San'at-o-Tijarat* deals with matters of indus-try and trade and 'helps members with their business problems'.[40] Elections will take place for the different positions on the *Aamala* in each local mosque. The *Ahmadi* involved in these elections, and candidates for positions, must be full *chanda*-paying members, that is those who pay fees according to the prescribed rate. As well as the numerous committees mentioned above there is also an international *Shura* which consists of elected representatives of *Tahrik-I-jadid* and *Sadr Anjuman*. This *Shura*, originally held in Pakistan, is now held in the UK after the annual *Jalsa Salana*. Being a foreign mission, and with the central headquarters at Rabwah, Pakistan, the UK *Jama'at* is placed in a branch known as *Tahrik-I-jadid* [new scheme]. The *Tahrik-I-jadid*, created by the second *Khalifa* in 1934, deals with problems relating to Islamic missions abroad. Led by the Director or *Wakilut Tabshir*, the *Tahrik-I-jadid* is in charge of all *Jama'ats* outside Pakistan and sends missionaries to other countries, opens new missions and mosques and publishes translations of the Quran and other literature. During the time of the fourth *Khalifa* a further *Tabshir* was appointed just for the UK.

Taking Bradford in West Yorkshire, England, as a typical exam-ple of *Ahmadiyya* organisation, the *Jama'at* in that area is part of the North East region which consists of groups meeting at Hartlepool, Huddersfield, Humberside, Keighley, Leeds, Sheffield and Spen Valley.[41] The North East region is served by two missionaries, or *Imam*s; one based at Huddersfield and Naseem Ahmad Bajwa at the Bradford mosque. The regional *Amir*, Bilal Atkinson, a retired police officer who converted to Islam several years ago, has jurisdic-tion over the region and is responsible to the national committee

---

40 Ibid.

41 *Regional Annual Report: North East Region, 2001/2002*, Bradford: *Ahmadiyyah Muslim Association*, 2002.

or *Shura*. Each local *Jama'at* holds its monthly *Amila* and general meetings which submits regular reports to the regional *Amir*. From the 1970s onwards the *Ahmadiyya Jama'at* was established with its *Ansarullah* [auxiliary organisation for men over forty years of age], the *Khuddam* [organisation for men aged fifteen to forty], and the *Lajna* [organisations for women]. As stated above, elections are held for President and membership of the Executive Committee, which makes the important decisions in the running of a mosque. Women also have an elected President. The process of filling posts is democratic, but qualified. Local members can choose their own candidates but the final selection is made at the highest level of the movement by the *Khalifa*. A name is put forward which is then seconded. Both the proposer and seconder must vote for that person. Everyone must vote and each person only has one vote. Canvassing is strictly prohibited. All names for the various posts are then submitted to the national *Amir* with a report of the meeting. The *Amir* will discuss with the *Khalifa*, who will have the final word on selection. It is important to note that the person who received the most votes by the members of the local *Jama'at* may not be elected if he is not accepted by the *Khalifa*; the *Khalifa* has the right to choose the second or third-placed person or even the person who received no votes. His word is final. As such 'a person who has gained the most votes does not automatically get elected'. As one writer remarks 'the election by the members is to show *Huzur* [the *Khalifa*] and *Amir Sahib* what is the recommendation of the members, but that is all'.[42]

As well as the UK *Majlis Aamala* there is the department of *Qada*, 'a court dealing with matters of a civil nature for the members'. If anything is referred to the *Qada* for decision, then it must be in writing that all the parties concerned agree to abide by the decision of the *Qada*. The *Amir* will then ensure that the decision is implemented. The appointment of the *Qadu* is made by names recommended by the *Amir* to the *Khalifa*. The Bradford *Jama'at* is one of fifty-five branches of the *Ahmadiyya Jama'at* in the UK, thirteen of which have mosques. A local branch is established when there are at least three members in an area. Every branch, attached to the nearest mosque,

---

42 Tahir Selby, *Al-Baseerat*, (October 1993), op.cit., p. 6.

will have books, pamphlets and other literature for the purpose of nurturing members and *tabligh*.

As indicated above, like other religious movements, the *Ahmadiyya Jama'at* expects loyalty, obedience and dedication from its members, both male and female. Members of the *Khuddam*, for instance, make the *Khuddam-ul-Ahmadiyya*, or pledge, to be 'ready to sacrifice my life, wealth, time and honour for the sake of my faith, country and nation'.[43] Also he pledges to be 'ready to offer any sacrifice for guarding the Institution of *Khalifatul-e-Ahmadiyya*' and to abide by any '*maroof* [decision] made by the *Khalifa*.[44] Each *Ahmadi* regards the *Jama'at* as a well organised institution, a 'brotherhood' of enthusiastic followers, dedicated to the expansion of the movement.

Tahir Selby, a former paint-sprayer in London, converted to the movement in the 1980s, later became an *Ahmadi Imam* and missionary. Speaking on 'the responsibilities of new *Ahmadis*' at the *Tarbiyyati* forum held at the Bradford mosque in October 1996, he told those present that 'their main responsibility was to develop their relationship with Allah', and reminded them 'about their responsibilities of *Chanda*, sacrifice and obedience to those in authority'.[45] 'The *Jama'at* must ensure', declared Selby, 'that the system of *Muakhat* [brotherhood] is working'.[46] Each member of the *Jama'at* must obey and follow the *Nizam-e-Jama'at*, the rules and regulations of the movement, and the discipline of the community. As Tahir Selby stated on another occasion,[47] although it is not expected that every member knows all the rules of the movement, there is 'one golden rule that is taught from childhood ... that rule is obedience to those in authority'. 'This golden rule', he continued, 'must also be installed into every new member'. It involves 'obedience to the *Amir* / President, respect of the *Amir*, and their right to disagree respectfully and convey their disagreement to the *Amir* himself or to the higher

43 Khuddam News, *Al-Bareesat*, (February 1997), p. 8.
44 Khuddam News, op.cit.
45 *Al-Baseerat*, (October 1996), p. 5.
46 *Al-Baseerat*, (October 1996), op.cit.
47 At the Educational Seminar held at Manchester on 26 September 1993, see *Al-Baseerat*, (November 1994), p. 3.

authorities without any bad blood flowing between them'. As such the *Amir* 'must be held in respect, not only in respect, but he should be treated with love, like a father, like the head of the family'. The *Ahmadi*, declared Selby, must also 'respect anyone [the *Amir*] places in authority above, whether he is a local President, a Secretary or even chosen to be in charge of a group who are on a journey'.[48] Selby pointed out that an *Ahmadi* has 'the right to disagree in principle' but that right means to disagree respectfully [sic]'. As Selby concludes:

> We are told by Allah that we must obey anyone in authority above us un-less they go against Allah and the Holy Quran. For instance, we must obey our parents, but if they tell us that we should not be Muslims, then we can disobey them.

The *Ahmadiyya Jama'at* is, to a great extent, a self-financing or-ganisation. Each member is expected to contribute regularly about 1/16 of his monthly income, some give as much as 1/3.[49] As one *Ahmadi* missionary stated: 'the *Ahmadiyya Jama'at* lays a lot of stress on the sacrifice of time and money'.[50] *Ahmadi*, like Muslims gener-ally, are reminded in the *hadiths* that 'he who spends in the cause of Allah has his reward seven hundred times'.[51] Mirza Ghulam Ahmad, directly warned his followers: 'if someone does not make a pledge [of money], he should be excommunicated, he is a hypocrite and has a darkened heart'.[52] 'Whether present or not present', he declared, 'you should inform your brothers about *chanda,* you should include even your weak brothers in *chanda*'.[53] The movement flourishes, not only on the gifts of the wealthy within the *Jama'at,* but on the small amounts given by the majority. As one *Ahmadi* remarked: 'Oceans are formed from drops'.[54] With the National Finance Department of the movement stating the level of giving of *chanda* [either com-pulsory or voluntary], a ledger is kept of the 'name and promise of

---

48 *Al-Baseerat*, (November 1994), op.cit., p. 3.

49 *Al-Baseerat*, (July 1995), p.2.

50 Tahir Selby, *Al-Baseerat*, (October 1993), p. 7.

51 *Hadiths* known as Tirmidhi.

52 cited by Zirvi, *Welcome to Ahmadiyyat*, op.cit., p. 388.

53 *Malfoozat, al-hakam*, vol. 7 no. 24, (July 1903), p. 8.

54 Karimullah Zirvi, *Welcome to Ahmadiyyat*, op.cit., p. 388.

chanda' of every member. As one *Ahmadi Imam* wrote: 'We do not have any oil fields lying around' therefore 'each member is asked to contribute 1/16th of their monthly earnings, known as C*handa Aam'*, and 1/10th of income received during any one month in the previous year'. Similarly C*handa Jalsa Salana*, 'one tenth of one month's net income' used to meet the expenses of the annual *Jalsa* at Islamabad, Surrey, is 'one of the compulsory *chandas* and must be paid'.[55] The *Khuddam Chanda*, another form of compulsory giving 'is used for general running costs of *Khuddam-u-Ahmadiyya'*. This giving 'is payable by all *Khuddam'*. 'The rate of *chanda* is 1% of your net monthly income [i.e., income after deducting tax]. Minimum payment is £5.00 per month for earning members and £3.00 per month for non-earning members'.[56] Similarly, other organisations within the *Jama'at* have their own rates of *chanda*. The *Atfal Chanda*, 'used to fund *Atfal* events, [is] payable by all *Atfal'* or 'parents of *Atfal* may pay on behalf of their children, ... the rate of *chanda* is £1 per month'. Similarly, the *Ijtema chanda*, '3% of your net income payable once a year, the minimum rate is £15 per year for earning members and £5 for non-earning members' is 'used to pay for the national *Ijtema* [and] must be paid by all *Khuddam* and *Atfal* regardless of whether they attend the event'. There is also *chanda tehrik-I-jadid*, money which is used for the building of mosques and mission houses, and for the propagation of Islam throughout the world. *Ahmadi* facing hardship may give '*chandas* at a reduced rate, but only after obtaining the permission of the *Khalifatul Masih* [*Khalifa*]'.[57] There is the *Fitrana*, £1 per person payable by all members including children during the month of *Ramadan* and before the saying of the *Eid* prayer. There is also the *Eid* fund, £5 per person paid by earning members only. If a member cannot keep the fast during *Ramadan* he is expected to pay the *Fidiya*, a payment of £45. At the present time voluntary, rather than compulsory contributions, include the Gambia Fund which 'is used to support the propagation of Islam in Gambia' and the *Tariq chanda*

---

55 Tahir Selby, 'The Importance of Chanda', *Ahmadiyya Bulletin*, (July/August 1999), p. 8.

56 Zirvi, *Welcome to Ahmadiyyat*, op.cit., p. 391.

57 Zirvi, ibid., p. 391.

'to pay for the production and distribution of *Tariq* magazine', the rate of this *chanda* being '50 pence per month'. Members can also pay *sadaqa*, a voluntary donation for the poor and needy. Payment of *chanda* does not relieve the *Ahmadi* from his duty to pay *zakat* 'on disposable assets above specific thresholds which have remained in his hands beyond one year'.[58] As in life, so in death, as indicated earlier, an *Ahmadi* is expected to become a *musi* [testator] making a contribution by *wasiyyat* or will, leaving between 1/10 to a 1/3 of his estate to the movement. Although it is recognised that such giving represents 'a huge financial burden on the members', it is believed that givers 'will be amply rewarded not only in this life by benefiting from such functions, but also Allah will reward them greatly for their sacrifices'.[59] When the work, and commitment, of the *Ahmadi* is assessed one can clearly see the justification of the *Ahmadi* claim: 'We are like an army, a work force of ants'.

---

58 Ibid., p. 169.
59 Tahir Selby, *Al Baseerat*, (October 1993), op.cit., p. 7.

5
'THE REMEMBRANCE OF ALLAH'
LIFE IN THE MOSQUE

There are over 1,000 mosques in Britain, about fifty-five of which can be found in Bradford. Some of these mosques are small affairs in terraced houses; others are former schools, warehouses, chapels, and other buildings purchased and converted into Muslim worship centres, while an increasing number are purpose-built structures, ornate and impressive in their traditional architectural design. An excursion around Bradford, either by car or by foot, reveals the imposing edifices of purpose-built mosques, buildings paid for by individual donations or Saudi petro-dollars, such as the Hanfia Mosque on Carlisle Road, Manningham, or the new mosque erected on derelict land, overlooking Drewton Street near the city centre. The main mosque in the lower section of the Leeds Road area, now occupying two buildings, is Abu Bakr, belonging to the *Deobandi* tradition: one building a former Police station, the other, standing less than a hundred yards away, an imposing new mosque constructed on nearby Steadman Terrace. With two minarets, a large green dome and classical arches leading to the main doorway, the new Abu Bakr mosque, completed at the start of the new millennium on elevated land overlooking most of Bradford 3, is a visual affirmation of the glory, pride and permanence of British Islam.

Baitul Hamd, the *Ahmadi* mosque on Leeds Road was originally a Victorian bath house. Lying in the shadow of the new Abu Bakr mosque, it has provided the four hundred or so *Ahmadi* residing in the Bradford area with a worship centre for the past twenty-five years.

ISLAM AND THE AHMADIYYA JAMAʿAT

It is a plain, practical building, unlike other *Ahmadi* mosques: the Al Aqsa Mosque at Rabwah, Pakistan, where I had joined 20,000 wor-shippers for *Juma* prayers; the Aqsa Mosque at Qadian, India, with its *Minaratul Masih*, a 105 foot high minaret, or the Baitul Futuh Mosque in London, one of the largest mosques in Western Europe, costing 15 million pounds to build. Much to the chagrin of other Muslim groups in the city, the *Ahmadi* have commenced work on a new mosque in Bradford, a three-storey building on an elevated site near the East Ward Labour Club in Rees Way, off Otley Road. Costing an estimated £2 million, and having the seating capacity for 1,000 worshippers. Once completed [possibly by Spring 2008], the building will be one of, if not the biggest, mosque in Bradford.

The mosque, with its *Mullahs* and *madrassahs*, is the nerve centre of Islam. The *Ahmadi*, like Muslims generally, exist in a plurality of worlds, moving daily between competing and often contradictory plausibility structures. He is compelled by necessity, especially within a multicultural society, to rub shoulders day by day with other 'world views', views which challenge and threaten the very basis of his faith. In a secular society that often appears apathetic, if not hostile to that which is different, the mosque provides the *Ahmadi* with a support-ive community: an epistemological, emotional and psychological back-up system which will support the individual believer, *as long as he obeys the rules*. Whether *Ahmadi* or mainstream Islam, the teach-ing and activities that take place in the mosque affirm and reiterate the Muslim's world view. Those who attend the mosque receive the knowledge that gives justification and explanation for fundamental beliefs and practices; beliefs and practices usually misunderstood, if not distorted, by the wider society. The mosque, in various ways therefore, provides a 'plausibility structure'; specific practices, rituals, and legitimations that maintain the believer's faith. It provides the social consensus, social networks, the 'legitimations', and all other 'pious practices'. It provides everything needed, from daily prayer to ritual ablutions, to give the adherent a sense of identity, a sense of well being, a warm feeling of being on the 'inside' of an experience from which the outside world is excluded. It provides a sense of being one of those who 'know' while the bulk of people outside, remain igno-rant and unknowing. A member's life therefore revolves around the activities of the mosque. His friends will mainly be fellow Muslims. He sees the world through the framework of the *Jama'at*, the *Ummah* and its ideology. Just as most Christian Churches have Scouts, Boys Brigade, Sunday School, Caravaners, Mum's and Toddlers, Bible study Groups, Coffee Mornings and numerous other activities, so the mosque provides a variety of meetings and activities to foster a sense of belonging within the group, and to prepare each member for life in what is generally perceived to be an irreligious society.

The mosque, for all Muslims, is primarily a place of prayer, a sanctuary where the believer acknowledges the *hakimiyyah*, the sovereignty, of Allah. It is a place of transcendence and immanence; a place where the Muslim is reminded of the omnipotence, the 'otherworldliness' of God, and the idea that the divine can be known, and loved, in the individual heart. Worship is central to a Muslim's life. 'And I have not created the *jinn* and the men', announces Allah, 'but that they may worship Me'.[1] Elsewhere the Quran declares: 'Thee alone do we worship, and Thee alone do we implore for help. Guide us in the straight path'.[2] As such to be an *Ahmadi*, as to be a Muslim of any of the numerous groups that make up the worldwide *Ummah*, is to submit to Allah and worship him. Prayer is one of the most important ways of worshipping God. As one *Ahmadi* remarked, 'the performance of *namaz* [prayer], at home and at the mosque, is the life-blood of the community, the very oxygen we breath'. It is regarded as a believer's 'link with God, our means of communicating with Allah and developing our relationship with Allah'.[3] The observance of the five daily prayers is a fundamental pillar of the Islamic faith. It is believed that prayer, especially collective prayer, will gain the greatest spiritual reward. 'Communal prayer', it is argued, 'is twenty seven times better than the prayer of a man alone in his house'.[4] Therefore, Muslims are exhorted to 'gather together, for the wolf picks off only the sheep

---

1 Quran, 51:57.

2 Quran 1:5, 6.

3 Tahir Selby, addressing a *seerat-un-Nabi* meeting at the Bradford mosque, 12 October 1991, reported in *Al-Baseerat*, (November 1991), p. 4.

4 *Hadith*, Bukhari, cited by Selby, *Al-Baseerat*, (November 1991), op.cit.

that stand alone'.[5] The value of congregational prayer in establishing the strength of the *Ummah* has not gone unnoticed by members of the *ulema*, the religious scholars within Islam. Mawdudi, the founder of the *Jama'at-i-Islami*, whose works can be found in the homes of Muslims all over Britain, emphasised how: 'the prayer is central to the establishment of this collective strength. Congregational Prayer five times a day, the Friday congregation, the congregation of two 'Id festivals – all these together make you like a strong wall and create in you that singleness of purpose, cohesiveness and real unity, which are necessary to make you helpers of each other in the cause of Allah in your day-to-day lives'.[6] It is believed that on the Day of Judgement the first question asked by Allah will be about the believer's observance of prayer. The faithful are taught how the observance of prayer creates 'consciousness of God [and] being in His presence, His love and His fear, [thereby gaining the] strength to avoid whatever may displease Him'.[7] Of particular importance for any Muslim is *Juma* prayers, the prayers at midday on Friday. Such prayers are obligatory for every male Muslim. 'Oh ye who believe', declares the Quran, 'when the call is made for Prayer on Friday, hasten to the remembrance of Allah, and leave off all business. That is best for you, if you only knew'.[8] Muslims are taught that special *sawab* [favour] or *baraka* [blessing] can be gained for attending *Juma* prayers. 'If a Muslim spends Friday in the remembrance of God Almighty, supplicating before his Lord', remarked one *Ahmadi*, 'he is abundantly rewarded by Allah'.[9] As taught in the *hadith* it is assumed that attendance at such prayers, and silent listening to the *Khutba*, [the sermon after such prayers] will result in the forgiveness of a man's sins 'since the previous Friday, and three days more'.[10] According to *Bukhari*, one of

---

5 Selby, *Al-Baseerat*, ibid.

6 K. Murad (ed.) Sayyid A. Mawdudi, *Let us be Muslims*, Leicester: The Islamic Foundation, 2000, p. 151.

7 Mawdudi, *Let us be Muslims*, op.cit., p. 149.

8 Quran 62:10.

9 Notes on Friday *Juma* prayers', *Al-Baseerat*, (September, 1994), p. 3.

10 The tradition of Abu Hurairah, quoting the words of Muhammad, *Muslim*, cited by *Al-Baseerat*, (September, 1994), op.cit.

the main collections of *hadiths*, 'when it is a Friday the angels stand at
the gate of the mosque and keep on writing the names of the persons
coming to the mosque …'. It is argued that the first to arrive will
receive the greatest blessing while those who arrive late, missing the
Khutba, it will be as if they never attended.[11] The routine for attendance at such prayers has remained the same for centuries. If work
and other circumstances permit, Muslims are to take a bath, dress in
clean clothes and assemble in the worship area of the mosque. Those
who are ill, blind or disabled, those on a journey, and women, are
exempt from the obligation of attending the prayer at the mosque.
In such cases prayer must be offered at another time instead. Regular
attendance at *Juma* prayers has benefits for the individual believer
and for the *Jama'at* as a whole. Fazal Dad, the Head *Imam* at the
Abu Bakr mosque, during one of two lengthy meetings I had with
him, informed me how gathering at the mosque at any time, but
particularly at midday on Friday, gives the men, and women, 'an
opportunity to meet together to discuss and solve their individual
as well as community problems'. Gathering together once a week,
he explained, 'develops unity, co-operation and cohesiveness among
Muslims' and also a 'demonstration of Islamic equality'. It serves as a
focal point of education and control where 'the *Imam* [has] a chance
to advise all Muslims at the same time on urgent matters that face
them'. His sermon 'gives them guidance in Islamic teachings'.

On many occasions I attended *Juma* prayers at the *Ahmadi* mosque
in Bradford, and occasionally at other mosques in the Bradford area.
Removing my shoes in the entrance hall, and placing them on the
shoe rack by the door, then quietly sitting on the floor at the back
of the worship hall, I would observe the *Ahmadi* at prayer. Usually
the *Muezzin* will give the *adhan*, the call to prayer, to the local community. However, the *Ahmadi* give the *Adhan* inside the mosque, so
as not to annoy other Muslims. This can be performed by any pious
member but, as would be expected in any religious organisation, is
usually carried out by the main official, in this case the *Imam*, Naseem
Bajwa. Worshippers would enter the hall, having performed *wudu*,

---

11 Bukhari quoted by the Fourth *Khalifa*, *khutba* delivered in August 1991,
   cited in *Al-Baseerat*, (September 1991), p. 2.

[ceremonial washing] in the adjacent wash room, and join with the other worshippers forming neat rows in front of the *Qibla* wall.[12] A variety of headwear, mainly white traditional *topis, tarbooshes, takias, Sindi* hats of varying colours, black *Nehru* hats or even western style base-ball caps, advertising Nike, Puma or some other popular make of sports gear, provided the appropriate head covering. The men would arrive, greeting each other with a delicate kiss on each cheek. Others embraced each other enthusiastically as though they were long-lost friends, finally united. They would then stand in rows, shoulder to shoulder. As Mawdudi explains: 'no one is higher or lower in status than his neighbour. In the Divine court, in the presence of God, you all belong to one class, you all have the same status. Nobody feels polluted if a fellow-worshipper's hand or body touches him. We are all equally pure because we are all human beings. We are all slaves of one God and believers in one *Din* [religion or way of life]'.[13] Late-comers would arrive and, instead of making their way to the front row, quietly sit down wherever possible, offering two *raka'ats*, [prostrations]. It is expected that such late arrivals will perform the complete prayers on their own once the *Imam* has finished leading the prayers. It is expected that a worshipper, rather than running in haste to arrive at the mosque on time, should proceed calmly and join the meeting at the stage of his arrival making up what they had missed later.[14] As I sat and watched, various members of the *Jama'at* would arrive and, on seeing me, *salaamed* and shook my hand, before making their way to the front of the hall. One or two of the elderly men, heavy with years, sat on chairs next to the walls, clinging to the radiators, instead of joining the other men on the floor. At the appointed time *Imam* Bajwa, standing in front of the *minbar* (pulpit) from which the *Imam* delivers sermons facing the direction of Mecca, and having raised his hands and touched the lobes of his ears, would cry out in Arabic:

---

12 The *Qibla* is the wall facing Mecca. It contains the *mihrab*, a niche, indicating the direction of the *Ka'aba*, the cube-shaped shrine in Mecca.

13 Mawdudi, *Let us be Muslims*, op.cit., p.169.

14 Karimullah Zirvi, *Welcome to Ahmadiyyat,*, Silver Springs, USA: *Ahmadiyyat Movement in Islam*, 2002, p. 84f.

Allah akbar, Allah is great, Allah is great,
I bear witness that there is none worthy
of worship except Allah. I bear witness
that Muhammad is the messenger of Allah,
come to prayer, come to prayer,
come to prosperity, come to prosperity,
Allah is the greatest, Allah is the greatest of all,
there is none worthy of worship except Allah.

An elaborate sequence of prayers and genuflexions would take place as the worshippers praise their God. The group collectively recite a prayer, followed by the recitation of the *Iqamat* [the call to prayer with a slight addition] by the *Imam*. During *salat* each worshipper will enter certain postures: *qiyam* or standing, *ruku,* bowing, *sajdah,* prostration and *qa'dah,* sitting. As each posture is performed the worshipper will recite in Arabic certain Quranic verses or phrases. The *Imam* will recite *Al-Fatihah,* [the opening *Surah* of the Quran] followed by the rest of the congregation. Having stood, knelt, or bowed in different places around the room, the worshippers, on hearing the *Iqamat,* assemble themselves in neat rows behind the *Imam*. A few verses of the Quran are read aloud by the *Imam* while everyone else remains silent, because, as the Quran directs: 'When the Quran is recited, give ear to it and keep silence, that you may be shown mercy'.[15] As such those attending are expected to listen attentively. Any form of conversation is strictly prohibited. I watched them carefully, sensing the holiness of the place, and I was aware that they were happy, in complete accord with themselves, united in an act of collective worship. The *Khutba* or sermon that follows the prayers, usually delivered by the *Imam,* has two parts. In the first part, which can be given in any language, the *Att'-awwuz* [a prayer containing the words; 'I seek refuge with God from Satan the accursed'] and *Al-Fatihah* are recited. The *Imam* advises the congregation to act on the commandments of Allah, reminding them of the duties to be performed by all good Muslims. The *khutba* can also deal with any other matter of importance. During my many visits to the *Ahmadi* mosque I heard *Khutbas* on various subjects such as *jihad,* the Iraqi war, giving financially to the mosque and other, more

15 Quran 7:205.

mundane matters. Once this first section of the *Khutba* is completed the *Imam* will sit down briefly before beginning the second part, the *Khutbah Thaniyya*, which is in Arabic, when again, a solemn silence will descend on the hall. At the end of the *Khutba* the *Imam*, having recited the *Iqamah*, leads the congregation into prayers by performing two *raka'ats*. The congregation disperses, each man returning to the usual duties of the day.

There is no priesthood in Islam. Each Muslim is regarded as being responsible for his own actions and decisions. However there have always been individuals within the *Ummah* who devote their lives to the study and practice of their faith, and, because of their *taqwa* [righteousness], are appointed to lead the faithful in worship. It is expected that such *Imam*s 'must be the best in character, piety and righteousness. He must have the greater knowledge of Islam, especially the Quran, than others'.[16] It is also assumed that 'an *Imam* should be liked and respected by the majority of the congregation'.[17] Unlike a priest within the Roman Catholic or Orthodox traditions in Christianity the *Imam* in a mosque does not claim to be an intermediary between humans and God. Although greatly respected, an *Imam* is first amongst equals. Mahmood, a regular worshipper at the *Ahmadi* mosque explained how, 'If an *Imam* is not present, any male member of the congregation who has knowledge of the Quran can take a service, but it's usually someone older, wiser, more respected'. All members of the mosque are trained for this. '*Imam*s are not tyrants', remarked Mahmood with a wry smile on his face, 'sometimes the people of a mosque can get rid of him'. He explained how if an *Imam* is guilty of impropriety, or the congregation lose confidence in him, he may be removed. He also told me that the *Imam* himself, for health or personal reasons, has the right to resign. As one writer remarks: 'in this there is no shame, nor should selfishness prevent him from doing so'.[18] Under the instruction of the *Imam*, and interaction with the collective ethos of the *Jama'at* generally, the members assimilate the ideology of the group. Such assimilation of 'orthodox'

---

16 Mawdudi, *Let us be Muslims*, op.cit., p. 172.

17 Ibid., p. 172.

18 Ibid, p. 173.

teaching guides the members, enabling them to adopt acceptable behaviour, and to interpret what occurs in the world outside the safety of the organisation. Many Muslims, *Ahmadi* and mainstream alike, are confused by the issues raised by modern secular society: is it right to go to discos, the cinema, have relationships with non-believers? They look to their leaders for advice, and guidance. The *Imam*, like the prophet Muhammad, is the example to emulate. He is a venerated figure, respected for his learning and piety. The Muslims who invited me to attend the Byrom Street Mosque, young men in their early twenties, manifested deep respect, almost adoration for their *Imam*s, elderly non-English speaking clerics, otherworldly and wise. However, in talking to Muslims in the Bradford area I sensed amongst some Muslims a deep feeling of disillusionment towards the local *Imam*s. Some Muslims are concerned at the cultural and generational differences between *Imam*s and the members of their congregations, differences which invariably influence the *Imam*'s role and image within the *Ummah*. There is often tension between the older and younger generations. Some see the *ulema* as too conservative, supporting the policies of whatever government is in office, rather than criticising those policies. The members of the committee controlling the mosque are usually elderly, always male, and usually the original migrants to the city. Younger Muslims often see such men as too traditional, 'out of touch', more knowledgeable about the practice of Islam in rural Pakistan than the problems facing Muslims in secular Britain. Others criticise the *ulema* for getting involved in local feuds rather than providing strong and effective leadership. I heard no criticisms, and sensed no undercurrents of dissent, against the leadership amongst members of the *Ahmadiyya Jama'at*. It was not that the *Ahmadi* I met with deliberately concealed such feelings from me, for they spoke to me openly on every subject, even the most personal things, occasionally matters considered *haram* [forbidden] or *makrou* [frowned upon but tolerated] by their leaders. The leaders within the *Ahmadi* organisation are genuinely respected, if not loved, as men appointed by God to guide.

The Imam of the *Baitul Hamd* Mosque, Naseem Ahmad Bajwa, living in the mission quarters of the mosque [a self contained flat at the front of the building] is the missionary in charge, not only

of the Bradford *Jama'at* but also the groups meeting at Huddersfield, Halifax, Scunthorpe, Keighley, Leeds, Sheffield, Hartlepool
and Spen valley. He and his family moved to Bradford in August
2001. A tall, lean man in his mid-fifties, although looking much
younger, Naseem was always immaculately dressed in a well ironed
shalwar kameez, or a salubrious black *sherwani* jacket, and either a
Jinnah or traditional Afghan hat on his head. *Imam* Bajwa, typical of *Imam*s generally, leads the five daily prayers and delivers the
khutba [sermon] at Friday prayers. He gives lectures and talks to the
community; distributes literature; visits the sick, the needy, widows,
orphans and those recently bereaved; offers counselling and advice;
performs marriages and funerals; organises and attends religious
and social functions and reports to the *Khalifa*, the Head of his sect.
His wife, Mrs Rashiqa Bajwa and his daughter teach the Quran to
the children and women, and [as is normal in an Asian household]
perform the numerous other [mainly domestic] daily duties. *Imam*
Bajwa is a rare mixture of decency, serenity and wisdom, a man of
sincere piety: upright and honest. Nothing was too much trouble for
him in assisting me to gain information on the *Ahmadiyya Jama'at*. I
really looked forward to, and enjoyed, my times at the mosque when
we would talk in his office or I would sit at a desk in another room,
reading through back copies of *Al-Baseerat*. He would always take
pride in offering me hospitality. As I worked on my laptop computer
he would always appear with a tray laden with fruit, a cup of tea and
samosas or some other delicacy. At other times he would take me
through to his private living accommodation and offer me food prepared beforehand by his wife. We would talk for long periods of time
on all aspects of Islam and Christianity: aware of our differences, yet
also the similarities in our beliefs. Looking at me through his silver-
rimmed spectacles, and with an unfeigned and touching humility, he
would share his life with me: his days at Shahid College in Pakistan,
his family in Birmingham, his times of persecution when preaching
on the streets of Bradford and other cities, and his *hajj* to Mecca, one
of the highlights of his life undertaken in 2004. There was a gentle
amiability about the man, nothing of the pomposity and arrogance
often manifested by those placed in positions of authority in various
religious institutions. On one occasion Naseem gave me a ring, a sil-

ver ring worn by most *Ahmadi* men, on which is inscribed in Arabic the words spoken by Allah to Ahmad; 'is Allah not sufficient for His servant'. I believe I have his friendship for life.

Although *salat* [*namaz*] has a central place in a Muslim's life, in the desire to proselytise, and nurture the faithful, numerous other events and activities are organised at the mosque throughout the year. Believing, as *Imam* Bajwa remarked, that Islam 'covers every area of life', activities are held for all age groups within the *Jama'at*. *Atfal* and *Nasirat* groups [girls and boys aged seven to fifteen], like other age groups within the *Jama'at*, meet weekly, and are trained in their faith and prepared to defend it by argument to outsiders. At a typical *Tarbiyyat* week [moral training, held regularly in each district], as well as fun, sports competitions, and 'the ever popular tuck-shop', lectures are given on a variety of subjects, including: sections of the Quran, prayer, and the differences between Islam and Christianity. These are followed by tests on each lecture. Each child follows a syllabus of study, graduating at different stages of their development.[19] The emphasis at such meetings is on recreation as well as study: swimming and football are arranged for the *Atfal* at the local sports centre on alternate Saturdays.

A typical week at the *Ahmadi* mosque involves meetings for other groups as well as *Atfal* and *Nasirat*. The *Khuddam*, [males between sixteen and forty]; *Ansar*, [men over forty] and the *Lajna*, [women sixteen and above] also meet regularly. Occasional meetings are held for the 'young *Khuddam*', males aged fifteen to twenty-five, and the 'young *Lajna*', for women under fifteen years of age; such meetings are usually highly didactic in nature. Members of the *Jama'at* are involved in various activities which take place at localities away from the mosque. The *Ansar* and other groups for example have their annual *Shura*, or Conference, in London. All other national gatherings of the other sub-groups are held at Islamabad in Surrey. As well as meetings held in London, regional gatherings are organised at other local mosques such as that at Spen Valley, Keighley or Scunthorpe. At such regional meetings issues relevant to that particular group are

---

19 See *Al-Baseerat*, (January 1993), p. 14 and also details given in a 'Report on events of 1993', *Al-Baseerat* (January 1994), pp. 2-6.

discussed, often with the advice and help of national leaders travelling up from London specifically to attend that gathering.

Special annual events occur at the *Ahmadi* mosque such as the *Musleh Maud* day, usually held on 20 February, celebrating the occasion when the founder of the movement, Mirza Ghulam Ahmad, claimed to have had a revelation predicting the birth of his son. Other days include *Siratun Nabi*, a day remembering the exemplary character of the prophet Muhammad; *Masih Maud* Day on 23 March, on which the *Ahmadi* remember when Ahmad first declared himself to be the promised Messiah; *Khilafat Day* on 27 May celebrating the significance of *Khalifate* and Religious Founders Day, a propaganda and promotional event, when people of other faiths are invited to talk about their religion and its founder. The most important event on the *Ahmadi* calendar however, especially in terms of public relations and bridge-building with the local community and wider non-Muslim society, is the *Eid Milan* party. By *waqar-i-amal* [the dignity of labour] the mosque is cleaned and decorated, by an enthusiastic team of volunteer workers. Tables are set up and the hall is decorated with posters and banners. On the occasion itself volunteers, usually from the *Khuddam*, undertake car park duty; members of the *Atfal* perform cloakroom duties, looking after coats and shoes; others carry out the registration, meet the guests and escort them to their places. The event is filmed and relayed to another room where the women are segregated.

The *Eid Milan* Party in 2002, typical of other years, was attended by over 600 people including over 200 guests.[20] Certain dignitaries attended including John Battle, MP and faith adviser to the Prime Minister; the Rt. Rev., David Smith, the Bishop of Bradford; Cllr. Margaret Eaton the Leader of Bradford Council; Ian Stewart, Chief Executive of Bradford Council,; Cllr Ghazanfer Khaliq, the Lord Mayor of Bradford; Terry Rooney MP and other leaders of various faiths from across the region. The event began in the traditional manner with *ti'awat* and *nazm*, the recitation of the Quran in Arabic and a prayer, by *Imam* Bajwa, followed by an English translation. Bari Malik, as President of the Bradford *Ahmadiyya Jama'at* then

---

20 Sunday 17 March, 2002.

gave a welcoming speech, followed by short addresses by some of the afore-mentioned guests. Charity work being an important aspect of the life of the *Ahmadi*, a giant card-board cheque of £1000 was made to the Lord Mayor for his 'Lord Mayor's Appeal'. The chief guest, John Battle MP, addressing the function, spoke about the 11 September and the riots that had taken place in Bradford in July the same year. He stressed the importance of building bridges and strengthening community relations while pin-pointing the role of religion in modern society. The same themes were then reiterated by Bilal Atkinson, who spoke in his capacity as regional *Amir* of the *Ahmadiyya Jama'at*. The guests then enjoyed a meal consisting of starters of Onion Bhajees or Chicken Tikka with mint sauce followed by a selection of pilau rice with chickpeas, lamb curry, dhal, vegetable curry with salad and sweet rice as the main course. As one of the invited guests on that occasion I can justifiably affirm that the event, particularly the meal, was enjoyed by all.

For the *Ahmadi*, as for Muslims generally, the year centres on the main religious festivals, particularly *Ramadan*. *Ramadan* is celebrated as 'the [month] in which the Quran was revealed as a guidance for mankind with clear proofs of guidance and discrimination [between right and wrong]'.[21] During this festival, from the first day of the sacred month to the appearance of the *Shawwal* moon, it is compulsory for every sane adult Muslim, whether male or female, to fast. From sunrise to sunset, [or as tradition states, from the time a white thread can be distinguished from a black one], no food or drink is to be consumed, a person must abstain from smoking, sexual intercourse, unkind thoughts and quarrelling. Exemptions to this may include pregnant women, mothers suckling young babies, people with serious illness, travelers and children. These however have to complete their missing fasts as soon as possible after the festival ends, and certainly before the next *Ramadan*. This abstinence from all food, drink, and sexual relations during the hours of daylight is regarded as a sacred duty. Not only is it a commandment given in the Quran but it is believed that 'to be moderate in eating and drinking and to bear hunger and thirst are necessary for the purification of the

---

21 Quran 2:185.

spirit and promote the capacity for visions'.[22] Obviously it is a time of discipline and self restraint for the Muslim. The Islamic calendar consists of twelve lunar months, consequently *Ramadan* occurs at different times each year. As Naseer, one member of the Bradford *Jama'at*, ruefully remarked: 'if the holy festival falls in the summer months we have such long days in which we must fast. Although still difficult, it is much easier to fulfil our obligations in winter when daylight hours are so short'. Members of the *Jama'at* are reminded that in fasting, as in all other spiritual activities, the worshipper must have the correct *niyyat* or intention. 'Before beginning a fast', advises the editor of *Al-Baseerat*, 'you must first make an intention to fast'.[23] Simply to fast is not enough, the mind and the heart must be focused on God. The festival of *Ramadan* comes to an end at the sighting of the New Moon, when the festival of *Eid-ul-fitr* takes place. Although Muslims fast throughout *Ramadan*, they also fast at other times, such as during *chilla*, [voluntary periods of forty days] but also on Thursdays. Thursday is regarded as being especially holy because it is believed that on this day the angels present an account of an individual's actions to Allah. Therefore fasting may gain *sawab* or favour, and persuade the angels to present a more favourable report to God.

On one night in the month of *Ramadan*, *Lailat al-kadr*, otherwise known as 'The Night of Power', it is believed that Muhammad received his first revelation from the Angel Gabriel.[24] As a way of celebrating this night some members of the *Jama'at* will observe *Itikaf*, a form of retreat when, during the last ten days of the festival a person who can afford to, will leave his usual everyday duties to stay in the mosque, concentrating totally on God.[25] During *Ramadan* in 2003 [27 October–26 November] I was invited by *Imam* Bajwa to join with such *Mu'takifins*, [the name given to those undertaking

---

22 Mirza Ghulam Ahmad, speech given at the Annual Conference, 1906, cited in *Al-Baseerat*, front page, (March, 1990).

23 *Al-Baseerat*, (March 1990), p. 3.

24 The Night of Power, the 27th night of the month of *Ramadan*, is described in Quran 97.

25 K. Zirvi, *Welcome to Ahmadiyyat*, op.cit., pp. 153-4.

the retreat] and observe what went on during *Itikaf.* On a cold and windy November morning, I awoke at 4.15 am, and made my way to the mosque, where *Imam* Bajwa and a group of about six other men had already gathered round a table covered with food, the *sehri* meal, the last meal before dawn. It is a time of blessing, preparation and bonding between men who share a similar devotion to God. Despite the early hour, and the howling wind outside making the doors to the worship area creak and groan, the conversation was animated. As we consumed cornflakes, chappati, dhal, and strong tea we discussed the arrival of President George Bush to the UK, the political situation in Pakistan and her neighbour India and other issues making the headlines in the news. With breakfast finished, at the set time, *Fajr*, the early morning prayers, began. Numerous other men, those who did not gather for the *sehri* meal, and not being able to observe *Itikaf*, arrived at the mosque, and on entering the worship area performed the required *rakas.* On this particular morning about thirty men assembled in rows, facing the *Qibla* wall, and went through the ritual of prayer. The *Dar-ul-Quran*, the portion of the Quran for that day was read and *Imam* Bajwa, reading in English, passed comment on *Surah* 2:186-7, explaining the need for fasting. Prayers over, and most of the congregation having gone off to their homes or places of employment, I sat and chatted with those that remained: men intent on gaining favour with God. The main hall had the appearance of a hospital ward, with make-shift curtains erected in such a way to form separate cubicles, providing a certain measure of privacy for each *Mu'takifin* to sleep, pray or read. During this time of voluntary retreat it is not allowed for the *Mu'takifin* to leave the mosque 'except for a genuine pious purpose and for the basic physical needs'.[26] Food, clean clothes and other needs are therefore provided by their families during their stay in the mosque. During the long intervals between the usual times of *namaz* the men spent their time catching up on sleep, praying or reading the Quran. As *Imam* Bajwa informed me: 'if possible it is desirable for us to read one chapter a day and try to complete the reading of the Holy Quran by the end of *Ramadan*'. With the sound of snoring coming from the worship room, and the

---

26 Zirvi, *Welcome to Ahmadiyyat*, ibid., p. 153.

roof groaning with the force of the wind outside, I sat at my lap-top computer at a table set up for that purpose in the entrance hall, taking notes from back copies of *Al-Baseerat*. The usual times of prayer were observed during the day when, just as at *Fajr*, other men arrived to join the *Mu'takifin*. After the sun had set the fast is broken and the *iftari* meal takes place. With relish, I joined in with the other men, eating the permissible food spread out on plates on a cloth covering the floor. With the performance of *Maghrib* [prayers immediately after the sun has set] and *Isha*, [prayers offered 'when dusk has finally disappeared, giving way to the darkness of night'] the day ended.[27] I stayed for some time, talking with the men who, for that day, had been my companions, the objects of my respectful scrutiny. As preparations were made for sleep and more prayer and another days fasting, I rejected an invitation to stay the night, quietly packed away my things and disappeared into the cold and darkness of the night. I knew my limits.

Throughout the period of *Ramadan*, it is the usual practice to hold *Dars ul Hadith* [talks on the traditions about the prophet] each day after *Fajr* prayers. A portion of the Quran [the Quran being divided into thirty sections so that the entire book will be read by the end of the month] is read by different members of the *Jama'at*. At weekends during *Ramadan* the *Khalifah's Dars ul Quran* are presented on the *Ahmadi* satellite TV channel. These practices signify the place of the Quran in the life of Muslims generally. Accepting it as 'the Holy Word of Allah conveyed to the Holy Prophet Muhammad by Divine revelation, over the period of twenty-two years, five months and fourteen days (610-632AD)', the Quran is believed to be infallible and inerrant.[28] Ignoring the textual problems that exist concerning the original collection of the traditions that went into the formalisation of the Quran under *Khalifa* Uthman,[29] it is argued 'in every religious book you will find mistakes except the Quran'. 'No one has found a mistake in the Quran in 1,400 years' declared one leading

---

27 Ibid., p. 100.

28 Ibid., p. 173.

29 The third *Khalifa* (d.656 AD), or successor, following the death of Muhammad.

member of the *ulema*.[30] As Sheik Anwar Bady, *Imam* at the London Central Mosque, remarked: 'no single word was added or omitted from the Quran. It's correct – it's the same as revealed from Allah'.[31] Applying either a figurative or literal, but uncritical, interpretation, the *Ahmadi* similarly assert 'the Holy Quran is the book of Allah. No other word is more definite and absolutely certain than the Word of God. It is clear from impurities of doubts and suspicions'.[32] Believing in its divine source and nature, for any Muslim the Quran is 'a detailed exposition of all things, and guidance and a mercy to a people who believe'.[33] They proudly assert how 'the wine of our spiritual knowledge is from the cup of the Book of God which is called the Quran'. As such it is taken for granted that the Quran 'contains a complete code of teaching and laws suitable to the needs of every age and provides the means for the spiritual and moral development of all mankind'.[34] As the Quran itself states it is 'an Exhortation from your Lord and a healing for whatever disease there is in the hearts, and guidance and a mercy to the believers'.[35] To ignore the Quran is to jeopardise one's spiritual well-being in this present life and one's eternal destiny. Ahmad declared to his followers: 'even a footstep's separation from that luminous Book is, with us, *kufr*, damnation and ruin'.[36] With these points in mind the *Ahmadi* do not simply read the Quran, they savour it. They recite the words aloud because for them it is the actual word of God, existing with Allah since the very beginning of time. The term Quran means 'recitation'. As such Muslims argue it is meant to be recited, read out loud, giving a sense of the divine. One *Ahmadi* told me how the beauty of the Arabic words have a mesmeric effect upon his mind, making him feel as though

---

30 The words of Abdul Kalam, Muslim cleric, cited by the *Daily Telegraph*, (27 March 2004).

31 *Daily telegraph*, (27 March 2004), op.cit.

32 Zirvi, *Welcome to Ahmadiyyat*, op.cit., p. 170.

33 Quran 12:111.

34 Zirvi, op.cit., p. 173.

35 Quran 10:58.

36 The words of Mirza Ghulam Ahmad, *Malfoozat*, vol. 1, p. 408, cited in *Al Baseerat*, (September 1992), front cover.

he was actually in the presence of Allah. For the *Ahmadi*, as with Muslims generally, reading and learning the Quran, with the duty of fasting, are essential activities in the daily walk with God.

Within the *Ahmadiyya Jama'at* medicine is seen as an integral element of religion. 'Allah has given us cures for the body as well as the soul', remarked Khalid, an elderly *Pathan*, one of the earliest members of the Huddersfield *Jama'at*. An important part of *Ahmadiyya* life in the mosque is the practice of homeopathy, the method of treating illness by the use of a small amount of a drug that, in healthy persons, produces symptoms similar to those of the disease being treated. Believing in a holistic approach to health problems, a combination of drugs, herbs, diet, prayer and counselling are offered for the cure of physical and mental ills. Within each *Ahmadi* community a Secretary of homeopathy is appointed, to specialise in the dispensing of such drugs, herbs and remedies. There is usually a small room or cupboard in each mosque where medicines and herbs are stored and dispensed. Mirza Ghulam Ahmad had been known for his knowledge of medicine. The second *Khalifa* was similarly interested in medicine and studied allopathic treatments. The fourth *Khalifa* was also a firm believer, if not an acknowledged expert, in homeopathic medicine. During his *Khalifate* he received hundreds of requests from *Ahmadi* and non-*Ahmadi* inquirers seeking advice on appropriate medicines for various ailments.

In May 2005 I visited the *Ahmadi* responsible for homeopathy in the Bradford *Jama'at*. An appointment had been made for my friend, Mustafa, a civil servant in Bradford, a lapsed Muslim. Mustafa had, three years previously, suffered a hernia while lifting stones in his back garden. Surgery had led to further complications resulting in four other operations. Mustafa, finding no relief to his pain, and no answers to explain the problems he experienced, had tried several consultants, even acupuncture, for a remedy. I had told him of the *Ahmadi* and their penchant for homeopathy and having an open mind, and feeling understandably frustrated with conventional medicine, he decided to give it a try. We went at the appointed time, not to the mosque which was the usual place for meeting with such a man, but to the Secretary's home. We knocked on the door of his basic cottage. Muhammad [a useful pseudonym for him], a man who looked to be in his late fifties, whom we later learned was close to seventy, answered the door and invited us in. The one room downstairs, almost spartan in appearance, contained a sofa, chairs, and a television set. The other articles in the room were tools for the trade used by Muhammad in his role as Secretary of homeopathy; a large fridge containing medicines, a large stand holding herbs that didn't need to be kept cold, and bookcases holding rows of medical journals, texts and notes. Another *Ahmadi*, Zafar, was waiting inside. In an atmosphere of friendliness and genuine concern we entered conversation. After some time Zafar left, allowing Mustafa the opportunity to discuss his medical problem privately with Muhammad. After listening intently for sometime, and asking the relevant questions, Muhammad suggested the problem that Mustafa had was appendicitis. Mustafa confirmed that this was the diagnosis put forward by at least one of the specialists he had been seeing at the local hospital. 'It is the guidance of God, not me', Muhammad replied modestly. He began to give general advice to Mustafa. 'Leave off cucumbers altogether, hard to digest' he said. 'Eat only simple food; fresh chapatti is good, but do not use bread with yeast, it causes arthritis— use wholemeal instead'. Looking intently at Mustafa through his round, silver-rimmed glasses Muhammad advised: 'always peel apples, salad is beneficial; carrots are good for the eyes, they also prevent inflammation, ulcers in the tummy and nervous troubles; avoid tinned food and things that cause gases. Avoid meat'. He began to explain some of the herbs he used. I knew from previous reading about the *Ahmadi* that the wide selection of herbs used includes *Carduus Marianus*, which is given for various ailments but particularly liver problems, and *Atropa Belladonna*, otherwise known as Deadly Nightshade, used for abdominal pains, ear problems, fever, headaches, coughs, colds and toothache. Similarities can be drawn between the dispensers of homeopathy in the *Ahmadiyya Jama'at* and the practice of *hakim*, the untrained doctors, or herbalists, who prescribe various remedies to cure most illnesses within the mainstream Islamic community. I had come across such *hakim*, not only in villages and towns in Pakistan, but in the Asian communities of Bradford, Huddersfield and other British towns. They were respected, even revered figures, particularly within the immigrant communities from rural Pakistan and Bangladesh.

Muhammad told us that he had become interested in medicine over forty years ago while living in the Punjab. In 1962 his daughter had developed typhoid fever. The doctor offered him a medicine costing fifteen rupees, a large sum of money at that time. Muhammad rushed home and gave the medicine to his ailing daughter but, to his surprise and grief, found her worse the next morning. On his way to see the doctor again he met a friend, a railway worker, who told him of a herbalist, an old man, who lived just down the road. Muhammad, eager to see his daughter well again, ran to the herbalist and persuaded him to visit his home. Having checked the girl's pulse and temperature, the old man prescribed a very small quantity of a liquid from a small bottle. He charged Muhammad only a fraction of what the doctor had charged for his medicine. The daughter got better during the night and was fully recovered by the morning. Although the cure of his daughter had a great influence in his thinking about medicine, the event that finally turned Muhammad's interest totally to homeopathy occurred some time later. Muhammad owned a large number of hens but one day they all became very ill, some dying. He questioned a homeopath about the problem. The homeopath gave him the same herb which had cured his daughter. Not believing that the same medicine could be used on both humans and animals, yet desperate to save his hens, Muhammad reluctantly applied the herbs. The hens recovered. Muhammad told us that from that time he had never doubted the effects of homeopathic remedies, and began to acquire his considerable knowledge about the subject. 'If I have a problem in assessing the right medicine to use', he said laughingly, 'I ring up my son who is a fully qualified doctor in Pakistan'.

At the end of the session, and once the medicine had been given, Mustafa offered to pay for his treatment. 'There is no charge for such remedies', said Muhammad holding up his hands, 'if we can help we will'. In doing this Muhammad was following the practice of the *Ahmadi* generally. They wish no slur on the *Ahmadi* faith. They do not want the *Ahmadi* likened to many *hakim* in the Asian community who charge a fee and make a handsome living curing other people's illnesses. Muhammad reminded us of the practice of the fourth *Ah-*

madi Khalifa who died in 2003. 'He was an expert in homeopathy;' he informed us with pride, 'he used to treat people free of charge from all over the world'. As one of the *Khalifa's* biographers remarked, he received 'a hundred or more letters a day from people describing their symptoms and asking him to prescribe a homeopathic medicine for them. Most requests are naturally from *Ahmadis*, but there are many people who have heard of the success of his treatments and have asked if he will prescribe for them'.[37] Some weeks later I asked Mustafa if the medicine had worked. For him the herbs had not worked and the health problems persist. However, others that I spoke to about 'the *Ahmadi* way', both *Ahmadi* and non-*Ahmadi*, were confident of the cure brought about by the medicine they received.

An important aspect of the life of the mosque is the organising and disciplining of its members. *Ahmadi,* similar to Muslims generally, proclaim a strict moral code. 'Whosoever does not wholly and completely keep away from every sin and every evil action, like wine, gambling, looking lustfully at women, dishonesty, bribes, and from every kind of illegal gratification', declared Ahmad, 'he is not of my community'.[38] Following the teaching of the Quran, it is expected that members of the *Jama'at* will 'shun all that is vain, and when they spend they do not waste'. Requiring all members to 'refrain from following un-Islamic customs and lustful inclinations' the third *Khalifa* emphasised how 'it is the duty of every *Ahmadi* family to uproot all bad practices from their homes and throw them out'.[39] In 1934 the second *Khalifa* announced what later became known as the 'New Scheme', a scheme to encourage the spirit of sacrifice of the *Ahmadi* people and to develop their spirituality.[40] Various demands were made, some of which are not observed by the *Ahmadi* today, such as the prohibition on visiting the cinema, theatres, circuses, and

---

37 Iain Adamson, *A Man of God: The Astonishing Story of His Holiness Khalifatul Masih IV,* Bristol: George Shepherd Publishers, 1991, p. 264.

38 Mirza Ghulam Ahmad, 'Conditions of Initiation', cited in *Al-Baseerat,* (December 1991), p. 2.

39 See *Al-Baseerat,* (December 1991), p. 2.

40 The New Scheme was pronounced compulsory by the *Khalifa* in 1937.

places of amusement generally.[41] As described in Chapter Eight on family life, *Ahmadi* are not averse to attending such leisure centres, several *Ahmadi* enjoying 'nights out' to watch a film or go to a football match.

Other prohibitions, which may seem petty and puritanical to some, are applied to wedding celebrations. *Ahmadi* are forbidden, for example: to give or eat 'cooked food on the occasion of a marriage'; to 'give fireworks display[s]' or to 'spend money on dancers and musicians'.[42] The practice of *Mehndi*, common amongst Muslims generally, of staining the bride's hands and feet with henna at a marriage, is seen as being 'contrary to Islam'. Similarly the practice of *sehra*, the wearing of a chaplet or wreath by the bride and bridegroom at a wedding, is regarded as 'a bad innovation'. As Ahmad stated, such a practice 'is tantamount to turning a man into a horse'.[43] Dancing at weddings is seen as 'a manifestly evil habit which once allowed will be impossible to stop and is bound to lead to moral bankruptcy'.[44] In 1991 the *Khalifa* 'instructed that all members of the *Jama'at* should be given notice that he will not participate in any marriage function, i.e. *Nikah* [marriage ceremony], *Rukhstana* [wedding reception], or *Walima* [wedding party given for friends and family], unless the parties concerned give written undertaking that they will strictly observe the tenets of Islam in respect of these functions and will eschew any custom or practice forbidden under the discipline of *Jama'at Ahmadiyya*'.[45] If anyone refused to do this it was recommended that 'he or she should be advised to leave the discipline of the *Jama'at* and act independently'.

---

41 *Al-Baseerat*, (December 1991), op.cit., p. 2.

42 'Wedding Guidelines', summary of rules relating to 'undesirable and innovative practices' issued by the Sho'ba Rishta, Nazarat Islaho-Irshad, Rabwah, in *Al-Baseerat*, (December 1991), ibid., pp. 2-3. The prohibition of giving or eating 'cooked food on the occasion of a marriage' was originally put forward to protect poorer members of the *Jama'at* in Pakistan who could never compete with the sumptious meals presented at weddings by wealthier members. 'Cooked food' in this context refers to food provided by outside caterers.

43 Ibid.

44 Ibid.

45 The words of Mirza Ghulam Ahmad, *Kashti-Nooh*, pp. 9-10, cited by *Al Baseerat*, (July 1992), p. 1. See Iain Adamson, *Man of God*, op.cit., p. 31.

There is a set procedure for resolving disputes between members of the community. As mentioned previously, *Ahmadi* are expected to take their disagreements before the *Darul Qada*, internal courts, on the basis of *Sharia'h* law. Such courts are free of charge.[46] Only civil matters, not required by the laws of the land, can be heard by such courts. In a mosque the *qadi*, or judge, can pronounce *fatawah* [legal opinions] or *mas'ala*, lesser legal decisions. 'As a member of the Community', declared Tahir Selby, 'we have the right to rectify what we consider to have been done wrongly or report it to a higher authority'.[47] The recommended procedure in settling disputes, as Selby explains, 'is to send a copy of the disagreement to the person you have the disagreement with'. However if the disagreement cannot be resolved amicably between the two parties concerned the matter should be taken to higher authority: first the Secretary of the mosque, then the regional *Amir* and lastly the national *Amir*. Selby stresses the importance of sending 'a copy to the person we are disagreeing with' for 'this is the spirit which we develop into *Ahmadis*, not just to understand the rules, but to submit to *Nizam-e-Jama'at* in accordance to the spirit underlying these rules'.[48] Each *Jama'at* has its own *Islahi* committee which is 'responsible for identifying moral dangers before they affect the *Jama'at*. They also endeavour to deal with any ills among *Jama'at* members'.[49] Such committees are regionally based so 'that members can have access to them more readily'. 'Members of the *Jama'at*', remarks Selby, 'can contact any of the *Islahi* Committee members... for counselling', which 'is provided in complete confidence' and 'lady counsellors are also available'.

Ahmadiyyat, like Islam generally, can appear strict in its administration of punishment. For example the *Ahmadi* recognise the cutting off of hands as a Quranic punishment prescribed for theft.[50] In an attempt to soften the apparent harshness of such punishment it is suggested that 'the Holy Quran makes it quite clear that this drastic measure

---

46 Karimullah Zirvi, *Welcome to Ahmadiyyat*, op.cit., p. 373.
47 *Al-Baseerat*, (December 1991), op.cit., p. 2.
48 Ibid.
49 Ibid.
50 Quran 5:39.

should be meted out only to habitual and totally incorrigible and unrepentant offenders'.[51] It is further argued that 'the proof of the pudding is in the eating' for, while crime statistics soar in cities such as London, New York or Los Angeles, 'in Mecca for example, where the cutting off of hands is inflicted, on average no more than three or four times a year, theft of any kind is a very rare crime'.[52] The harshest punishment for offenders within the *Jama'at* in Britain is expulsion. 'The main punishment for someone going away from the rules of the community', states Tahir Selby, 'is to be expelled from the *Nizam-e-Jama'at*, to be no longer a member of the *Ahmadiyya* Community'.[53] Expulsion of a member 'can only be imposed by the *Khalifa*'.

The following reports of internal discipline illustrate the procedure of expulsion of members from the *Jama'at*. The 1993 edition of *Al-Baseerat* refers to Muhammad 1 (the name changed for reasons of confidentiality). It states how 'the person named who is presently residing in Bradford, UK, arrived in England in 1988 in breach of *Nizam-e-Jama'at*'. Although the offence committed is not mentioned we are informed that Muhammad 1 'was repeatedly requested to comply with the code of discipline of the *Ahmadiyya Jama'at* and to return to Pakistan and was informed that if he wished to return to England he might do so through *Nizam-e-Jama'at*'. 'Unfortunately', concludes the report, 'he failed to comply with the instructions of *Nizam-e-Jama'at* and therefore, with the approval of *Hadhrat* Khalifatul Masih IV, he has been expelled from the *Ahmadiyya Jama'at*'.[54] Another person, Muhammad 2 'violated the code of discipline of *Ahmadiyya Jama'at* when he came to England to attend *Jalsa Salana* 1986'. This time we are informed that the offender had 'stayed on [in England] to seek asylum in this country'. Consequently 'he was... expelled from the *Jama'at*'. However in this instance the miscreant was 'asked to return to Pakistan and seek pardon' from the *Khalifa*. The report states how Muhammad 2 'has since complied with the

---

51 'Common Misconceptions', *The Muslim Herald*, (April 1982), p. 8.

52 *The Muslim Herald*, (April 1982), op.cit., p. 8.

53 *Al-Baseerat*, (October 1993), p. 3.

54 Islahi Committee report, *Ahmadiyya Bulletin*, (December 2002/January 2003), p.8.

instructions of *Nizam-e-Jama'at* and the *Khalifa* 'has very kindly forgiven him'. While driving down to London with Dr Muhammad Iqbal [a member of the Bradford *Jama'at*] to celebrate the opening of the *Baitul Futuh* Mosque in October 1993, my companion informed me that as far as he could remember there had been about three expulsions from the Bradford *Jama'at* during the previous ten or fifteen years: one for marrying outside the community, one for selling items in his shop believed to be *haram*, the third offence he could not recall. Despite several requests, I was never given official accounts of disciplinary action against members of the *Jama'at*, nor statistics relating to the number of expulsions.

6
AHMADI BELIEF AND TEACHING

The *Ahmadi*, like Muslims generally, believe in 'the five fundamental acts of worship in Islam', acts usually designated as the five pillars of Islam.[1] Reference has already been made to the importance of these acts: *shahada, salat, zakat, sawm* and *hajj* in Islam. Similarly, the *Ahmadi* notion of '*iman* or belief, and '*Amal*, deeds and practice, is to a great extent identical to the belief and practice of most mainstream Muslims. In particular *tawhid*, 'the absolute oneness of God', is seen by the *Ahmadi* as 'the most important and the cardinal principle of Islam'.[2] In accordance with Islamic theology generally, the *Ahmadi* acknowledge the existence of Angels, 'spiritual beings who are assigned various duties by God and carry them out as commanded by Him';[3] believe in 'the revealed books', namely the *Tawrat* [Torah], *Zabur* [Psalms of David], *Injil* [Gospel of Jesus] and the Quran; accept 'all the prophets or Messengers sent by God Almighty and revere them';[4] and believe in 'the idea of *akhirah*, judgement day, when every Muslim will be judged and asked to give an account'.

---

1   Waheed Ahmad, *A Book of Religious Knowledge for Ahmadi Muslims*, Athens, Ohio: Fazl-I-umar Press, 1988, p. 38.

2   Karimullah Zirvi, *Welcome to Ahmadiyyat: The true Islam*, Silver Springs, USA: Ahmadiyya Movement in Islam, 2002, op.cit., p. 53.

3   W. Ahmad, *A Book of Religious Knowledge*, op.cit., p. 21. It is relevant to point out that the *Ahmadi* follow the *Hijri Shmasi* calendar, based on a solar cycle, in contrast to the lunar calendar used by mainstream Islam. See Zirvi, *Welcome to Ahmadiyyat*, op.cit., p. 486, this calendar was introduced for *Ahmadi* usage by the second *Khalifa* in 1938.

4   Zirvi, *Welcome to Ahmadiyyat*, ibid., p. 67.

Like Muslims worldwide, the *Ahmadi* teach that 'every human being will be raised after death, and will be held answerable to God with regards to the life he had led here on earth'.[5] Linked with the idea of *akhirah* is the notion of *taqdir*, the law of nature, the divine decree, which is believed to control 'the eventual outcome of all actions in the universe'. As such, *Ahmadi* and mainstream Muslims alike maintain that 'man is given free will to choose the course' he will follow, and therefore 'we will be judged on the basis of our intentions and deeds on the Day of judgement'.[6] These beliefs are regarded by the *Ahmadi* as 'the foundation of Islam, hidden from the view but supporting the superstructure of Islamic actions'.[7] Presenting themselves as *Sunni* Muslims, the *Ahmadi* declare, 'there is none worthy of worship except God, and Muhammad is the Messenger of God'.

Although declaring themselves to be orthodox in practice and belief, the *Ahmadi* are not accepted as such by mainstream Muslims. As briefly mentioned in Chapter Two, the reason for this rejection centres mainly on the issue of prophet-hood and whether or not there can be prophecy after the prophet. The Qadiani *Ahmadi* teach that although Muhammad was the greatest of the prophets, prophecy did not end with him. This is one of several important points on which the Qadiani *Ahmadi* disagree with the beliefs of the Lahori group. The Lahori group accept Muhammad as the last and the greatest of the Prophets, arguing that no prophet can come after him. They regard Mirza Ghulam Ahmad as *Mujaddid* [reformer] and a prophet in a metaphysical sense only, just as members of various branches of mainstream Islam regard saints or holy men as prophets. For mainstream Muslims, belief in the unique status of Muhammad as the last of the prophets is sacrosanct to the faith. Consequently the Qadiani teaching on prophet-hood is regarded by Muslims generally, not only as wrong, but as 'the most dangerous – of all the conspiracies hatched against Islam in modern times' giving rise to 'wide-spread mental chaos amongst the *Ummah*'.[8] For

---

5   Zirvi, ibid., p. 71.

6   Ibid., p. 72.

7   W. Ahmad, *A Book of Religious Knowledge*, op.cit., p.16.

8   Sayyid A. Mawdudi, *Finality of Prophethood*, Lahore: Islamic Publications,

this reason the Lahori *Ahmadi*, always eager to completely distance themselves from the Qadiani, emphasize with alacrity how Mawdudi, 'the most systematic thinker of modern Islam',[9] although rejecting the Qadiani *Ahmadi* as heretics and non-Muslim because of their teaching on prophet-hood, classed the Lahori *Ahmadi* as Muslims, with the proviso that it is 'expedient policy not to encourage them because it is a path to assisting Qadianism'.[10]

The majority of Muslims believe that the idea of the finality of prophet-hood 'has been unequivocally announced in the Holy Quran'.[11] Reference is made to *Surah* 33:41, which declares how 'Muhammad is not the father of any of your men, but *he is* the Messenger of Allah, and the Seal of the Prophets'.[12] The Arabic phrase *Khataman nabiyeen*, as found in this verse, is usually taken to mean that Muhammad is the 'Seal of the Prophets', the greatest and the last of the prophets sent by God. As such, with Muhammad, it is

---

1975, Foreword.

9   W. C. Smith, *Islam in Modern History*, Princeton: Princeton University Press, 1957, p. 234.

10   In a letter written by Mawdudi, dated 25 March 1938, he stated: 'In my opinion the Qadiani group is excluded from Islam, but the *Ahmadi* (Lahori) group is included within Islam. However, I consider it inadvisable to co-operate with this group or to encourage them because after becoming *Ahmadi* a man becomes very close to Qadianism ... As to the educated people from among the *Ahmadis* (the Lahori *Ahmadi*) who are adhering to this unreasonable position, we cannot issue any *fatwa* (ruling) against them on the basis of the *Sharia'h* because they are denying the prophethood of Mirza. But we are bound to conclude either that they are adhering to their past errors and are guilty of obstinacy, or that they are denying the prophet-hood of Mirza with some reservation of mind, or lastly there is some flaw in their minds making them unable to realize the contradiction in their position. In any case, although we appreciate the work they are doing in support of Islam, we consider it expedient policy not to encourage them because it is a path to assisting Qadianism'. See the entire letter in Urdu and English, http: //www.muslim. org/movement /mawdudi/letter. htm, accessed 14 August 2007.

11   M. Fadil Khan, *Hadhrat Pir Meher Ali Shah of Golra Sharif*, Lahore: n.p., 1989, p. 81.

12   For reasons explained earlier this verse is 33:41 in the Farid translation of the Quran while in other translations it is the previous verse.

suggested, 'the door to formal prophet-hood was closed forever'.[13] As well as the Quran, support for such an interpretation is also found in certain *hadith* where Muhammad is recorded as saying: 'I am the last of the prophets. There will be no prophet after me'.[14] On another occasion, comparing prophet-hood to a beautiful house, Muhammad is reported to have said: 'I am the last brick in the house. I am the last of the prophets'.[15] *Bukhari*, usually regarded as the most authoritative of the *hadiths*, records Muhammad as teaching: 'the tribes of Israel were guided by prophets. When a prophet passed away, another prophet succeeded him. But no prophet will come after me: only *Khalifas* will succeed me'.[16] Elsewhere Muhammad declares: 'the line of prophets has come to an end in me'.[17] Abdullah Yusuf Ali, a well known translator and commentator of the Quran, expressed the mainstream teaching on Muhammad well when he wrote: 'When a document is sealed, it is complete, and there can be no further addition. The Holy Prophet Muhammad closed the long line of Messengers. Allah's teaching is and will always be continuous but there has been and will be no Prophet after Muhammad'. As such, concludes Ali, 'this is not an arbitrary matter. It is a decree full of knowledge and wisdom'.[18]

A long line of Muslim thinkers, going back to the Medieval period and earlier, reject the idea of prophecy after the prophet. Ibn-i-Jarir Tabari, [d. 923 AD] in his Quranic commentary, declared how Muhammad 'has closed and sealed the prophet-hood and the door [of prophet-hood] shall not open for anyone till the end of the world'.[19] Al Ghazali [d. 1111 AD], the 'influential *Ashari* theologian,

---

13   Khan, *Hadhrat Pir Meher Ali Shah of Golra Sharif*, op.cit., p. 5.

14   See *Mishkat-ul-Masabih*, Kitab-ul-Fitan, ch. 2 cited by Sayyid A. Mawdudi, *The Finality of Prophethood*, Lahore: Islamic Publications, 1975, p. 10.

15   Bukhari, *Kitab-ul-Manaqib*, chapter entitled 'Last of the prophets', see Mawdudi, op.cit., p. 13.

16   Bhukhari, *Kitab-ul-Manaqib*, cited by Mawdudi, ibid.

17   Muslim, *Tirmidhi, Ibn Majah*, cited by Mawdudi, ibid., p. 14.

18   Abdullah Yusuf Ali, *The Holy Quran: Text, translation and Commentary*, Maryland, USA: Amana Corporation, 1989, fn 3731 for *Surah* 33:40.

19   Ibn-i-Jarir Tabari, Commentary on the Holy Quran, vol. 22, p. 12 cited by Mawdudi, ibid., p. 15.

jurist, and mystic',[20] stated how 'the entire *Ummah* by a consensus of opinion recognises that the words "No prophet shall come after him", and the context of the traditions, suggest that the Holy Prophet meant that "no Prophet, nor messenger shall follow him"'. 'Furthermore', he continued, 'the *Ummah* is agreed on the point that the above words of the Holy Prophet leave no scope for a different interpretation than given to it by the consensus of the *Ummah*, and he who would not join the consensus is no more than a dissident'.[21] Ibn Kathir, writing in the fourteenth century, vehemently asserted that 'anyone who lays a claim to prophet-hood after Muhammad is a liar, a disruptionist, an impostor, depraved and a seducer, despite his wondrous jugglery and magical feats'.[22] Mawdudi, expressing similar sentiments to Ibn Kathir, argued that those who deny *Khata-man nabiyeen* are 'hypocrites'; 'mischief-mongers' and 'mischievous people'.[23] As he stated; 'a glance through the history of Islam from the first century up to the modern times reveals to us the fact that the *ulema* of all periods in every Islamic country of the world are unanimous in their conviction that no new prophet can be raised after Muhammad'.[24] In his book, *The Finality of Prophethood*, specifically written to refute *Ahmadi* teaching, Mawdudi remarked: 'no messenger nor even a prophet charged with the mission of carrying out reforms in the sphere of law or society which might have been omitted [God forbid] during the lifetime of Muhammad [PBUH] will ever succeed him'. Prophecy, he argued, and continuation of it is an 'infidel custom' brought to an end by Allah. 'Had he not done away with this custom', reasons Mawdudi, 'there would arise no man comparable in status to Prophet Muhammad who could accomplish the task'.[25]

---

20   John L. Esposito, *The Oxford Dictionary of Islam*, Oxford: Oxford University Press, 2003, sv.

21   Al-Ghazali, cited by Maududi, *The Finality of Prophethood*, op.cit., p. 12.

22   *Commentary*, vol. 3, pp. 493-4. cited by Mawdudi, ibid.

23   Mawdudi, ibid., p. 17.

24   Ibid., p. 25.

25   Ibid., p. 4.

The *Ahmadi* 'believe firmly, fervently, without any ambiguity or reservation, and with all their heart and soul' that Muhammad 'was and will ever remain the greatest Prophet of all times – past, present and future – and his *Sharia'h* will remain unaltered and the guiding code and law for mankind till Doomsday'.[26] They believe Muhammad to have been 'the last *law-bearing* prophet who brought the perfect and final Divine law and guidance to mankind and that he was the best of all the prophets and the perfect exemplar who came to mankind with all the Divine blessings'.[27] 'Our belief, which we hold in this life here on earth and to which we will continue to adhere firmly till the time we pass on to the next world', declared Ahmad, 'is that our spiritual leader and master, Muhammad[sa], is the Seal of the Prophets and the Best of Messengers. At his hands', continues Ahmad, 'religion has been perfected and blessing of Allah has been consummated which leads man to the right path and further on to God Himself'.[28] Therefore, the *Ahmadi* affirm with other Muslims that:

The Holy Prophet[sa] is the most perfect of all the Prophets; he is the seal of the prophets and Adornment of the Prophets. All the excellences of prophet-hood found their utmost expression in him and he was handed the key to all greatness and superiority, viz., his divine ordinance [*Sharia'h*], ie., the Holy Quran and the holy Prophet's precept [*sunnah*] will continue to reign till the end of time and will encompass every nook and cranny of the world ... So the Holy Prophet[sa] is the bearer of the final *Sharia'h* and the final preceptor who must be obeyed. He was final to all the prophets: in the *physical* as well as the *spiritual* sense ... With his advent the spiritual munificence of all other prophets came to an end, but his own spiritual munificence will continue till the end of time. And all those spiritual benefits and blessings which the followers of the previous prophets used to receive, will now be delivered, in manifold strength, exclusively at the bounteous hand of the Holy Prophet till the end of time. In short, we in every sense – physical as

---

26 Zirvi, *Welcome to Ahmadiyyat*, op.cit. p. 285.

27 M. Dabbous, *Al-Baseerat*, (December 1992), p. 6.

28 *Izala-e-Auhaam, Roohaani Khazaa*, vol. 3, pp. 169-170, cited in *Mahzarnama: the Memorandum, Submission by the Ahmadiyya Muslim Jama'at to the National Assembly of Pakistan regarding its basic tenets*, trans. by Saleem-ur-rehman, Ghana: n.p., 1999, reprinted Islamabad: Islam International Publications, UK, 2003, p. 22..

well as real, spiritual as well as exegetical – affirm that the Holy Prophet[sa] is the seal of the prophets.[29]

'The concept of the Finality of the Holy Prophet Muhammad' is, for the *Ahmadi*, 'unique and peerless in its comprehensive beauty'.[30] Ahmad regarded it as 'a colossal calumny' that his critics should accuse him and his followers of disbelieving 'the Messenger of Allah[sa] to be *Khataman nabiyeen*'.[31] He vehemently asserted his belief that, in the person of Muhammad 'every excellence reached its end. No doubt, every Prophet came to an end'.[32] In a poem written in Persian he described Muhammad as 'the best of prophets and the best of creation' and how 'every prophet-hood has found its culmination in him'.[33] As such, opines Ahmad, 'it is from him that we drink every water that is; and it is from him that every man who is satiated has received his satisfaction'. In a flurry of poetic praise for the Prophet, Ahmad muses how 'it is from him that we get every light and perfection'. He insists that 'it is impossible to attain union with the eternal Beloved independently of him'. He writes how 'whatever that Messenger of the Lord said about angels and the life to come is from God ... and any Muslim who denies it is deserving of the curse of God'. 'All his miracles', declares Ahmad, 'are right and true, and he who denies them is under the curse of God'.

However, although the *Ahmadi* agree that after Muhammad 'there can be no independent Prophet with a new law or code', to the chagrin of mainstream Muslims, the *Ahmadi* claim there can be lesser prophets.[34] The *Ahmadi* teach that the age in which prophets brought new law has ended but there have been, and will be, non-legislative, *zilli* [shadowy] prophets. As regards the usually held view that Muhammad 'put an end to prophets', the *Ahmadi* maintain that Muhammad 'put an end to all prophets in respect of the excellences of Prophethood'. By this they mean that 'compared to all other prophets he was

---

29   *Mahzarnama: the Memorandum*, op.cit., p. 27-8.

30   *Memorandum*, ibid., p. 69.

31   Ahmad, *Tajaliyyat-I-Ilahiyya*, pp. 24-5 cited in *Memorandum*, ibid.

32   *Taudheeh-e-Maraam, Roohaani Khazaa'*, vol. 3, p. 62 cited in *Memorandum*, ibid., p. 108.

33   Memorandum, ibid., p. 34. The words of Mirza Ghulam Ahmad as contained in a Persian poem, cited by Sher Ali, 'Differences Between *Ahmadis* and Non-*Ahmadis*', *Review of Religions*, (April, 1991), p. 24.

34   Memorandum, ibid., p. 108.

higher in the level of perfection, more elevated and more eminent'.[35] Also, 'his true grandeur is that, in him, not only the Prophet-hood but all possible spiritual excellences also reached the end limits'. The phrase *Khataman nabiyeen* is interpreted by the *Ahmadi* to mean that Muhammad is the spiritual father even of prophets, and therefore, such lesser prophets cannot be independent prophets but ones that bear 'the seal of his allegiance and spiritual fatherhood'.[36] In other words *Khataman nabiyeen* is to be understood, not as meaning 'the last of all prophets', but as 'father of Prophets', the greatest and best of all prophets, and the last law-bearing prophet. As such it is claimed that there can be spiritual sons of Muhammad [Ahmad himself claiming to be such a son] who will be prophets bearing the 'seal of his allegiance and obedience'. Believing that prophet-hood is 'the best of all the Divine blessings', it is claimed that Muhammad 'could not come to deprive humanity of this great blessing, but on the contrary he came to teach his true followers how to attain to this exalted spiritual station'. It is further suggested by the *Ahmadi* that Muhammad was appointed 'the Possessor of Seal', that is Allah 'gave Him the seal, for the dissemination of [His] perfection, which was certainly not given to any other prophet'.[37] It is a cardinal tenet of *Ahmadi* belief that 'following [Muhammad] imbues a lesser prophet with the excellences of Prophet-hood, and [Muhammad's] 'spiritual attention is Prophet-carving'. The *Ahmadi* maintain that this conception of Prophet-hood can be held by the orthodox Muslim 'without implying any damage to the Seal of Prophet-hood'.[38]

In searching for Quranic or *hadith* support for their interpretation of 'prophet-hood' the *Ahmadi* refer to *Surah* 4:70 where it states: 'and whoso obeys Allah and *this* Messenger shall be among those on whom Allah has bestowed His blessings – the Prophets, the Truthful, the Martyrs and the Righteous'. On the basis of this verse the *Ahmadi* conclude that 'anybody who obeys Allah and the Holy Prophet can

---

35   Haqeeqatul Wahi, Roohaani Khazaa'in, vol. 22, p. 100, *Memorandum*, ibid., p. 108.

36   Dabbous, *Al-Baseerat*, (December 1992), op.cit., p. 7.

37   Dabbous, ibid., p. 7.

38   *Memorandum*, op.cit, p. 31.

attain one of these four exalted spiritual stations and can be counted among the Prophets, the Truthful, the Martyrs or the Righteous'.[39] The *Ahmadi* rely heavily on a tradition in which A'isha, the youngest and apparently the favourite wife of Muhammad, stated: 'say [that the Prophet is] the seal of the prophets and do not say that there is no prophet after him'.[40] Similarly, much is made of the *hadith* in which Muhammad, on the death of his infant son Ibrahim, said 'had he lived he certainly would have become a true prophet'. With cogent reasoning, it is argued that 'the title *Khataman nabiyeen* is not an impediment to anyone becoming a true prophet', for if such an interpretation was implied, 'then [Muhammad] would have said on this occasion: even if my son Ibrahim had remained alive, he still could not have become a prophet, because I am *Khataman nabiyeen*'. The *Ahmadi* point out that, instead of making such a statement, the prophet 'conveyed the following: 'Although I am *Khataman nabiyeen*, but had my son remained alive he would certainly have become a Prophet'. 'In other words', argue the *Ahmadi*, 'what stood in the way of Ibrahim's becoming a Prophet was his death not the existence of the verse of *Khataman nabiyeen*'.[41] In the light of the relevant Quranic texts and *hadith* the *Ahmadi* conclude: 'it becomes plainly obvious that after the Holy Prophet[sa], the advent of new Law-bearing Prophets, or Prophets in their own right, is closed. However, there does exist the possibility of such a prophet who would be an *Ummati* prophet and an obedient follower of *Sharia'h* of the Holy Prophet[sa]'.[42]

The *Ahmadiyya Jama'at* teaches that there are three types of prophet-hood within Islam: law-bearing prophets such as Moses and Muhammad; non-law bearing prophets, and the third type, a person upon whom prophet-hood is bestowed due to his allegiance to a law-bearing prophet as a reflection of his light and excellences. Ahmad is accepted as *Ummati Nabi* [a subordinate prophet] and is believed to

---

39 Al-Suyuti, Commentary, *Durr-I-Manthur*, vol. 5, p. 204, cited by Friedmann, *Prophecy Continuous: Aspects of Ahmadi Religious Thought and its Medieval Background*, op.cit., p. 63. I have relied heavily on Friedmann in writing up this section.

40 *Memorandum*, ibid., p. 112.

41 Ibid., p. 115.

42 Ibid., p. 112.

be '*Imam Mahdi* and Promised Messiah who was prophesied by the prophet Muhammad'. He is regarded as 'a law-bearer', 'subservient to every word of *Sharia'h* of the Holy Prophet Muhammad[sa]', and one 'who teaches and implements the same'.[43] Ahmad professed himself to be one of the *muhaddathun*, [inspired persons], 'people who are spoken to'. Some *Sufis* believe there is little difference between *nabi* and *muhaddath*. Others argue the two are differentiated by *taklif*, the imposition of new law.[44] Generally within Islam it is believed that *muhaddath* receive *ilham*, divine communication, speaking the truth without being a prophet.[45] Ahmad, as *muhaddath*, claimed to have had a revelation in which he was told: 'we have made you Jesus the son of Mary'. On the basis of this revelation, and their interpretation of the Quran, the *Ahmadi* assert that 'a fully devoted Muslim can attain to the station of Prophet-hood'. It is argued that Ahmad achieved this state and 'proved to the whole world that even today anybody can attain this exalted station provided that he follows perfectly in the steps of the Holy Prophet of Islam'.[46]

There appears to have been a gradual change in Ahmad's views about his own personal status. In his earlier works, although denying prophet-hood, he declared: 'I am, indeed, inspired and a warner from Allah'.[47] He later supported the doctrine of *Khataman nabiyeen* stating that anyone who rejected it was 'faithless and outside the pale of Islam'. From the time of the beginning of the *Ahmadiyya Jama'at Ahmadi* were challenged by other Muslims as to who, or what, they had pledged allegiance: was it to a *nabi* [prophet] or a *rasul* [messenger], or both? Ahmad himself contributed towards the confusion arising in this matter, stating on at least one occasion: 'I am not a Prophet and have brought no book'.[48] As he stated, these two words – *nabi* and *rasul* – 'occur in my revelations not once or twice

43   Friedmann, op.cit., pp. 88f.
44   Ibid., p. 91.
45   *Izala-yi awham*, cited by Friedmann, ibid., p. 132.
46   Ibid., pp. 88f.
47   Mirza Ghulam Ahmad, *A Misunderstanding Removed*, Rabwah, Pakistan: The Oriental & Religious Publishing Co.,1901, p. 2.
48   Ahmad, *A Misunderstanding Removed*, op.cit., p. 2.

but hundreds of times'.[49] However, despite these and other denials of prophet-hood, in other works such as the *Braheen-i-Ahmadi-yya*, Ahmad declared: 'I certainly am a Prophet in the sense [that] I have been endowed with the knowledge of the unseen'.[50] When opponents point to the Quranic declaration that Muhammad is 'the Messenger of Allah and the seal of the prophets' [Quran 33:41][51] Ahmad rejected the idea of the finality of prophet-hood suggesting 'the divine gift of prophecy will remain withheld from the world till the end of time'.[52] He claimed he was a prophet, *sirat-i-siddiqui*, one who is totally annihilated in the love of the prophet Muhammad. He claimed to 'wear the mantle of prophet-hood which is nothing but a part of the Holy Prophet's own prophet-hood'. Consequently, declared Ahmad, I am 'therefore, a prophet not for self-exaltation but for the glorification of the Holy Prophet'. He declared himself to be merely Muhammad's 'shadow reflecting all his qualities in his person and acknowledging his debt to him'.[53] Defining *nabi* as 'one who proclaims the knowledge of the Unseen from God', and arguing that 'a *nabi* must necessarily be a *rasul* [messenger]', he again stated that he was a prophet. However, drawing a distinction between the uniqueness of Muhammad and himself he suggested 'that no prophet can come after the Holy Prophet till the end of time with an independent law'.[54] Although denying that he was the 'bearer of new law nor an independent Prophet' Ahmad claimed that God 'has sent me as the Promised Messiah', and that he was 'God's vicegerent on earth'.[55] Ahmad described his relationship to Muhammad in terms of total absorption of two personalities, declaring that he had lost 'his whole being in that of the prophet, wiping out the least trace of sepa-rateness', consequently reflecting 'in his person all the beauties and

---

49   Ibid., p. 11.

50   Ibid., p. 4.

51   As stated previously (see note two, chapter one) in other translations of the Quran used by mainstream Muslims the reference would be *Surah* 33:40.

52   Ibid., p. 4.

53   Ibid., pp. 4, 5.

54   Ibid., p.6.

55   Ibid., p. 10.

excellences of the Holy Prophet like a clear mirror'.[56] He had become a 'reflex of Muhammad and his alter-ego'. Elsewhere he reassured his followers: 'It should be remembered that I have never hesitated to claim prophet-hood and Messiahship in this sense of the word'. On another occasion Ahmad declared: 'When I have myself witnessed the clear fulfilment of about 150 prophecies, how can I refuse to call myself a Prophet or Messenger of Allah?'[57]

Although the *Ahmadi* teaching on the 'seal of the prophet', and Ahmad's claims to prophet-hood, is important, particularly by way of explaining the animosity that many mainstream Muslims have towards the movement, it is only one of several doctrines characterising *Ahmadi* belief. It would be fair to say that the *Ahmadi*, in terms of doctrine, ritual and practice, have much in common with Muslims generally. However, there are several other differences between *Ahmadi* and main-stream Muslims which must be discussed if an accurate picture of the movement is to be presented. As stated above, concerning the power and the attributes of God, *Ahmadi*, similar to other Muslims, emphasize *tawhid,* the idea of divine oneness/unity and *hakimiyyah*, the absolute sovereignty of Allah. Believing in *shirk*, that it is a sin to associate God with anything else,[58] *Ahmadi* proclaim Allah to be a perfect being, the creator, the living God. The prayer is always on *Ahmadi* lips, *La ilaha illallah*, 'there is none worthy of worship except Allah'. However, the *Ahmadi* disagree with the accepted view on how Allah communicates with His people. Mainstream Muslims generally believe that God can see and hear His subjects, but does not speak directly to them. They believe that God spoke to people in the past but that has now ceased. In contrast, the *Ahmadi* argue, just as God 'spoke in the past, he still speaks today to his true servants, [as] none of his powers can ever stop functioning'.[59] Stressing the intimacy of the believer's relationship with God,

---

56 Ibid., pp, 7, 9.

57 Mainstream Muslims accuse *Ahmadi* of the sin of *shirk* because *Ahmadi* believe in the divine nature of their founder.

58 See John L. Esposito, *The Oxford Dictionary of Islam*, Oxford University Press, 2003, sv.

59 Dabbous, *Al-Baseerat*, (December 1992), op.cit., pp. 2-7.

as seen in the Quranic reminder that Allah is nearer to us than even our jugular vein,[60] the *Ahmadi* explain that God hears our requests and can answer them directly. Although recognising that 'the Holy Quran... contains all the Divine Guidance that man might possibly need till the end of time', the *Ahmadi* teach the necessity of the direct 'help of God to show' a person 'the correct way of following its teaching'.[61] They therefore emphasise that 'no one can know his creator properly unless he has a *living relationship* with him'. The *Ahmadi* therefore emphasise the realisation of *ma'rifat*, the individual believer attaining an experimental knowledge of God. It is believed that by devotion and piety an individual can attain *'ilm*, practical knowledge of the divine. Such intimate knowledge of God is taught by *Sufis* 'to describe mystical intuitive knowledge, knowledge of spiritual truth as reached through ecstatic experiences rather than revealed or rationally acquired', but frowned upon by mainstream *ulema*.[62]

The *Ahmadi*, keen to convey the image of rationality and reasonableness,[63] criticise many of the practices of mainstream Muslims as superstition, even nonsense. In particular *Ahmadi* look askance at certain popular practices such as the consultation with, and reverence of, *pirs* or holy men. They ridicule the use of *taweez* and other amulets to ward off the *evil eye* [the envy and malice of others] and belief in harmful *jinn* [spirits made out of fire which can interfere in a person's life]. Many Muslims, especially those from rural areas of the Asian sub-continent, cling to the beliefs and practices associated with their place of origin. Consequently many, especially those belonging to the *Barelwi* tradition, in contrast to the more conservative *Deobandi*, have recourse to *Pirs, Chachasti* [one who is holier than *ulema*] or even *'ajûza* [old women, medicine women, herbalists] to seek help and advice, or visit the shrines of holy men to gain *baraka* or blessing. Such phenomena are to be found throughout the *Ummah* worldwide.

---

60 Quran 50:17.

61 Dabbous, *Al-Baseerat*, op.cit., pp. 2-7.

62 Ibid., p. 7.

63 *Imam* Bajwa stated to me how the *Ahmadi* are educated, rational, logical people who reject the superstitions and fairy tales believed by other Muslims; private conversation, *Ahmadiyya* mosque, Leeds Road, Bradford, March 2002.

The reverence for *Pirs*, practiced in Pakistan, India and Bangladesh, is matched by the veneration of *marabout*, *Sufi* holy men or saints, in Morocco, Tunisia and other North African countries. The *Ahmadi*, as with various strands of mainstream Islam, regard such practices and beliefs as *bidat*, harmful innovations which have crept into the faith, mainly from Hinduism. *Pirs* are written off as charlatans, who, instead of contributing to the spiritual development of fellow Muslims, are accused of capitalising on ignorance and the need of many ordinary Muslims for spiritual and physical healing. *Imam* Bajwa, in one of our many conversations together, told me how one Asian woman had gone to the *Ahmadi* mosque in Birmingham by mistake, thinking it was the *Barelwi* mosque nearby. She told the *Imam* how her husband was maltreating her and how he had got *taweez* to act against her amulets. She asked for help. To her surprise Bajwa told her that belief in *taweez* was mere superstition and un-Quranic. The woman, shocked at the advice given, remonstrated, stating that she had been to the mosque before and had been given different advice. Bajwa told her that she had not been before and that she must be referring to the mosque up the road. The woman left, never to return. *Imam* Bajwa explained to me how the use of *taweez* in the *Ummah* is 'big business', with each *Imam* 'having a huge potential to earn a lot of money in his role as spiritual adviser'. He lamented how the *Ahmadi* rejection of such practices is one of the reasons why many Muslims persecute the movement. 'The existence of the *Ahmadi Jama'at*, and its rejection of such superstitious practices', declared Bajwa, 'is a great financial threat to the official hierarchy within Islam'.

Despite the official stance of the *Jama'at* against folk religion and superstition, at grassroots level many *Ahmadi* find it hard to relinquish the beliefs they held before they took *bai'at*. In my personal observation of the *Ahmadi* it was quite obvious that like Muslims generally, they use sayings or mantras to ward off harm or evil. For example if an *Ahmadi* sees someone 'suffering affliction' and recites 'Praise be to Allah, who has kept me free from affliction He has brought on him, and has shown me favour above many whom he created', it is believed 'that affliction, whatever it may be, will not smite him'.[64] Like other Muslims, *Ahmadi* adopt the usual practice of uttering '*bismillah*', 'thanks be to God', before they leave the home, arrive back at their house, eat their food or before they go to bed. It is a commonly held belief amongst the *Ahmadi* that the recitation of verse 131 of *Al-Shu'ara, Surah 26*, 'protects one from harmful insect bites and stings'.[65] Although *Ahmadi* recognise the fact that the 'evil eye' is referred to by Muhammad in a *hadith*, as *Imam* Bajwa remarked, 'we believe that it cannot harm those who trust in God for the divine will always prevails'. Although not using amulets in this way, most *Ahmadi* will use the phrase '*ma'sha'allah*', 'what God has willed', in their every day speech. It implies that all glory goes to God, not the person who possesses something to be envied or who has achieved something of merit. I have attended family social occasions when someone has passed comment about the beauty of a child or baby and the *Ahmadi* mother has responded with the phrase '*ma'sha'allah*'. When asked for an explanation for the use of this phrase I was informed that the evil eye is averted as the user of the phrase denies all praise, and claims all praise should go to Allah alone. When faced with problems *Ahmadi* will offer *Istikharah* prayers, prayers asking for guidance. I was told by several *Ahmadi* how God answered such prayers in the form of dreams, signs or a sense of well-being. Although not used in a superstitious way, many *Ahmadi* will wear a distinctive ring on the second finger of the right hand bearing the phrase in Arabic: 'Is Allah not sufficient for His servant?' Rather than being seen as possessing *baraka*, or spiritual power, the ring is regarded as a constant reminder that Allah provides the believer's needs.

Several *Ahmadi*, in Britain and abroad, openly affirmed to me their belief that 'Allah has angels who go about on the roads seeking those who remember Allah'.[66] As taught in the Quran, *Ahmadi* believe in the *Mala'ikah*: angels, spiritual beings such as Gabriel and Michael, messengers created and sent by God to implement his commands,

---

64   *Muslim Herald*, (November 1975), p. 19.

65   A belief stated by the fourth *Khalifa* in his Friday sermons; see *Ahmadiyya Bulletin*, (July/August, 2002).

66   The *Muslim Herald*, op.cit., p. 16.

to take revelations to the prophets, administer punishment and keep records of our deeds.[67] It is part of *Ahmadi* teaching that angels have been 'entrusted [with] the control, management and supervision of the affairs of the physical world' and 'to carry God's messages and Will to His servants'. All Muslims accept the existence of angels, believing them to be beings devoted to the service of God. In contrast to mainstream Muslims however, who believe that angels used to bring God's messages to men but this role has now ceased, *Ahmadi* emphasise the revelatory function of angels in communicating God's will not only to prophets, but to any true believer, today. *Ahmadi* do believe in ghosts but not in the idea of 'the spirit of a dead person living around us and haunting a house'. They believe in 'a form of life which is ethereal and that can make itself appear to people as an apparition'.[68]

Concerning *jinn, Ahmadi* reject the belief held by many mainstream Muslims that *jinn* are evil spirits. Basing their views mainly on *Al-Jinn*, the seventy-second *Surah* of the Quran, *Ahmadi* interpret the Arabic word *jinn* as meaning 'a class of human beings... the great and the powerful',[69] the 'big or influential men' of the world,[70] who 'often remain aloof from the common people and do not mix with them'.[71] As Mirza Tahir Ahmad, the fourth *Khalifa* of the *Ahmadiyya* movement stated, regarding many mainstream Muslims: 'their concept of *jinn* [genie] as a ghostlike creature is largely superstitious'. 'Such superstitions', he continued, 'would have us believe that the *jinn* possess a mixture of part human and part hobgoblin characteristics, which can adopt as many shapes and forms as they please'.[72] In reference to the popular belief in the power of *jinn* to possess or destroy people Ahmad reassured members of the *Jama'at* that there

---

67   See Quran 22:76, 41:31, 66:7, 39:76.

68   Hazoors question & answer column, *Ahmadiyya Bulletin*, (September 2002), p. 14.

69   M. G. Farid (ed.) *The Holy Quran: Arabic Text with English Translation and Short Commentary*, Islam International Publications Ltd, Islamabad, Surrey, 1994, Al:Jinn, 72:1-2, fn, p. 900.

70   Farid, *Quran*, op.cit., fn, p. 3139.

71   Ibid., fn, 910.

72   Mirza T. Ahmad, *Revelation, Rationality, Knowledge and Truth*, Islamabad, Surrey: Islam International Publications Ltd, 1998, p. 342.

is nothing in the Quran to support this 'superstitious human fantasy'. The word *jinn*, he maintained, refers to 'anything which lies beyond the reach of common sight or is invisible to the unaided naked eye'. According to Mirza Tahir Ahmad therefore, this includes snakes that hide in rocks, women who observe segregation, and chieftains who keep their distance from the people or the inhabitants of remote mountain areas.[73] *Ahmadi* believe that *jinn* are human and not divine, and contrary to popular Islamic belief they suggest that *jinn* have a fiery temperament rather than being made from fire.[74] There are, according to the *Ahmadi*, two types of such *jinn*. Firstly there are those important people who are righteous, either believers in Islam or God-fearers generally, who use their power for good. Secondly there are the arrogant, those who reject the Quran and use their power and influence in a wrong way. It is also argued that in the Quran the word *jinn* is used in one verse to refer to certain groups of 'Jews of Nasibin' who, 'apprehensive of the Meccan's opposition, ... met the Holy Prophet at night and after listening to the Quran and to the Holy Prophet's discourse, they became converted to Islam and carried the new message to their people who also readily accepted it'.[75] In another context *jinn* refers to 'Unitarian Christians'.[76] Elsewhere Mirza Tahir Ahmad gave the rather interesting interpretation of *jinn* as 'invisible organisms, which feed on rotting bones, dung etc.,' such as 'bacteria and viruses'.[77]

As indicated previously the *Ahmadi* place much emphasis on the significance of dreams as a means of divine communication. Mirza Ghulam Ahmad, the founder of the *Ahmadiyya Jama'at*, claimed to

---

73 Ahmad, *Revelation*, op.cit., p. 363.

74 For a full appraisal of the *Ahmadi* teaching about *jinn* see Ahmad, ibid., pp. 339-52, 363-67.

75 Farid, *Quran*, op.cit., Al Jinn, 72:1-2, fn, 3137, Ahmad, ibid., pp. 363-7.

76 Farid, *Quran*, ibid., Al Jinn, 72:1-2, fn, 3137.

77 An argument expressed by Mirza Tahir Ahmad on the basis of a tradition relating to the prophet in which he admonishes his followers for using dried up lumps of dung and the bones of dead animals for cleaning themselves after attending to a call of nature. According to Ahmad, the prophet, in referring to *jinn*, was actually referring to harmful bacteria. See *Revelation*, op.cit., pp. 363-364.

have had dreams in which he foresaw, amongst other things, the outbreak of the First World War, deaths of opponents and the spreading
of the *Ahmadiyyat* across the world. Later *Khalifas* have continued to
make similar claims. In addressing the *Jalsa Salana* in July 1994 the
fourth *Khalifa*, Mirza Tahir Ahmad, while speaking about conversion targets, referred to a dream he had had 'concerning the Franco-
phone countries [French speaking African countries]', stating 'that a
change would take place'. The *Khalifa* remarked how the dream had
been fulfilled. 'Last year', he stated, 'there was a change from 100's to
1000's [of conversions], but this year there has been around 150,000
people accepting *Ahmadiyyat*'.[78] Other *Ahmadi* talk of *Kushoof*, waking visions, in which they saw 'liquid like honey that an angel had
given to his father';[79] 'a baby boy and the name of that boy and how
this was fulfilled',[80] or, as one *Ahmadi* stated in Qadian 'the death
of Mrs Gandhi'.[81] Many *Ahmadi* claim to have had dreams predicting the tragic end of President Bhutto.[82] Dr Muhammad Iqbal, a
member of the Bradford *Jama'at*, while taking me in his car to the
Jalsa Salana of 2003, remarked how he had had dreams fore-telling
'the *Khalifa's* migration to London, the Gulf war, [and] the passing
of [his] PhD'.

The *Ahmadi*, like followers of any sectarian group, view the world
according to their own particular mind-set. They approach life believing that their religious views are true, and their God is totally
in control. Accepting the *kibriyai* [greatness] and the *mutakabbir*
[exaltedness] of Allah, the intervention of God in history and world
events will, according to the *Ahmadi*, bring about unquestionable
success, and ultimate victory, for the movement. Everything that

---

78 *Al-Baseerat*, (August 1994), pp. 2-3.

79 A vision claimed by Professor Soofi Basharat, reported by Tahir Selby
at a *tabligh* Seminar held at the Bradford mosque, cited in *Al- Baseerat*,
(August 1991), p. 5. No interpretation was given in the report of this
vision.

80 Narrated by Tahir Selby, *Al-Baseerat*, (August 1991), op.cit., p. 5.

81 Indira Gandhi, who became Prime Minister of India in 1980, was
assassinated by her own Sikh bodyguard in 1984 as they resented her use
of troops to remove malcontents from the Golden temple.

82 *Al-Baseerat*, (August 1991), op.cit., p. 5.

human beings do comes under the scrutiny of God. God is seen as *Al-Jabbar*, the one who subdues, the one who exalts the humble and degrades the proud.[83] As such, it is maintained that God has created His world according to certain moralistic laws: that the righteous are blessed and the unrighteous punished. Divine retribution is seen as the vindicator of truth and a reward for patient endurance in the face of unjustified persecution. Members of the *Ahmadiyya* community accept, and are consoled and comforted by the belief, that opponents of the movement will not only face Divine punishment for their actions in the after-life, but they will face *hawia*, 'death or utter disgrace', in this life. The fourth *Khalifa*, while describing the martyrdom of one *Ahmadi*, told of the horrendous details of his murder but ended with the consolatory note; 'his murderers met a sorry end'.[84] President Bhutto's removal from office in the *coup d'etat* in July 1977, and his trial and execution, were seen as vindication of *Ahmadi* claims, and punishment of an offender who had persecuted the movement. Similarly, with the death of General Zia-ul-Haq, on 17 August 1988, another persecutor of *Ahmadiyyat*, the *Ahmadi* declared with vindictive exuberance how he was dramatically 'blown from the sky' in a plane crash which 'they still have not been able to find out what caused it, whereas the movement he was trying to destroy now broadcasts their message through satellite television all over the world and continues to get larger and larger, stronger and stronger'.[85] The *Ahmadi* believe that Zia's death was brought about due to a *mubahalah* [a challenge in which, it is argued, God vindicates the claims of the just] pronounced by the fourth *Khalifa* on 17 August 1988 and a prediction that General Zia would soon be punished. When news of the death of Zia occurred later that day the *Khalifa* declared: 'It is the wrath of God'.[86]

---

83   The teaching of the fourth *Khalifa*, cited in 'Friday Sermons of the fourth Khalifa', in *Ahmadiyya Bulletin*, (July/August 2002), op.cit., p. 4.

84   *Hazoor's Friday Sermons*, *Ahmadiyya Bulletin*, (July/August 1999), p. 5. The *Khalifa* was describing the martyrdom of Dr Muhammad Ahmad Shaheed.

85   *Al-Baseerat*, (April 1994), p. 3.

86   Iain Adamson, *A Man of God, The Life of his Holiness Khalifatul Masih IV*, Bristol: George Shepherd Publishers, 1991, p. 11.

As with a literal interpretation of the biblical text which teaches that Christians are at war with spiritual 'principalities and powers',[87] so the *Ahmadi*, similar to mainstream Islam, believe in Satanic powers working, albeit in vain, against the forces of good in the world. Ahmad reminded his followers how 'Satan has implanted in' the hearts of their opponents evil lies, and consequently 'all kind of calumny and slander is admissible and not just admissible, rather it is [seen as] a righteous act'.[88] But Ahmad, anticipating such opposition, encouraged his followers with the rhetoric of an Old Testament prophet: 'Now God will only keep safe the community of the virtuous and He will destroy the other'. When talking of divine judgement Ahmad stated, 'When the appointee is accused of falsehood and refuted beyond reason then just as the farmer sharpens the sickle at harvest time, Allah the Exalted also prepares for those who make accusations of falsehood'.[89] The fourth *Khalifa*, during a question and answer session in London, in 1996, referred to Abdullah Atham, a critic and contemporary of Mirza Ghulam Ahmad, who questioned Mirza's claim to prophet-hood. With unmasked enthusiasm the *Khalifa* declared how Atham, as punishment for his disbelief, and for his criticisms of the founder of the *Ahmadiyya* faith, 'lived practically in Hell'. He described how Atham, previously the vehement opponent of *Ahmadiyyat*, due to the judgement of Allah, ran 'from place to place ... repeating that he had never meant any abuses against the holy prophet', and 'began to see snakes and scorpions and images all around him'.[90] In a *khutba* delivered at the London mosque in September 2003, the fifth *Khalifa* of the *Ahmadiyya* community referred to 'the recent unrefined commotion raised by some religious

---

87 The Apostle Paul, writing to the Christians at Ephesus, reminded them that 'we are not contending against flesh and blood, but against the principalities, against the powers, against the world rulers of this present darkness, against the spiritual hosts of wickedness in the heavenly places', see Ephesians 6:12.

88 *Hadhrat* Mirza Ghulam Ahmad, *Malfoozat*, Lahore: n.p., vol. 3, p. 237.

89 Ahmad, *Malfoozat*, op.cit..

90 The words of *Hadhrat* Khalifatul Masih IV, during a question and answer session at London, on 26 February, 1996, see *Ahmadiyya Bulletin*, (December 2002/January 2003), pp. 10-2.

scholars in Pakistan' regarding the claims of the *Ahmadi* founder. Encouraging the *Ahmadi* in that country 'to be patient and steadfast' he declared how 'when man does not speak up, that is when God speaks up', adding that 'in the past' they had 'seen our adversaries crushed to pieces'.[91]

Concerning *Ahmadiyyat* and other faiths, the *Ahmadi* regard themselves as 'the movement to unite all religions'.[92] Although believing that it alone is 'the true Islam', and that Ahmad was sent to bring all peoples back to the true path, the *Ahmadiyya* movement teaches that no single faith, race or people has a monopoly on truth. It is further emphasised that no one can be forced to accept Islam, as the Quran states: 'there is no compulsion in religion'.[93] True peace, it is argued, is born within the soul as each person finds a relationship with God. *Ahmadi*, mainly due to their desire to 'promote good will and harmony between Muslims and non-Muslim people', 'revere as prophets all those great men whom a larger section of humanity has accepted as heavenly messengers or avatars'. The movement acknowledges 'Zoroaster, Buddha, Krishna and Rama Chandra [as] divine messengers who guided their people to the right path' and 'honour them as such'.[94] Although the *Ahmadi*, as with other Muslims, believe that the teachings of these other faiths 'may have been tampered with or they may be misinterpreted', it is agreed that 'the teachings which these holy men gave, according to the need of their times and the requirements of the respective peoples, were based on Divine revelation'. However, just as these prophets were raised by God to point people to true religion, the *Ahmadi* believe that in the last age 'the religious universality of Islam points to the fact that the Divine reformer of the latter days will appear within the religion

---

91   *Khutba* delivered on 12 September 2003, *Ahmadiyya Bulletin*, (January 2004), p. 7.

92   See the title of the book by Iain Adamson, *Ahmad: The Guided One: A Life of the Holy Founder of the Movement to Unite All Religions*, Islamabad, UK, op.cit. Publications, n.d.

93   Quran 2:257.

94   '*Ahmadiyyat: The True Islam*', Leaflet, Millennium Gift Series No. 8, printed by the Ahmadiyya Muslim Association UK; see also *Takmil-I-Tabligh*, leaflet issued by Mirza Ghulam Ahmad, 12 January 1889.

of Islam'. This divine reformer, in the opinion of the *Ahmadi*, is of course Mirza Ghulam Ahmad. Although the *Ahmadi* claim to recognize all religions as valid they also proclaim an exclusivism on truth. They refer to 'Christianity and other evils', and describe Christianity as a 'polytheistic religion'.[95] Christianity, it is argued, like other faiths is corrupted by *shirk*, associating God with other things, and Christians have 'interpolated their revealed books'.[96] Christians, in believing Jesus to be the Son of God, and the Holy Spirit as the third person of a divine trinity, are regarded as *Mushrik*, those guilty of *shirk*.[97] As stated in Chapter One, although the *Ahmadi* agree with Muslims generally that Jesus was born of the Virgin Mary, they reject the teaching of mainstream Islam that Jesus did not die but was taken up into heaven, arguing instead that he travelled extensively in the East, eventually dying in Kashmir. As with Islam generally, the *Ahmadi* teach that 'Christians distorted their beliefs after the death of Jesus and certainly not during his lifetime'.[98] Concerning the Christian teaching of the *Parousia*, the second coming of Jesus before judgement day, the *Ahmadi* believe this was fulfilled in the person of Mirza Ghulam Ahmad.

Although expressing respect for other faiths, *Ahmadi* regard unbelievers as *kafir*, believing 'these are they who have bartered guidance for error'.[99] As one *Ahmadi* writes: 'Christian doctrine is a misrepresentation', Christians 'have used the manoeuvre of deception to the extreme and their damnation lends support to the belief that they are "anti-Christ" who have altered and distorted the Holy Books . . .'.[100] 'By unscrupulously modifying the heavenly books' it is claimed that Christians 'have enthroned a human being as God'. As the fourth

95   N. A. Faruqui, *Ahmadiyyat: in the service of Islam*, Lahore: *Ahmadiyya Anjuman* Isha'at Islam, 1983, pp. 42, 4.

96   Faruqui, *Ahmadiyyat: in the service of Islam*, op.cit., p. 45.

97   Bashir A. Rafiq, *Truth about Ahmadiyyat*, n.d., p. 20, see www.alislam.org/html.

98   Rafiq, op.cit., pp. 20, 21.

99   Quran 2:17.

100 Rafiq, ibid., pp. 20, 21.

Khalifa wrote, 'Christianity' is nothing less than 'A journey from facts to fiction'.[101]

Ahmadi, similar to most other sects, have a distinct eschatological framework based upon Quranic teaching. Using Muhammad's words in *Surah Al-Nasr* 110, where the prophet refers to 'men entering the religion of Allah in troops', *Ahmadi* believe in a great revival of religion in the last days 'when billions of people will enter *Ahmadiyyat*—the true Islam'.[102] Mirza Ghulam Ahmad predicted an age when Christians would become confused because 'none of them shall ever see Jesus, son of Mary, coming down from heaven'.[103] According to Ahmad, God shall cause 'great consternation in their minds and they shall know then that the period of the dominance of the cross has also passed away and the way of life has changed completely…'. 'Then in dismay', he declares, 'the wise among them shall forsake this belief and three centuries from now shall not have passed when those who await the coming of Jesus son of Mary, whether they be Muslims or Christians, shall relinquish altogether this conception'. When this happens, argued Ahmad 'then shall prevail only one religion over the whole world and there shall be only one religious Leader'.[104] At that time, According to Ahmad, Allah:

will make my movement spread all over the earth; and He would make my followers prevail over all other sects; and the members of my movement will attain to such perfection in knowledge and comprehension that, with the light of their truth and signs, they would make their opponents dumb in defeat; and all peoples shall drink from this fountain; and this movement shall grow with great vigour, and thrive, till it embraced the whole earth'.[105]

---

101 The title of a book written by the fourth *Khalifa*, *Christianity, A journey from Facts to Fiction*, Islamabad, Surrey: Ahmadiyya Muslim Publications, 1994.

102 Mirza Ghulam Ahmad, *Malfoozat*, op.cit., vol. 2, p. 253.

103 Farid, Holy Quran, op.cit., 15:28, fn, 1494.

104 Ibid., 72:1-2, fn, 3137.

105 Ibid., fn, 92.

7
AHMADIYYAT: INTEGRATION AND THE PRESERVATION OF FAITH

The heat was oppressive, unusually so for London. It brought a smile to my face to talk later with Nasir who, having come from Pakistan to visit his two sons living in the United Kingdom, complained of the warmth of an English summer. He remarked how, while in England, he preferred to walk in the evenings when it was cooler. The large rotating fan on the ceiling, and all the windows open, didn't seem to have much of an effect on the temperature of the room. I sat on a high-backed chair with about sixteen other men, and several boys, most of them sitting silently cross-legged on the floor. Regularly wiping our foreheads with our handkerchiefs, we listened intently to the speaker, Dr Zahid Aziz, urbane and eloquent, explain the nature of a true follower of Islam. He spoke of submission to Allah and the necessity of true piety rather than the mere following of rules and regulations. As he spoke I occasionally glanced around the room. An archway led from the lounge, where we sat, into a dining area where a number of women, some veiled others not, similarly sat in silence. What looked like a settee, conveniently placed under the archway, formed a barrier enforcing segregation, fulfilling *purdah*. I looked at my companions; men of differing ages, some first generation immigrants, others born and bred in Britain. The older men, wearing jackets, shirt and ties, the younger clad in jeans and open-necked short-sleeved shirts, all concentrating on the speaker's words.

Zahid finished his address. His place was taken by an elderly woman, who had been sitting in the adjacent room. Wearing a

151

long Asian dress, sunglasses, and with a veil covering her head, this woman, whom I later learnt was Azia Khan, the General Secretary of the UK branch of this particular Islamic movement, introduced me to the group and invited me to give a few words. With alacrity I walked to the lectern placed by the settee under the archway and, after thanking them for their invitation, I explained my interest in Islam. I spoke of the need to remove the stereotypes of Islam that had been created by the media since 9/11, and the need to remind the West of the true nature of Islamic teaching. I invited questions and to my delight both men and women shared their thoughts with me. I had been in various mosques before, and attended different meetings and events, where the women were totally separated from the men. Usually at such events the speaker's message would be relayed by PA system to the women sitting in an enclosed adjacent room. At such meetings the women would not make eye contact with any unfamiliar man. A handshake would be forbidden. But here it was open and informal. One young woman [I think she said she was a social worker] came to me after the meeting, shook my hand, and entered into convivial chat. Speaking in a cockney accent she told me of her pride in being Muslim, but also of being British. 'Yes, we pray, we have a strict moral code, our religion is our life', she confessed, 'but I believe we have integrated well with non-Muslims in this city'. This woman, like other members of the Muslim faith, lived in the community, and wanted to be part of that community. Mrs Khan brought things to a conclusion. I returned to my seat as the men began to stand in rows in order to perform *namaz*, the obligatory prayers for that time of the day.

The house, the property of the Lahori *Ahmadi*, was a large Edwardian three-storey end-terrace, situated in Brent. I was later taken on a guided tour by Mrs Khan. She informed me how the building served as the main worship area for the Lahori *Ahmadi* in the London area, a movement numbering only about 250 members throughout England. It consisted of a kitchen [large enough to cater for the needs of those attending the regular meetings held there], offices, sleeping rooms for visitors and the living quarters for the house-keeper who maintained the property. Mrs Khan, articulate, undemonstrative and welcoming, told me how this house-keeper's husband had previously been the resident *Imam* but, as has happened to so many *Ahmadi*, he was killed by other Muslims whilst visiting Guyana.[1] She now lives in the house alone, keeping the premises clean and tidy. Mrs Khan told me how the Lahori *Ahmadi* worshipping at this site had tried to get the house registered as a mosque. Permission had been granted originally but, with a new council and objections from certain sources [especially local Muslims], permission was later withdrawn. 'But we are happy', she said smiling, 'we have the freedom to worship as we will, even if this building is recognized as a mosque or not'.

As described above, the Lahori *Ahmadi*, living, working and worshipping in London, have integrated well into the wider society yet managed, to a great extent, to preserve their identity, beliefs and faith. The same can be said of the Qadiani *Ahmadi*. 'No one wants to be an outsider, or an outcast or left out', wrote one young *Ahmadi* in *Al-Baseerat*, the official Magazine of the movement.[2] 'We fear the consequences of not conforming to society', remarked another member of the sect; 'We fear being left isolated and rejected by others'.[3] However, although recognising the need to integrate there is also an understandable fear of the compromise of faith that such integration may, and does, bring. Although, as Waseem Ahmad opined, 'there are many admirable aspects of the western culture', he strongly reminded his co-religionists how 'we must also retain our religious integrity which forms the cornerstone of our religious beliefs'.[4] Aware of the harmful influence that secularism can have on religion Waseem advised other members of his community: 'we should keep it [the dominant culture] in context relative to our own religious beliefs'.[5] For the *Ahmadi*, as with the followers of any strict religious sect, the allurements of a secular, free, western society are ubiquitous

---

1   The persecution faced by the *Ahmadi* is discussed in detail in chapter eleven.

2   Mansoora Haque, 'The Impact of Western Culture', *Ahmadiyya Bulletin*, (January 2004), p. 21.

3   Sadiya Ayaz, 'Alcoholism and Drug-Taking', *Ahmadiyya Bulletin*, (September 2002), p. 19.

4   'Problems Faced by Young Muslims Growing up in a Western Society', *Al-Baseerat*, (March 1993), p. 4.

5   *Al-Baseerat*, (March 1993), op. cit.

and strong. 'We are often faced with numerous temptations from our peer groups that we find difficult to reject', complained another *Ahmadi*.[6] 'Throughout school/college education', Waseem explained, 'we are taught a different way of thinking to that which we are taught at home'.[7] Problems at school relate to 'ideas on male and female segregation, dress sense, our attitude towards other people...'. As Waseem stated, 'we are surrounded by establishments offering us alcohol or hamburgers ... there are betting shops, casinos, strip-joints, tickets for Leeds United matches, all of which infringe our religious beliefs'.[8] The problems caused by integration were clearly seen in the issues raised by 'Parenting Classes' held by the *Jama'at* throughout the United Kingdom in 2002. Most of the problems discussed at such classes related to parental concern about the views and practices of the younger generation. Common themes included the availability of harmful material on the internet: 'fashion versus religion', 'lack of marriage prospects for girls', 'pre-marital relationships' and 'social trends'.[9] Although, in many ways the problems faced by parents and children in the *Ahmadiyya* community mirror those of families in the wider non-Muslim society, for the *Ahmadi* such problems present a threat to the very existence of the sect.

According to the *Ahmadi*, [mainstream Muslims and many Christians as well], Britain has been undergoing a steady, if not rapid, moral decline throughout the twentieth century. 'After the 2nd World War', declared Tahir Selby, 'the youth [of Britain] found new independence and they started rebelling against their fathers'.[10] Continuing to apply what some might regard as a gross generalisation

---

6   Sadiya Ayaz, 'Alcoholism and Drug-Taking', op. cit., p. 19.

7   *Al-Baseerat*, (March 1993), op. cit.

8   Ibid. Being puzzled about his concern over 'tickets for Leeds United' I managed to contact Waseem Ahmad and talk with him on these issues. He explained to me that the article was originally given as a lecture to young boys at the mosque. The comment about Leeds United was a joke to make the address more interesting. He himself has been a season ticket holder with Bradford City F. C. for several years and sees no compromise of his faith to see a football match.

9   *Ahmadiyya Bulletin*, (December 2002/January 2003), op. cit., p. 23.

10   The words of Tahir Selby, 'Prepare yourself for the New century', in *Al-Baseerat: Centenary Thanksgiving Number*, (August 1989), pp. 11-2.

of post-war British society, Selby argued how such youth 'became "Teddy Boys" and roamed the streets creating trouble. They in turn became fathers and their children became the "free love" society of the sixties. That generation in turn became parents and the decline in society continued right up to the present generation'. Consequently, remarked Selby, 'now in England you have an irreligious, immoral society, where children beat up their teachers!'.[11] Such thoughts are shared by other members of the movement. 'Alcohol intake is part of Western culture', remarked Mansoor Ahmad Shah, 'excessive materialism, gambling, free mixing of the sexes, sexual licentiousness, cohabitation outside marriage, women parading semi-naked, exhibiting their physical beauty, open display of kissing and the scarcity of modesty are some distinct features of the current emancipated Western culture'.[12] The *Ahmadi* maintain that 'the modern values of the West, devoid of morals and based on material benefits and self-interest are not only detrimental, but are in fact self-destructive'. As such it is argued, 'if trends are maintained, it will be these very modern traditions themselves that will bring down the edifice of modern culture'.[13] In referring to Western societies generally Ahmad Shah laments how:

Rights of the individual are being so stressed upon that even when there is a dire need in training their children, parents cannot even lightly punish them. On the other hand children think nothing of disrespecting their teachers. The moment they hit the ages of sixteen or eighteen they are independent of their parents. Yearning to see their offspring, many an old parent passes away in old people's homes or hospitals. In the West the idea that sex is a natural emotion and should therefore be satiated without any hindrance is gathering influence as a trend. When expressing opinion on this subject in particular, the traditional feminine bashfulness is becoming a thing of the Past. It is proudly considered to be a candid expression of honesty to declare one's indulgence in sin, audacious conversation, nudity, brazenness, displaying one's body etc. Many such similar aspects that were considered immoral some 60, 70 years ago today symbolise the culture.[14]

---

11   Tahir Selby, *Al-Baseerat: Centenary Thanksgiving Number*, op. cit., p. 12.

12   Mansoor Ahmad Shah, 'Social Integration', *The Review of Religions*, (February1997), p. 14.

13   Ahmad Shah, 'Social Integration', op. cit., p. 14.

14   Ibid., p. 14.

With the *Ahmadi*, as with other ethnic groups living in Britain, we see internal dissent and cultural adjustment, tensions between older patterns of life and 'new' forms of social behaviour. This conflict has led to the clarifying and hardening of boundaries between religious communities and the larger society, and a defining of sectarian positions within a religion. Many members of the *Ahmadiyya Jama'at*, in their daily interaction with mainstream British society, have undergone cognitive bargaining, partial 'compromise', resulting in a degree of conformity to 'western' values usually deemed unacceptable to the faith. During the period in which I was allowed to observe the *Ahmadiyya* movement in Bradford I was aware of certain members, usually the young, 'hitting the city centre' in their sports cars on a Saturday night, with the aim, as one *Ahmadi* remarked, of 'clubbing' and 'pulling'. One *Ahmadi*, a married man with teenage children, made no secret of his regular sessions surfing the internet for 'glamour websites'. He confided in me how, on one occasion, he had had a sexual relationship with a female relative living in the nearby town of Huddersfield. The same *Ahmadi* informed me how he and some of his male relatives [free from the control of the *Imam*] would occasionally travel to Germany, spending weekends visiting the red light area of Hamburg. I was occasionally invited to the homes of different *Ahmadi* families where we would watch James Bond films or other Hollywood blockbusters, regarded by the leadership within the movement as harmful and wrong. Riaz, an *Ahmadi* in his midtwenties with whom I had a particular friendship, similarly revealed traits of such ethical and cognitive dissonance. Fully participating in the activities of the mosque, attending prayers as often as work commitments would permit, he was a real 'film buff' going to see almost any film that was released. As with *Ahmadi* generally he rejected the 'pub-culture' associated with British society and, as would be expected, regarded alcohol and immorality as *haram* [forbidden]. However there was a real contradiction between what he believed to be *haram* and what he regarded as being acceptable behaviour in everyday life. Although rigid in his views of *purdah*, the covering and segregation of women, he was not averse to seeing the glamorous, if not sexual, portrayal of women on 'the big screen'. He regularly attended the cinema watching films with violence and sexual scenes yet regarded such actions as reprehensible in real life. As early as the 1970s the third *Khalifa*, concerned about such compromise by members of the *Jama'at*, remarked: 'So the times have changed and I am sorry to remark that in some directions they have changed for the worse'.[15] Looking askance at the use of lip-stick by *Ahmadi* women, he referred to the former days at Qadian when 'there were [no] more than ten women ... who used lipstick'. 'Now', he declared, 'there would hardly be 10 of them who do not use it'. 'Such women may be small in number', opined the *Khalifa*, 'but their attitude is enough to cause a stir in our community, and some of our branches are clamouring for taking disciplinary action against them'. He expressed his hope 'that the ladies may make amends themselves' before it was necessary to take 'any drastic step against them'.[16]

Although, as discussed in chapter four, discipline is an integral element of maintaining the cohesion of the community, the *Ahmadi* see the solution to such problems in the use of correct teaching and the example set by pious parents and elder members of the group. The *Ahmadi* stress the need 'to teach young Muslims the virtues of Islam and to demonstrate a better way of life'.[17] Compulsion is usually seen as being counter-productive. 'To force youngsters to do something they don't want to do', argued the editor of the *Ahmadiyya Bulletin* in 1999 'will only bring about resentment'.[18] Instead of compulsion the pursuit of *taqwa* [righteousness] is seen as the means of keeping the faithful on the straight and narrow. 'The institution of *salat* must be inculcated into them', declared the editor, and '*Jama'ats* must also make sure that arrangements are made for the teaching of the holy Quran'.[19] As Naseem Bajwa once remarked to me: 'truth is truth; once people are told it they will walk in it'.

---

15 'Lajna on the March', an address by *Hadhrat Hafiz* Mirza Nasir Ahmad, Khalifatul Masih III, *Muslim Herald*, (December 1975/January 1976), p.18.

16 'Lajna on the March', op. cit., p. 18.

17 Report on the 20th Majlis Shura UK, *Ahmadiyya Bulletin*, (July/August 1999), p. 10.

18 *Ahmadiyya Bulletin*, (July/August 1999), p. 11.

19 Ibid., p. 11.

The need to integrate is recognised by all levels of the *Ahmadi* hierarchy. 'It is imperative that we assimilate ourselves in the society that is our host', announced Mirza Tahir Ahmad, the fourth *Khalifa.*[20] Such assimilation is regarded as a mutual exchange of the best attributes of the two societies concerned rather than a oneway process in which the immigrant community relinquishes its own culture and beliefs in favour of the dominant society. Speaking on the subject of 'social integration' during his address to the annual convention of the Norweigan *Ahmadiyya* Community in October 1996, the fourth *Khalifa* emphasised how, although assimilation is imperative, 'the extent of this assimilation is a most significant issue [for] assimilation connotes combining the capacities of two sides in a way that enables to foster a capacity that is replete with the excellent attributes of both'.[21] 'As a consequence of this', he remarked—the fusion of the 'excellent attributes' of the host society and those of the minority groups living within it—'a society should emerge that is more attractive and delightful than before'. 'This', he declared, 'is the objective that the *Ahmadiyya* Community should keep in view'. 'Such assimilation', he continued, 'does not mean that those aspects that have become detrimental to' the host society [such as immorality and irreligion] 'should be adopted' by the minority group. 'Adopting them' he argued 'would cause you to become like them. If you enforce your own negative characteristics on them then you will be in the wrong...'. Therefore, concluded the fourth *Khalifa*, 'when I speak of assimilation, I speak of an assimilation of values, not absorption brought about by blindly following each other. Thus the thing to watch out for is that the exchange is of exquisiteness and not of unsightliness'.[22]

Such interaction [or 'assimilation'] between the members of the *Ahmadiyya Jama'at* and the host society, although extensive, is circumscribed. With any such minority group there is always the danger of either surrendering to the cultural claims of the dominant society

---

20   Stated at a *Khuddam* student seminar, Bradford, 1 March 1997, cited by *Khuddam* News, *Al-Baseerat*, (March 1997), p. 10.

21   Introduction, *Ahmadiyya Muslim Association, North East, 2001-2003, Annual Report*, Bradford: n.p., p. 3.

22   *Ahmadiyya Muslim Association, North East, 2001-2003, Annual Report*, ibid.

or defying such claims. The *Ahmadi*, without 'surrendering' to a society deemed to be godless, and manifesting a benign defiance, have 'mixed' professionally, but not socially, with those outside their faith. For business, educational and especially evangelistic purposes the *Ahmadi* 'mix' with any social group that will reciprocate. However, although commendable, it is a limited integration, mainly motivated by soteriological and proselytising factors. 'We are here', said one *Ahmadi*, 'to bring everyone to accept the truth'. In the eight years or so that I have been associated with the *Ahmadi* it appears that they mainly mix socially only with other *Ahmadi*. Apart from several students who had non-Muslim and main-stream Muslim friends [and this was frowned upon by parents and elders] the *Ahmadi* are still a community within a community, clinging together for support, legitimation, and the common purpose of evangelism. Such a selective integrative stance is hardly surprising given the opposition the *Ahmadi* face from main-stream Muslims and the inclusivist-monopolistic claims of their own faith. To argue, as they do, that mainstream Muslims are not true Muslims unless they accept the claims of Mirza Ghulam Ahmad will hardly endear the *Ahmadi* to the wider Muslim community. Although wishing to become identified with the host society, by conversion of it rather than absorption by it, the *Ahmadi* maintain an ethnic horizon by their life-style, their language value-orientation, and of course by religious affiliation.

Despite the fact that many *Ahmadi* adopt Western dress, attend the cinema, follow local football teams and have become 'westernised' in certain ways, they retain codes of conduct and practice which communicates their ethnic distinctness. They judge their own behaviour, and that of their co-religionists, according to the value-standards that are particularly theirs. They are limited by their knowledge of society and their interpretation of its values, and by certain cognitive restraints, the main one being their belief that their world-view and morality is superior to that of the host society. In talking to the *Ahmadi*, and reading their literature, it becomes clear that their willingness to 'assimilate' is based, less on a desire to co-exist with others as equals, but more on a missiological imperative to spiritually redeem what they consider to be misled people from a corrupt and godless society. The *Ahmadi* mix, not so much to become British as such, but to convert the majority population to their 'world-view', to lead people to take *bai'at* and accept the *Ahmadi* faith. This observation is not made as a criticism of the *Ahmadi*, for in seeking converts, and wishing for the conversion of society to its own interpretation of truth, the *Ahmadi* are merely acting as all missionary-minded groups act. Most evangelical Christians want to convert society, if not the world, to Christ. The same is true of the Jehovah's Witnesses, the Mormons, and other movements characterised by an aggressive 'knocking-on-doors' approach to religion.

Out of a genuine feeling of loyalty to their place of residence, an understandable desire to present their faith in the best possible light, and the need for acceptance and support in the face of persecution from main-stream Muslims, the *Ahmadi* take every opportunity to present themselves as true British subjects, loyal to the Crown and obedient to the governing authorities. As its own official literature declares: '*Ahmadi* Muslims have earned the distinction of being a law-abiding, peaceful, persevering and benevolent community'.[23] With reference to immigrants who enter one country [in this context Western Europe] to escape the hostility of another the *Khalifa* stated: 'they have absolutely no right whatsoever to be disrespectful to the law of the land'.[24] People 'whom this country has treated with great goodwill for the simple reason that their own country had rejected them and they have been accepted and embraced here', he suggested, 'are duty bound to not only respect the law of the land but to assist and support them in all their efforts to stem the surge of lawlessness'. He declared how 'it is extremely important that the young, the old, men, women, and children of the *Ahmadiyya* Community all step forward and in a co-operative spirit present their services' to those in power in the host country. Such cultural exchange is made easier by the fact that the vast majority of *Ahmadi* [including women] have a very good grasp of English. The fourth *Khalifa*, in his Norwegian address, stated that the 'sense of isolation' experienced by most im-

---

23   'Problems Faced by Young Muslims Growing up in a Western Society', article in *Al-Baseerat*, (March 1993), op. cit., p. 12.

24   *Ahmadiyya Muslim Association, North East, 2001-2003, Annual Report,* op. cit., p. 3.

migrants 'mostly stems from, and is supported by, disagreement over languages'. 'Those who immigrate and settle in foreign lands and fence themselves in around their language', he argued, 'remain "foreigners" despite having lived in the new country for centuries and despite being its legal citizens'. By refusing to learn the language of the host country, he explained, 'defensive walls' are erected 'against the outside environment'. Although, reasoned the fourth *Khalifa* 'it is indeed fair to keep one's language alive, for through language one's cultural values that pertain to high morals, are kept alive, one does not have the right to live in a country as an alien, as if one is dumb and the flow of exchange of ideas between one and the local community ceases'.[25]

Due to their ability to speak English, coupled with a willingness to mix [particularly in the business world] with non-*Ahmadi*, the *Ahmadi* are more socially mobile than their co-religionists. As a general rule, many Muslims in the UK [particularly those belonging to the *Pathan* or *Mirpur* communities] are predominantly 'stable' lower class, intentionally or otherwise, preserving an almost ghetto mentality. In contrast to other ethnic groups, particularly Afro-Caribbean, the *Ahmadi* live up to mainstream norms of achievement. They are in many ways the Muslim bourgeoisie, the upwardly mobile integrationists with the same social aspirations of affluence, materialism, 'getting on', characterising members of the host society. As one *Ahmadi* remarked: 'why shouldn't we be successful at business. After all success is a clear sign that God has favoured you'.

Integration was a common theme in several of the discussions I had with Riaz. On one such occasion, in my house on Edderthorpe Street, he told me: 'Many Muslims living in the west, swayed and influenced by the views of ignorant, prejudicial *Mullahs* who teach them many wrong things about British society and non-Muslims, behave badly towards whites'. I asked him to explain. 'Many Muslims in this country', he replied, 'see British people as enemies of Islam, and resent them, and do not want harmony with them'. Riaz explained to me how *Ahmadi* teaching emphasises the need for true Muslims to be good, law-abiding citizens and to live peacefully with

---

25   Ibid.

everyone. He asked for a copy of the Quran. I obligingly went up-
stairs to the study and returned with one of several translations of
the Quran I had in my possession. Turning the pages over with the
confidence of someone who knew his holy book well, he drew my
attention to *Surah Al Maidah*, reading to me Muhammad's words:
'O ye who believe! Be steadfast in the cause of Allah, bearing witness
in equity; and let not a people's enmity incite you to act otherwise
than with justice. Be *always* just, that is nearer to righteousness. And
fear Allah. Surely Allah is aware of what you do'.[26] With alacrity
he turned to another verse; 'Allah forbids you not, respecting those
who have not fought against you on account of your religion, and
who have not driven you forth from your homes, that you be kind
to them, and act equitably towards them; surely Allah loves those
who are equitable'.[27] Similarly, turning to another text, he read: 'O
ye who believe! Let not one people deride another people, who may
be better than they, nor let women deride other women, who may
be better than they. Do not slander your own people, nor taunt each
other with nicknames. It is bad indeed to earn foul reputation after
professing the faith; and those who repent not are the wrongdoers'.[28]
He closed the Quran and respectfully placed it on the highest ledge
on the bookcase. 'Not only the Quran', he continued, 'but also in the
hadith there is much teaching on justice, living in peace with one
another, and tolerance'.

'Can you give me an example?' I asked enquiringly.

'Although *Maulvi sahib* [the name that *Ahmadi* give to their *Imam*]
will know the exact reference', he stated, 'I know that in his farewell
sermon Muhammad, peace be upon him, made it quite clear the way
we are supposed to live'.

'What did he say?', I asked with interest.

'Well, although I can't quote exactly' confessed Riaz, 'he said that
our God is one, and our father is one. As such he reminded us that
an Arab possesses no superiority over the non-Arab, nor does a non-
Arab over an Arab. He said that a white person has no superiority

---

26 Quran 5:9.

27 Quran 60:9.

28 Quran 49:11.

over the black or the black over the white. He finished his speech by saying that righteousness and integrity are the bases of distinction and preference'. I was impressed with his knowledge, and his conviction that many Muslims were failing to portray what he believed to be true Islam. He presented to me an Islam that flew in the face of the religion presented by Osama Bin Ladin, Ayman al-Zawahiri, Muhammad Atta and other leading figures of radical Islam. I asked him why other Muslims did not share the same view; surely they also read the Quran? A smile came over his face. 'Of course', he replied, 'all Muslims revere the Quran as the word of Allah revealed through his prophet Muhammad, peace be upon him. But very few Muslims read it for themselves. Some can even recite all or part of it by memory in Arabic not English', he remarked, 'but they do not understand the Arabic they learn by rote. Because of this they rely on the word of the *Mullah* to tell them what the Quran says and if you get a leader who is prejudiced against British society he will have a profound effect on the people he is leading'.

Because *khidmat-e-khalq* [welfare of people] is an important aspect of the religious life for *Ahmadi*, and also because of their strong desire to manifest the veracity of their truth claims and to integrate into the wider society, many activities are organised throughout the year for charitable causes. *Ansarullah*, male members of the *Jama'at*, are constantly reminded that 'they are the helpers of God, and in so being, they should set an example for their families, their neighbours and the communities in which they live'.[29] As one regional *Amir* declared; 'take an active role within your community, do not sit back and think you have done enough'.[30] As the editor of *Al-Baseerat* remarked: 'the majority of people living in this country regard Islam as a religion of violence and hatred instead of a religion of peace'. As such, a primary aim of the *Ahmadi Jama'at* is the organisation of Charity events where, as one *Ahmadi* stated, 'we are serving humanity; raising large sums of money for different charities, help[ing] to change the poor

29   *Al-Baseerat*, (March 1997), op. cit., p. 10.
30   Report by Bilal Atkinson, *Nazim Ansarullah*, Yorkshire region, cited in *Al-Baseerat*, (February 1997), p. 3.

image of Islam'.[31] Collections are often held at local stores such as Morrisons, collecting money for worthy causes.[32] Prayer vigils have been held to lift people's awareness of on-going atrocities in places such as Bosnia, Herzegovina and Rwanda, and to raise money for the innocent civilian populations involved in such crises. A glance at past editions of the *Ahmadi* newsletter, *Al-Baseerat,* reveals the special meetings held throughout the early '90s to assist Bosnian refugees living at the 'Springfield Bosnian Centre', Leeds, and the centre at 'Highfield', Batley. A food convoy was organised in April 1993 taking '10 tonnes of medicine and food' to the town of Tuzia, Bosnia.[33] In March of that year a vigil was held jointly by the Bradford, Spen Valley and Leeds *Jama'ats,* at Leeds Town Hall raising £2,500, while a second vigil, organised at York Minster, raised a further £1,000 for the Bosnian relief. Regular Marathon Walks are organised by the *Ahmadi* in different parts of the country and for different charitable causes. In 1989, so as to celebrate the centenary of the movement, the *Ahmadi* Youth organised a sponsored National Marathon Cycle ride, involving over 100 cyclists riding from Bradford to London. This Cycle ride raised £27,000 for the London Children's Hospital and the Great Ormond Street Hospital, which now has a new wing dedicated to the Youth of the *Ahmadiyya Jama'at.* In 1992 over 300 people took part in a National Charity Walk from Addingham to Otley and back, a twenty-six mile walk, raising £28,000 for charity. Regular contributions are made to the Lord Mayor's Appeal.

In times of national and local crisis the *Ahmadi* are keen to identify with the suffering and grief of others. A message of sympathy and an offer of financial help was sent to all those who suffered in the fire at Bradford City's Valley Parade Football Ground in 1985. The *Ahmadi* joined in the public grief expressed by the nation generally for the death of Lady Diana, Princess of Wales, in 1997. The *Jama'at* was instructed 'to take part in the two minute silence' that was held in her honour and sympathy cards were sent 'in accordance with the teachings of Islam'. The President of the *Jama'at,* Mr Abdul Bary

---

31   *Al-Baseerat,* (May 1997), editorial, p. 2.

32   *Al-Baseerat,* (May, 1993).

33   *Al-Baseerat,* (February 1997), p. 3.

Malik, and other members, 'signed the book of condolence at the Bradford Town Hall'.

Various activities, usually with a distinct public relations angle, are organised for humanitarian reasons. 'Humanitarian days' are held in local hospitals 'when all children on a paediatric ward will receive presents, perhaps consisting of chocolates, and will be visited and talked to by the *Jama'at* members'. As the official literature of the movement states: 'the intention is to invite the local press and then explain the occasion, whilst also displaying the charitable name of the *Jama'at*'.[34] The obvious need to organise events as public relations exercises is seen in the way *Ahmadi* are told to give blood. *Ahmadi* are reminded how 'it is better to organise *Jama'at* volunteers to donate blood in groups rather than individually, so that the staff and any other donators at the clinic are aware of an organised attempt by *Ahmadi* Muslims to donate blood'. Similarly the collection of food aid from supermarkets 'highlighted the *Jama'at* convoys to Bosnia and thus elevated the charitable name of the *Jama'at* to the public'.[35] Every year an *Eid Milan* Party is held at the mosque where people from all walks of life are invited, not only as an opportunity for *Ahmadis* to share their faith with others, but also as a gesture of friendship to the community in general. A cheque is given by the *Ahmadi* to a relevant charity, usually the Lord Mayor's appeal for that year. Understandably, the *Ahmadi* gain maximum publicity from such events. The *Yorkshire Post*, *Telegraph and Argus* and other local news papers are always informed by the public relations office of the *Jama'at* of any events taking place. At the *Eid Milan* party in 2003, I sat as one of 300 invited guests in the *Ahmadi* mosque, and as I watched Bary Malik shake the hand of Margaret Eaton, the Mayoress, and present her with an enlarged cardboard cheque for £1600, for the Lord Mayor's Appeal, I asked myself 'Would the *Ahmadi* still be doing this if they simply sent a cheque to the charity concerned, or even did it anonymously?'

Due to the educational and class background of most *Ahmadi*, the *Ahmadiyya Jama'at*, despite its relatively small size, has made a

---

34   *Al-Baseerat*, (February 1997), p. 3.

35   *Al-Baseerat*, (February 1997), op. cit.

significant contribution to the economy of most regions where its members settle. Taking Bradford as an example, with Amini textiles, Crown textiles, and Ahmad textiles, three of the most significant textile retailers in the area, the *Jama'at* has enjoyed a significant involvement in the commercial life of the city. One of the earliest immigrants in the borough, Rafi Mir, was a pioneer trader; he was one of the first wholesale greengrocers, establishing a trade in fruit and vegetables at the Old St James Market. One of the first Asian GPs in Bradford was Dr. N. U. Mir who helped to establish the Medical Centre on Horton Lane. *Ahmadis* have been influential in other aspects of Bradford life, as seen in the case of Abdul Bary Malik who has served as a Justice of the Peace since 1987, and has contributed significantly in various business and philanthropic enterprises in the Bradford area. He has also frequently spoken out, as seen in both local and national newspapers, on issues related to Bradford.

As its promotional literature declares, the *Ahmadiyya Jama'at* 'encourages interfaith dialogue' and diligently seeks to remove misunderstandings between all faiths'. Positive efforts are made to form links with every group within the local community. Activities are varied: football tournaments are held in the sports hall at the mosque. In July 1996 for example, the 'Leeds Road City Challenge Tournament' was held when boys under 14 invited other teams from the Muslim Association, Hindu Cultural Society, the Sikh *Gurdwara* and the Air Training Corps.[36] However, while it is to be welcomed, it would appear to some that this tolerance is really for the purpose of revealing the errors of other faiths and uniting all peoples within *Ahmadiyyat*. For example, *Ahmadi* believe that one of the aims of the *Jama'at* is 'to cleanse Muslims of the errors and superstitious customs that had crept into their beliefs and practices during fourteen centuries, and following Islam the way it was practised at the time of the Holy Prophet'.[37] *Ahmadi* see other faiths as distortions of truth; they are not recognised as valid in their own right. They are errors which need to be corrected and brought under the banner of

---

36   *Al-Baseerat*, (February 1997), ibid.

37   Karimullah Zirvi, *Welcome to Ahmadiyyat: The true Islam*, Ahmadiyya Movement in Islam, Silver Springs, USA, 2002, *passim*.

Ahmadiyyat. In establishing such correction the *Ahmadiyyat* 'encourages interfaith dialogue, diligently defends Islam and tries to correct misunderstandings about Islam in the west'. Such is clearly seen in the system of *Chanda waqf-i-jadid*, a scheme initiated by the second *Khalifa* in 1957, 'primarily to protect the public of Pakistan from Christian missionaries' efforts to convert them to Christianity, [and] to train villagers as missionaries for the propagation of Islam'.[38] As such, interfaith dialogue for the *Ahmadi* is not seen as a process of recognising the truth in other faiths, but as a means by which discussion can begin which, in the opinion of *Ahmadi*, will result in the exposure of the errors of other belief systems, and the establishment of the truth of the claims of the *Ahmadi* faith.

The *Ahmadi*, being a persecuted minority, keen to be acknowledged and gain support, are hardly in a position to get involved in politics. They do not see themselves as a politically-minded movement and as such, despite their high level of educational and financial influence within society, do not usually stand as Councillors or Members of Parliament. As the fourth *Khalifa* remarked: 'the Promised Messiah had always kept out of politics and had indicated that those who followed him should also keep out of direct involvement in politics'.[39] However, despite this 'no-politics rule', *Ahmadi* believe they are under a divine imperative to advise rulers on what is right for the people and to speak out against what is morally wrong. As the fourth *Khalifa* stated: 'moral guidance was the *Khalifa's* responsibility. Religion can never be totally disassociated from politics. It is the duty of all religions to keep reminding politicians of their moral obligation to mankind'.[40] As such the *Ahmadi*, despite fierce persecution by mainstream Muslims, were active in the inter-war years campaigning for an independent Muslim state in India. In Britain, and the Western world generally, the *Ahmadi* endeavour to 'influence opinion-makers through newspapers and the media' and 'get involved in social is-

---

38   Zirvi, op. cit., p. 410.

39   I. Adamson, *Man of God: The Astonishing Story of His Holiness Khalifatul Masih IV*, Bristol: George Shepherd Publishers, 1991, p. 83.

40   Adamson, op. cit., p. 83.

sues—the political face of Islam'.[41] In an attempt to 'change people's opinions,' *Ahmadi* students are encouraged to 'get involved in societies and committees in universities'. The *Ahmadi* have also occasionally been controversial when speaking out on key issues. In late 1987, and early in the following year, the *Ahmadi* Muslims of Bradford campaigned to have Friday made a holiday, thus enabling the devout to attend prayers at the mosque.[42] Believing that all Muslims should be allowed the same religious rights enjoyed by Christians and Jews, who enjoy a 'holiday' on Saturday and Sunday, they campaigned to get workers and school children the right to attend *Juma* prayers at the midday service on Friday. Members of the movement backed the campaign nationally by writing to the government, local authorities and industries. Bary Malik, the chief spokesman for the *Ahmadiyya Jama'at* in Bradford stated how: 'we are not asking for a whole day or even a half day off. The service usually starts at midday and would be over within an hour'. It was reasoned that 'workers could make up the hours in overtime and school children could do extra homework or alter their lunch hours'. Although recognising it as an important issue, local business leaders stated that 'making Friday a holiday is best decided by the individual companies because much will depend on things like shifts'.[43] The debate continues on this issue.

The *Ahmadi*, as indicated above, present an interesting paradigm of integration by a minority group in a multicultural society. Tendentious, organised, and disciplined, the *Ahmadiyya Jama'at*, despite its relatively small size, is becoming a valued section of society in Bradford and other European and American cities. As well as being generally well-educated, English-speaking, prosperous and keen to display a philanthropic spirit, with the aid of their satellite TV channel, the *Ahmadi* are capable of integrating into Western secular society, a process aided by a developed penchant for marketing and publicity. As a public relations exercise, and in an attempt to get their views over to the media, the *Jama'at*, following the events of 9/11, launched the *Islam Awareness Campaign*. This petered out. A more

---

41   *Ahmadiyya Bulletin*, (December 2002/January 2003), p. 20.

42   *Al-Baseerat*, (August 1996), p. 7

43   *Al-Baseerat*, (June 1996), p. 6.

comprehensive media structure was put in its place. The *National Media Cell* [NMC] was established. It consists of the Heads and deputy Heads of all the different media-related groups: *tabligh*, human rights, press and publicity, and others appointed by the *Amir*.[44] A co-ordinator keeps the *Amir* informed of media activities in the United Kingdom through regular reports. His main task is disseminating 'media-related information among the NMC and to make sure that the different media sub-groups are kept informed about each other's activities. This includes forwarding press releases to each member of the NMC. The NMC has a team of scanners which 'scans all media in the United Kingdom on a daily basis for news relating to Islam and *Ahmadiyyat*'.[45]

---

44 *Ahmadiyya Bulletin*, (December 2002/January 2003), p. 20.
45 *Ahmadiyya Bulletin*, (December 2002/January 2003), op. cit., p. 21.

8

WOMEN AND THE FAMILY

The role and status of women is just one of several controversial issues facing contemporary Islam. The image of Muslim women hidden beneath veils or *burqa* has caused some to see Islam as a male-dominated and misogynist faith, with Muslim women being submissive shadows of the men, 'prisoners in the four walls of the house', 'non-persons', people 'who have no rights ... living always under the domination of a man'.[1] Others however, usually adherents of the faith, argue that 'these notions are totally wrong, and based on ignorance rather than knowledge of Islam', and claim that 'women have a very important place in Islamic society ... and unlike a number of other religions Islam holds a woman in high esteem'.[2] As such, the wearing of *hijab* and *chador,* is seen as a model of freedom which challenges the alleged exploitation of women in the West. It is not within the scope of this present book to try and provide answers to these questions. However, a consideration of the *Ahmadi* teaching on women, marriage and family life, will provide interpretative insight into Islam generally, and the *Ahmadi* sect specifically.

The *Ahmadi*, similar to Muslims worldwide, firmly believe that 'no religion other than Islam presents such a [high] status for women'.[3] The official website of the Lahori *Ahmadi*, in presenting its teaching to

---

1   Ghulam Sarwar, *Islam: Beliefs and Teachings*, London: The Muslim Educational Trust, 1987, p. 166.

2   G. Sarwar, *Islam: Beliefs and Teachings*, op. cit., p. 166.

3   Karimullah Zirvi, *Welcome to Ahmadiyyat: The True Islam*, Silver Spring, USA: *Ahmadiyya* Movement in Islam, 2002, p. 437.

the general enquirer, declares the equality of the sexes arguing how 'Islam recognises the position of women to be equal to that of men, both from a maternal as well as spiritual point of view'.[4] 'No religion of the world', it asserts, 'accords as high a status to women as Islam, ... no other religious book and no other reformer have done a fraction of what the Holy Quran and the Holy Prophet have done to raise the status of women'. Justification for the claim that 'it is Islam which has really elevated the status of women', is found in the fact that in pre-Islamic Arabia 'women were sold as personal commodities [and] female children were buried alive because they were considered as a curse for the family'.[5] Islam brought such practices to an end and, as many Muslims assert, it was Muhammad who established women as being equal to men. 'Oh Mankind', declares the Quran, 'fear your God who created you from one soul and from the same soul created his mate'.[6] As such it is generally agreed that 'a woman's prayers are equal in value to that of a man and women can receive revelation from Allah'.[7]

Although the idea of equality is taught by the *Ahmadi*, as it is within Islam generally, some would argue, in relation to gender issues, that some are more equal than others. Such equality involves the assignment of roles and obligations, the privileging of each sex in the area that, it is assumed, most suits a man's nature or that of a woman. It is generally assumed by the *Ahmadi*, like other Muslims, that a woman is better suited to a maternal, domestic role, while the man, being stronger [physically], is the provider. The woman's crucial social role therefore is balanced by the male's slightly more important position as a leader. 'Men are in charge of women', declares the Quran, 'because Allah hath made the one of them to excel the other'.[8] As such 'good women are the obedient, guarding in secret that which

---

4   Sarah Ahmad, article, 'Position of Women in Islam', www.aaiil.org.

5   Zirvi, *Welcome to Ahmadiyyat*, op. cit., p. 433.

6   Quran 4:2.

7   Mrs Tahir Selby 'The Status of Women in Islam', *Al Baseerat*, (July 1993), p. 7.

8   Quran 4:34.

Allah has guarded'.[9] The *Ahmadi* present a patriarchal view of marriage and the family. 'The role of the wife', declared one leader within the *Jama'at*, 'is to raise the children and look after the home whilst the husband's is to go to work and provide for the family'.[10] If there are no children, or if the children are attending full time school then if the wife desires, she may go out to work 'with her husband's permission'. Although the man has divinely approved pre-eminence, it is assumed that both sexes have human rights and duties to an equal degree, and the rewards of the hereafter are available to men and women alike. Rather than being rulers over the women the *Ahmadi*, like Muslims generally, argue that men 'are given more responsibilities about taking care of the woman and [should] give them every possible protection'.[11] Consequently, it is recognised that a woman has the right of *nafaqa*, the right to be provided for. Concerning wives, the Quran reminds a man: 'they are a garment to you, and you are a garment to them'.[12] Reference is made to the words of Muhammad who, in emphasising one of the main roles of women as child-bearers and mothers, proclaimed: 'Paradise lies at the feet of your mothers'.[13] Many of the practices viewed by westerners which seem to show Muslim women in a bad light, such as the image of women as submissive, uneducated housewives are regarded by *Ahmadi* as *bidat*, 'un-Islamic customs which have crept into Islam over the years as it spread to different countries and adopted their customs'.[14]

Mirza Ghulam Ahmad had many things to say about women. He reminded the men within the sect that they 'should not think that women are something to be taken as very low and of no importance whatsoever'.[15] In reference to the way certain Muslims abused the

9   Quran 4:34.

10   Mrs Tahir Selby, *Al-Baseerat*, op. cit., p. 6.

11   Zirvi, *Welcome to Ahmadiyyat*, op. cit., p. 436.

12   Quran 4:3.

13   *Nisa'i* and *Baihaqi*. Two of the twelve *Amirs*/prophets appointed by Muhammad, *hadith* cited by Zirvi, *Welcome to Ahmadiyyat*, op. cit., p. 437.

14   Mrs Tahir Selby, 'The Status of Women in Islam', *Al-Baseerat*, op. cit., p. 6.

15   Mirza Ghulam Ahmad, *Malfoozat*, vol. II, p. 147, cited in 'Behaviour

Quranic text which allows a husband to 'beat his wife gently',[16] or those who relied on the *hadith* which reported Muhammad as advising that, if a man must beat his wife the beating should be such as to leave no mark on her body,[17] Ahmad stated that 'he who does not treat his wife nicely, cannot be called a righteous person'. 'He who quarrels with his wife and scolds her for every petty thing and beats her up', he continued, 'can certainly do no good to others'.[18] He emphasised how 'at times it so happens that a person is annoyed with his wife and beats her and as a result of that she gets hurt at some delicate part of her body and she passes away. It is to avoid this kind of thing that God says: *Aashiroo hunna bil ma'roof* [treat your wives well]'.[19] However, Ahmad then qualifies this advice by adding: 'of course if she [the wife] does something very undesirable, she may be given a warning'. Although there is no mention about the wife reprimanding the unfaithful or impious husband, or criticising *his* shortcomings, Ahmad declares: 'It is the duty of the man to tell the woman [the wife] that he will not like anything that is contrary to the religious commands, but at the same time he should also tell her that he is not so harsh and hardhearted that he should not overlook any of *her* shortcomings'.[20]

Claiming to be orthodox Muslims, *Ahmadi* observe *purdah*, the segregation of women from men. Literally meaning 'curtain' or 'veil', *purdah* refers to both segregation of the sexes, and Islamic dress for women.[21] 'Modesty and faith are joined closely together', declares *hadith*, 'if either of them is lost, the other goes also'. *Ahmadi* women, like all Muslim women, are supposed to have a sense of *sharam*: shame or shyness. As such the legs must not be shown. Muslim dress should always be modest, never attention-seeking. Women are expected to practice *hijab*, or *satr*, the covering of the body according to

towards wives', front page, *Al-Baseerat*, (July 1990).

16 Quran 4:35.
17 Tirmidhi & Muslim, cited by Farid, *Quran*, op. cit., fn., 601, p. 201.
18 *Malfoozat*, op. cit., p. 148 cited in *Al-Baseerat*, (July 1990), op. cit.
19 *Malfoozat*, ibid., p. 147.
20 Ibid.
21 Quran 33:59; J. Esposito, *Oxford Dictionary of Islam*, op. cit., sv.

standards of propriety and modesty. Although the wearing of *burqa* or *chador* [the full length garment covering a woman from head to foot] is seen by feminists [both Muslim and non-Muslim] as a symbol of backwardness, oppression, or inferiority, for many *Ahmadi* and mainstream Muslims alike it is regarded as an indication of Muslim identity, a sign of piety and modesty. The Quran instructs Muslim women to 'cast a veil over their private parts and dress modestly'.[22] Reference is made by the *Ahmadi* to other Quranic texts in which the prophet's wives and daughters are told to cover themselves as 'it is more likely that they will thus be distinguished and not molested'.[23]

Older women within the *Ahmadi Jama'at*, reflecting the views of the Asian community generally in Britain, wear traditional Asian dress, particularly the head covering. Although the younger women are educated and brought up to respect and practice the traditional customs of sobriety, some *Ahmadi* manifest 'deviant' behaviour by wearing make-up, jeans, high heels. This has caused considerable concern amongst the leaders of the *Jama'at*. Abdul Bary Malik, speaking at the monthly meeting of the Bradford mosque in September 1996, told the congregation how 'in Pakistan, the *Ahmadi* ladies were known for their *purdah*'.[24] As such, he stated, 'we must lead by example in this country otherwise girls will walk in the streets with nothing covering their heads'.[25] While talking with various leaders of the *Jama'at* during my stay at the *Ahmadi* international headquarters at Rabwah in 2004 I was made aware of the general concern about the adoption of western values by *Ahmadi* women in Europe, especially clothing and make-up,. 'This is the problem', remarked the editor of *Al-Fadl*, 'when we live in a society that does not fear God'. The third *Khalifa*, speaking in 1972, stressed that the observance of *purdah* 'does not mean that I want you to put on *burqa*, for the Holy Quran has nowhere enjoined so'.[26] However, such leniency is then

---

22   Quran 24:32.

23   Quran 33:60.

24   *Al-Baseerat*, (February 1997).

25   *Al-Baseerat*, op. cit.

26   'Lajna on the March', an address by *Hadhrat Hafiz* Mirza Nasir Ahmad, *Khalifatul Masih III*, *The Muslim Herald*, (December 1975/January 1976),

tempered with the directive: 'the Holy Quran forbids you to show even that much beauty of your person to anybody which you show to your father and father-in-law'.[27] It is expected within the *Jama'at* that women 'are to wear an outer and wrapping garment which should cover their heads and bosoms in such a manner that the garment should come down from the head to the bosom covering the whole body including the face'.[28] The rationale for this is that, when a woman 'goes about her business she may be spared the mental anguish of being stared at by persons of questionable character'. The value of *purdah*, according to *Ahmadiyyat*, is self evident to any moral person. As the third *Khalifa* remarked: 'Do you want to imitate the women of the West who have delivered illegitimate children in a number exceeding the total female population of Pakistan'. As well as women's clothing it is worth pointing out that modesty extends to eye contact and even handshaking. Many *Ahmadi* believe that men should not look directly at a woman, for the Quran instructs both men and women, to 'lower their gaze and guard their modesty'.[29] It is also believed by many *Ahmadi*, as a general rule of etiquette, men should only shake hands with men, women only with women.

It is interesting to note how, just as various stereotypes are held by white non-Muslims in the West regarding Islam, so Muslims tend to stereotype in their assessment of Western secular society. The arguments put forward by *Ahmadi* to justify the dress code required by women, as well as the Quranic texts outlined above, are based on generalisations and stereotypes of Western society, and women living within that society. For example it is generally assumed that all British people drink alcohol and go to night clubs at the weekend. When I have been in conversation with *Ahmadi* or mainstream Muslims and told them that I am tee-total and do not go 'clubbing', despite clear statements to the contrary, they have always assumed I am a Muslim. *Ahmadi*, like their co-religionists, also tend to assume that the majority of British women, not only drink to excess, but are

---

p. 19.

27   *The Muslim Herald*, (December 1975/January 1976), op. cit., p. 19.

28   Ibid.

29   Quran 24:32.

sexually immoral. Despite the fact that many western women would share the same abhorrence of exploitative nudity and gratuitous sex on Television and in advertising, and the excesses of club land, the unjustified assumption is made that all Western women 'sleep around' or 'parade their bodies' in 'cheap and tacky newspapers'. Reference has already been made in the previous chapter to the *Ahmadi* belief that, 'now in England you have an irreligious, immoral society, where children beat up their teachers!' and how 'the modern values of the West' are 'devoid of morals and based on material benefits and self-interest'.[30] In similar vein another *Ahmadi* writes:

When I look at the English women who tell me that I have no rights, I look at their so-called freedom. If being able to display my body in cheap and tacky newspapers is having freedom and respect then I would much rather have no rights. I feel sorry for my non-Muslim sisters as they are blind in believing that they have equal rights when they clearly do not.[31]

Clearly such a view of Western women is a stereotype which ignores the fact there are many non-Muslims in Britain who regard cohabitation, immorality and excessive drinking as wrong.

The *Ahmadi* are adamant in their belief that women within their sect enjoy greater freedom than non-Muslim women and women within mainstream Islam. As one writer remarked: 'most *Ahmadi* women are well educated, and active in many spheres of life, while maintaining their dignity through Islam'.[32] In conversation with Bary Malik at the Bradford mosque, he stressed how women within the movement have the same educational and career opportunities as the men. While at Rabwah, Pakistan, I was taken on a tour of the new *Ahmadi* hospital and introduced to the head surgeon, a woman who had trained in Britain: erudite, confident and affable. Most *Ahmadi* women, in contrast to many women in other strands of Islam, have driving licenses. The *Ahmadi* women I saw in Bradford, Birmingham, Leicester, Manchester, London and other British cities, drove

---

30 Mansoor Ahmad Shah, 'Social Integration', *The Review of Religions*, (February 1997), p. 14.

31 Mrs Selby, 'The Status of Women in Islam', *Al-Baseerat*, (July 1993), op. cit., p. 6.

32 The *Ahmadiyya Gazette*, (January 2002), pp. 17-9.

around freely, often on their own. Women mixed with men at family gatherings although the expected segregation of the sexes occurred at weddings and other social functions at the mosque. Women in the *Ahmadiyya* community appear to enjoy more power and influence, particularly in the family unit, than their counterparts in mainstream Islam. In my association with the *Ahmadi* I have seen men talk business with their wives, in front of me, asking for advice, if not permission to undertake certain business ventures. Such influence and authority by the woman is heightened when her relatives are wealthy, and through the *biradri* network, the husband needs cash for financial undertakings. Few *Ahmadi* women attend public houses or clubs. There are exceptions though. One Nigerian woman, a student in her early twenties, whom I met on the train returning from the *Jalsa Salana* at Islamabad, Tilford, in July 2003, spoke openly to me, a man, of her pleasure in attending discos [even nightclubs] although, as she said, the officials within the movement and her parents disliked this.

Although some *Ahmadi* women, particularly the younger Western women, seem to enjoy greater freedoms and rights than many of their co-religionists, for the majority of *Ahmadi* women theirs is a restricted world of limited contact, a world of hiding and concealment, a world carefully controlled by men. In the several years I have known *Imam* Bajwa, and attended the Bradford mosque for various functions or to carry out research, I have never had the opportunity to meet his wife or daughters. I occasionally had glimpses of a small middle aged woman, dressed in *hijab*, walking along the hall from the *Imam's* private quarters in the mosque to the main entrance, whom I presumed was his wife. One young woman, similarly dressed in *hijab*, whom I took to be one of his daughters, I met briefly in the main office in the mosque. She was typing on the computer with her back towards me. Realising that we were alone together in a room, sensing her embarrassment and fully aware of the requirements of *purdah*, I *salaamed* her and made a hasty retreat back out to the hall to wait for Naseem to appear. Whenever I enjoyed hospitality at the mosque with Naseem his wife would never join us; she would merely call down from the up-stairs kitchen when the food was ready. Similarly, in many *Ahmadi* homes the women remain separate from the men, preparing and serving the food while the men sit and talk.

As hinted at above such 'control' is justified on the grounds of protecting the woman, and the need to prevent immorality. 'I feel that the rule of segregation', declared one female convert to *Ahmadiyyat*, 'goes hand in hand with an old English saying "Prevention is better than cure"'.[33] She continued:

Segregation is a precautionary measure to prevent any kind of physical and indeed mental contact between men and women who are not married to each other. By cutting off all avenues of destruction you are safe-guarding the future. Allah is well aware that we are only human and that temptation of having a beautiful woman, or attractive man for that matter, in your presence could be very hard for you to not think impure thoughts.[34]

Segregation is taken to extraordinary lengths. In many *Ahmadi* homes there is a distinct absence of wedding photographs, or pictures showing wives and daughters, as it is deemed dishonourable for other men to see such things. At weddings and other social functions it is thought improper for men to video women. Furthermore a separate room is given over for videoing so that 'only those women who wished to be filmed would go to that area'.[35] In the interests of segregation women are usually allocated a separate room in the mosque away from the men for prayer, or encouraged to pray at home. The mosque in Bradford has two separate prayer rooms, one for either sex. This was the case with *Ahmadi* mosques at Rabwah, Qadian, Srinigar and other places around the world. At official functions such as *Eid Milan* Parties, or other occasions, the addresses are relayed to the women who gather separately away from the men in another room, by a PA system.

In various communities living in Britain, such as the Afro-Caribbean, Italian, German, Polish, or Latvian, marriage is seen by some within those communities as a significant element in the dilution of ethnicity. These communities, in allowing its members to marry outside that ethnic group, have inevitably seen a loss of cultural identity.

33   Mrs Tahir Selby, *Al-Baseerat*, (July 1993), op. cit.
34   Mrs Selby, ibid., p. 6.
35   'Monthly Meeting News' reported in *Al-Baseerat*, (January 1993), p. 2.

This is not the case generally however with other minority groups such as the Hindu, Sikh and Muslim communities, as marriage with 'outsiders' is at least discouraged, if not openly opposed. The *Ahmadiyya Jama'at*, like Islam generally, is endogamous in nature, forbidding marriage outside the community for women and allowing such marriages, only in exceptional circumstances, for men.[36] Strict rules specify what categories of persons are regarded as eligible marriage partners. 'This is the final word', declared *Masih-e-Mauood*, 'that to marry a girl to a non-*Ahmadi* boy is a sin'.[37] Other *Ahmadi* leaders have stated; 'No *Ahmadi* girl is allowed to marry a non-*Ahmadi* boy, except if permission is granted from the centre'.[38] Such permission, as Naseem Bajwa remarked, is rarely given. *Ahmadi* rules relating to marriage mirror the rules followed in mainstream Islam. Although marriage to an idolater is totally forbidden, men, but not women, may marry partners of the *Ahli-kitab* [people of the book], 'although it is not considered preferable'.[39] Ahmad explained that *Ahli-kitab* referred to Christians or Jews.[40] The *Ahmadi*, refusing to recognise the orthodoxy of other Muslims, also try to prevent unions between *Ahmadi* and mainstream believers. Riaz, typifying the stance adopted by *Ahmadi* generally, told me of one *Ahmadi*, a relative in Pakistan, who had fallen in love with a main-stream Muslim. Although the members of the *Ahmadiyya Jama'at* did not threaten to kill her or her lover, she was excommunicated from the community. Although not allowed to marry mother, father, sister, brother, aunts, or uncles, *Ahmadi*, as with Muslims generally, can, and do, marry cousins.[41]

Ahmadi and main-stream Muslims agree that 'the best form of marriage is an arranged marriage since the marriage partners have

---

36 Zirvi, *Welcome to Ahmadiyyat*, op. cit., p. 418.

37 Masih-e-Mauood, in a letter to an *Ahmadi* in Peelal, Gujarat, cited in *Al-Baseerat*, (June 1990), p. 4.

38 Tahir Selby while writing on the subject of *Nizam-e-Jamaat* in *Al-Baseerat*, (October 1993), p. 5.

39 Zirvi, *Welcome to Ahmadiyyat*, op. cit., p. 418. Marriage of Muslims to idolaters is forbidden in the Quran, 2:222.

40 Zirvi, ibid., p. 418.

41 Quran 4:23-24.

been chosen because they are best suited for one another'.[42] Although recognising that 'love marriages' do work the *Ahmadi* argue that 'since the couple have come together because of attraction and not because of suitability, there is a danger that the marriage will not work'.[43] It is stressed however 'that there is never any compulsion, and the choice is left to the parties concerned'. As such *nikah*, the announcement of marriage, cannot be performed if either party does not agree. Following *Sharia'h* law, the *Ahmadi* believe a woman must have the consent of her near male relatives [father or brother/s] before she can marry, and the bridegroom must give *haq mehr* to his wife [an agreed sum of money]. Due mainly to 'the lack of free mixing of the sexes in Islam, marriages are arranged by the child's parents'. [44] Following a tradition of the prophet Muhammad it is believed that parents, when choosing a suitable partner for their son, should consider four main qualities: her wealth [compatibility], the family background, her beauty and her piety.[45] It is argued, 'if the child was left with the choice, then the child could easily be blinded by love or looks etc., and overlook the vital ingredient of piety'. It is important to stress that the *Ahmadi* believe in arranged marriages, not forced marriages. As one *Ahmadi* woman explained: 'I would like to point out ... that where true Islamic law is observed, the children both, or girl, should NOT be forced into marriage'.[46]

So as 'to ensure that they understand Islam properly and have developed themselves ... no new *Ahmadi* can marry until they have been an *Ahmadi* for one year'.[47] Exceptions have been known with the permission of the *Khalifa*. This regulation 'gives a chance for the members to get to know the new convert properly'. From the time of *Masih-e-Mauood*, the second *Khalifa*, the *Jama'at* has kept 'a secret and confidential register' containing 'the names of boys and girls'. Therefore, 'if the parents of a girl are unable to find in their own

---

42   *Al-Baseerat*, (February 1990), p. 2.

43   *Al-Baseerat*, (February 1990), op. cit.

44   Mrs Selby, *Al-Baseerat*, (July 1993), op. cit., p. 6.

45   Al-Bukhari. ibid.

46   Ibid.

47   'Marriage and Family Seminar', *Al-Baseerat*, (July 1990), p. 2.

family a boy', and similarly, 'if a suitable girl is not available, in a situation like this, it would be incumbent upon parents to allow' the *Ahmadi* authorities 'to look for a suitable match among the members of [the] *Jama'at*.[48] The register, organised by the office of *Rishta Naata* [marriage bureau], is searched 'from among the people of the candidate's caste, if possible, or alternatively, among those who practice inter-marriages in accordance with their current custom'. The main consideration 'will be that the boy or the girl should be of good character and merit and also that he is dutiful'. This register is kept secret and information is given when the need arises.[49] Parents concerned about a suitable marriage partner for their child, continuing with their *Istikharah prayers* seeking Allah's blessings and guidance, submit details of their child to the *Rishta Naata* which searches the details of suitable candidates either in the UK or abroad. The parents will meet that partner and if they agree to the match they then ask their child if he or she agrees and a meeting of the child with the prospective partner, under supervision, will be arranged.[50]

Although it is claimed by some writers that the *Ahmadi* 'uphold polygamy and consider it to be in keeping with human [or should one say, male] nature',[51] I witnessed only the practice of monogamy wherever I met *Ahmadi* around the world. In Islam it is permitted for a man to have as many as four wives simultaneously, although such a practice is quite rare. I have heard of certain mainstream Muslims who have had one wife in Britain and one, or more, in Pakistan. Although rarely practiced by the *Ahmadi*, the community recognises the Quranic teaching on this matter.[52] To soften the controversial aspect of the teaching on marriage it is argued that there are terms and conditions set up to regulate its practice. As one *Ahmadi* remarked : 'marriage is the same, whether it is one wife or more, you should

---

48   Sayings of *Hadhrat Masih-e-Mauood*, in *Al-Baseerat*, (June 1990), p. 4.

49   Sayings of *Hadhrat Masih-e-Mauood*, in *Al-Baseerat*, op. cit.

50   Ibid., p. 2.

51   Y. Friedmann, *Prophecy Continuous: Aspects of Ahmadi religious thoughts and its Medieval background*, op. cit., p. 184.

52   Quran 4:3.

marry for companionship and to raise children'.[53] If a man decides on having another wife then 'she is to be treated exactly the same as the first'. A man should only consider taking another wife if:

1. his wife is severely disabled.
2. if his wife cannot produce children.
3. if your wife is old and you would like a younger wife.
4. if you take another wife for humanitarian reasons i.e. During a war many men die leaving widows who are not catered for by the government who have to go to work or turn to prostitution to support themselves and their children.

It is argued that if a man marries another woman for the right reasons 'then not only would your first wife be happy with that, but she might also choose the wife for you'.[54] In the opinion of one *Ahmadi*, polygamy 'would solve the rising adultery problem in this country. There would be no threat to the first wife if the husband took a second wife because, unlike with adulterous affaires, she would know who her husband was with, and that she was not going to be left in the lurch for the so-called "other woman"'.[55] The *Ahmadi*, again following Quranic teaching, allow divorce. 'Divorce is permitted in Islam by both parties. However it is stressed that this should be the last resort'. As Muhammad is reported as saying: 'divorce is of all permissible things most hateful in the eyes of Allah'.[56]

As stated above, the *Ahmadi*, as with Muslims generally, believe that the main purpose of marriage is to have children and bring them up in a good Muslim home. It is argued that Muhammad set a perfect example in marrying and raising a family. Parents should teach their children how to pray, the basic beliefs of Islam, the nature of right and wrong. They are to set a good example for their children to follow. As stated in a *hadith* quoted by *al'Timmidhi*, Muslims are reminded that 'no father can give his child anything better than good

---

53   Mrs Selby, *Al-Baseerat*, op. cit., p. 7.
54   Ibid.
55   Ibid.
56   Dawud, ibid.

manners'. As Naseem Bajwa remarked, 'we believe that children are a gift from God and we will be judged at the end of the world on how we have raised our children'. Riaz explained to me how, as well as sending his children 'to the mosque to learn the Quran in Arabic and learn about the faith, it is important to teach them at home, to perform *namaz*'. 'We say our prayers together as a family', he said. 'We teach our children at home what is *halal* and what is *haram*'. As with most other Asian groups the *Ahmadi* are characterized by *biradri*, the extended family, rather than the traditional nuclear family unit. As such, the members of a family have a network of relatives to support them through life, particularly once they reach old age. As Bary Malik remarked 'according to the Quran the truly wise are those who "bind up the ties of kinship", caring for their husband or wife, their children and their elder relatives'.[57]

The *Ahmadi* have the practice of *waqfi-nau*, literally meaning 'new dedication'. The scheme was created by the fourth *Khalifa* in April 1987 so that 'a great army of devoted children may be entering the next century free of the worldly desires but as slaves of the holy Prophet Muhammad Mustafa'.[58] Following this practice many *Ahmadi* write to the *Khalifa* just before the birth of their child. The *Khalifa* gives the child a name and a dedication number. The child is then devoted to God and trained as *waqfin*, devotees, 'ready to sacrifice their lives for the sake of God in a short period of time'.[59] At the age of sixteen the child is asked directly if she or he agrees with the practice. Up to 2002 over 20,500 children have been dedicated in this way.[60] This dedication procedure gives the child concerned a special status instilling in him or her the feeling that they have been chosen for a specific task. The Secretary in each *Jama'at* is responsible for aiding the parents in the training and upbringing of such children. Special classes are held for them. Weekly meetings

---

57 *Telegraph & Argus*, (22 February 1993).

58 The words of the fourth *Khalifa*, *Khutbah Jumu'ah*, 3 April 1987, cited by Zirvi, *Welcome to Ahmadiyyat*, op. cit., p. 383.

59 Zirvi, ibid., p. 383.

60 Zirvi states that in 2002 there were 20,515 *waqfin-I-Nau* children, 14,259 boys and 6,256 girls, see Zirvi, ibid., p. 383.

are held at *Ahmadi* mosques throughout the world for *waqfin*. In Britain, such *waqfin* are taught in Urdu one week, as it is the wish of the *Khalifa* that such children should be able to speak that language, while on the alternate week the class will be held in English. So as to create a potential army of well educated bi-lingual missionaries *waqfin* are taught world languages such as German, French, Danish or Spanish.[61] Many make visits to Rabwah, the *Ahmadi* headquaters in Pakistan, to become familiar with the structure and daily running of the movement. This practice of *Waqfi-nau is* regarded as an important element in maintaining the structure and discipline of the movement.

The *Ahmadi* family group functions in a similar way to Muslim families generally. During the eighteen months I lived on Edderthorpe Street I had the opportunity to spend time with several *Ahmadi* families, in particular the Umar family.[62] This family, which I believe to be typical of the majority of *Ahmadi* families living in Britain, was patriarchal in structure with Tariq, the husband, ostensibly the head with Fatima the wife, submissive and obedient. In this family, Fatima, typical of many women in the *Ahmadi Jama'at,* carries out the house-hold duties: cleaning, cooking and looking after the children. Fatima was not educated and her English was poor. Fatima possessed a driving license but Tariq did most of the driving, saying that his wife lacked the confidence to drive on British roads. To all outward appearances, Tariq did all the business and financial matters. However, it became clear on numerous occasions that he relied heavily on money from his wife and her relatives. On one occasion the conversation centred on money. With a wave of her hand Fatima ejaculated: 'I can get £100,000 today if I need it'. She then disappeared out of the room returning a few minutes later with fists full of money which she deposited on the coffee table in front of me. She then began to count it with considerable pride. Tariq was totally dependent on Fatima for his meals, washing, cleaning and all other

---

61 It must be stressed that not all *waqfin* become missionaries for the movement.

62 The surname Umar, and individual first names, are pseudonyms given for reasons of confidentiality.

domestic issues. On one occasion when I called round unannounced at his house I found Tariq alone. With great embarrassment he said he would offer me a cup of tea but he didn't know how to make one. 'Such work is woman's work anyway', he added. Fatima always dressed in the traditional Asian garb, occasionally wearing a head scarf but never the *hijab*. She would wear make-up and a heeled shoe underneath long trousers.

The two daughters in the Umar family went to a local Roman Catholic state school. The *Ahmadi* have no schools in the UK of their own. The Umar daughters, or other *Ahmadi* children, would not be allowed to attend one of several Islamic schools in the region, such as Feversham College, due to the refusal of mainstream Muslims to accept *Ahmadi* as fellow Muslims. Apparently the two girls in the Umar family were happy at the Roman Catholic school they attended. They claimed to mix freely with children from mainstream Islam and with non-Muslims, although I never witnessed such other children coming to the house. I asked Tariq why he had sent his girls to a Church school. 'They are happy, and I am happy', he replied. 'I feel they receive a good education and the discipline is good'.

A television, [and in many cases a video, DVD, and entertainment centre], is to be found in most *Ahmadi* homes. Tariq was proud of the expensive wide screen leisure centre which he had purchased, and which formed the focal point of the living room. Such technology was to be enjoyed; it brought the world into the home, a world of excitement, entertainment and information. For other *Ahmadi* television was yet another device bringing about the decline of Islamic faith, culture and spirituality. Others shared with me their concerns about the television: how it introduces 'Western poison' into the privacy of the home: a world of pop music and gyrating bodies; films and programs with adultery, fornication and explicit sex; advertisements with scantily dressed girls, images promoting loose morality, the breakdown of the family unit, rampant materialism. Tariq, less so Fatima, was quite liberal in the choice of programs and films that he would watch. Many programs on television, although watched by Tariq with other men who visited the house, would be switched off if the *Imam* unexpectedly arrived. As with many things in religion generally, whether it be Islam, Christianity or any other belief system, blatent contradictions often exist between faith and practice.

9

'THE PEN IS MIGHTIER THAN THE SWORD': AHMADIYYAT AND JIHAD

'Let there be no compulsion in religion'. This was the message of Naseem Bajwa, *Imam* at the *Ahmadiyya* mosque in Bradford, West Yorkshire, England. It was *Juma* prayers, midday prayers on Friday, the most important occasion of the week for Muslims. It was 1 November 2001, five weeks after the horrendous events of 9/11, events which had shocked the world and helped to reinforce the stereotype of Islam as a religion of violence. As a non-Muslim I sat as an observer, in respectful silence, at the back of the worship area of the mosque. About 100 Muslims, devout men, both old and young, sat with me listening intently to the words of the *khutba*, the Friday sermon, delivered by their congregational leader. *Imam* Bajwa, a tall, lean man in his mid-fifties [although looking much younger], dressed in a salubrious black *sherwani* jacket, and a *jinnah* hat on his head, solemnly addressed the rows of silent worshippers sitting on the floor before him. Speaking in English, and then Urdu, *Imam* Bajwa informed the congregation of a speech he had recently given elsewhere when a child had asked him directly: 'Are we for America or Osama bin Laden?' In a calm and dignified manner he reminded those present of the teaching of the Quran, how Islam stresses respect for life, the wickedness of killing innocent men, women and children and how suicide, [as in the case of extremists who hi-jack planes,] instead of gaining a place in paradise would merit the punishments of hell. *Jihad*, he explained, is to strive in the cause of God, to work for inner purification and righteousness, to win people to the faith,

189

not by compulsion or the sword, but by *da'wa*: preaching, inviting, and discussing. Referring to the teachings of Mirza Ghulam Ahmad, the founder of the *Ahmadiyya* community, and quoting the teaching of *Bukhari*, one of the most authoritative collections of traditions of the prophet, *Imam* Bajwa declared how, in the last age *Jihad* or Holy War, would be suspended and Muslims would win others to their faith by their lives of love, generosity and hospitality. Revealing a profound knowledge of the Quran and *hadith*, he explained various passages from both that clearly rejected the idea of aggressive, violent *Jihad*. Having elaborated his theme for about twenty minutes *Imam* Bajwa concluded, 'Tell your children, and those who cannot attend prayers at this time of day, that our faith is one of peace, tolerance and understanding'. *Imam* Bajwa's message, explaining the true nature of *Jihad*, was similar to the ideas I had heard first hand from the mouths of *Ahmadi* leaders in Lahore, Faisalabad, Qadian and other places throughout the Muslim world

The twentieth century has witnessed the rise of various figures within Islam: household names such as Osama bin Ladin, Ayman al-Zawāhirī, Abdullah 'Azzam, Abu Hamza, and others, who advocate an aggressive form of *Jihad*, not only against the West and secular society, but also against Muslims who are accused of failing to live according to the stipulations of *Sharia'h* law. In the light of the events of 9/11; the suicide bombings in London in July 2005, Madrid in March the previous year and numerous other bomb attacks by Islamists at various places around the world, *Jihad* has become the focus of debate for academics and non-academics alike. In the context of our present study, in order to understand the *Ahmadi* teaching on *Jihad*, its differences and similarities with the teaching of mainstream Muslims, it is necessary to consider the Islamic teaching on *Jihad* generally.

The Arabic word *Jihada*, found throughout the Quran, basically means 'striving', 'effort' or 'to try one's utmost'. As one writer declares 'the aim of *Jihad* [or struggle] is to earn the pleasure of Allah'.[1] It involves *fisabi'l illah*, the 'struggle in the cause of Allah'. Within the

---

1   Ghulam Sarwar, *Islam: Beliefs and Teachings,* London: Muslim Educational Trust, 2003, p. 15.

Muslim community generally *Jihad* is understood as meaning 'to work together towards what is right and to keep away from what is evil'. It is regarded as a 'joint effort to root out evil and establish truth'; 'to try one's utmost to see Truth prevail and Falsehood vanish from society'.[2]

A distinction is often drawn between *Jihadi Akbar*, the greater *Jihad*, and *Jihadi Asghar*, the lesser *Jihad*. *Jihadi Akbar* involves, not only the struggle by the individual believer against *nafs*, [the self] and the pursuit of *taqwa*, 'God consciousness', or inner righteousness, but it also involves the struggle against *dunya*, the lusts and evils of worldiness. It involves the promotion of *ilm*, [knowledge,] and *hiqmah*, [wisdom]; the establishing of what is *maruf*, [right], and the removing of *munkar*, [evil]; and the fight against social wrongs such as injustice, poverty, illiteracy, unfair trading and unemployment. *Jihadi Asghar*, the lesser *Jihad*, involves *qital*, the way of fighting and conflict, 'the physical battle in self-defence, also called Holy War'.

Rules of warfare [*siyar*] have developed within Islam similar to the Just War doctrine within Christianity. 'Fight in the way of Allah against those who fight you', declares the Quran, 'but do not transgress [limits]. Surely, Allah loves not the transgressors'.[3] On the strength of this and other Quranic texts Muslim jurists have taught that defensive, not aggressive, warfare is justified. 'Permission to take up arms', declares the Quran, 'is given to those against whom war is made, because they have been wronged'.[4] Elsewhere in the Quran Muslims are taught to defend themselves against those who have 'driven you out from of your homes', but kindness must be shown to those who have not attacked first.[5] Another passage of the Quran teaches that in the middle of a war, if the enemy want peace, then a treaty must be made.[6] A limit is set to war for, as the Quran states, 'And fight them until there is no persecution, and religion is *professed*

---

2   Sarwar, *Islam: Beliefs and Teachings*, op. cit., p. 81-2.
3   Quran 2:191 in the Farid translation, 2:190 in other mainstream translations.
4   Quran 22:40.
5   Quran 60:9.
6   Quran 8: 61, 62.

only for Allah. But if they desist, then *remember* that no hostility is allowed except against the wrongdoers'. [7] In one text, the Quran teaches that killing is so much against the divine fiat that Muhammad declared: 'whosoever killed a person [without justification] it shall be as if he had killed all mankind'.[8] Under such Islamic rules of conflict it was taught that war could only be declared by a legitimate authority, a duly appointed state not a private individual; there must be a call to the enemy to accept Islam first, or a treaty, before war is declared; non-combatants must not be attacked; and trees, crops and livestock must not be harmed. In other Quranic passages Muslims are told that, in war, holy places—including Churches and Synagogues—were to be respected.[9] Muslim Jurists divided the world into two realms: *Darul-harb*—the abode of war, the areas which are not ruled by Muslims, and which are often hostile to Islam—and *Darul-Islam*, the abode of Islam, where Muslim rule prevails. There is also *Darul-Sulh*, the house of truce, a non-Muslim country which has an agreement with the Muslims, or recognises an Islamic State as its ruler and pays *jizyah*, taxes. Islam also developed the idea of *harbi*, the rule of safe conduct whereby merchants and pilgrims were given *aman*, safe conduct.

During the 1400 years since the death of Muhammad there have been various other developments within the doctrine of *Jihad*. Classical *Sunni* tradition regarded an existing Muslim regime as legitimate as long as the ruler did not publicly reject Islam by preventing Muslims from practicing their faith. It was argued that even a bad ruler is better than *fitna*, [disorder, chaos]. As Ibn Hanbal, in the ninth century, remarked: 'you should obey the government and not rebel against it. If the ruler orders something which implies *ma'siya* [sin against God] you should neither obey or rebel. Do not support the *fitna*, neither by hand nor by your tongue'. [10] As such it

---

7   Quran 2:193,194.

8   Quran 5:33.

9   Quran 22:40, 41.

10   Ibn Hanbal, *kitab al-Sunna*, cited by Emmanuel Sivan, *Radical Islam: Medieval Theology and Modern Politics*, New Haven/London: Yale University Press, 1985, p. 91.

was argued that believers have no recognisable right to rebel even against an unjust ruler. Ibn Taymiyya [1268-1328 AD], dubbed 'the spiritual father of the Islamic revolution',[11] contradicting classical teaching, argued that *Jihad* should be waged against those who do not follow the teachings of Islam, and the unjust Muslim ruler must be opposed.[12] The Muslims of Taymiyya's day faced a dilemma: the Mongols had conquered all the lands of Islam east of Syria and had, by the thirteenth century, embraced *Sunni* Islam. As such the *ulema* of Syria and Egypt debated whether war could be fought against the Mongols who had become fellow Muslims. Taymiyya issued a famous *fatwa* against the Mongols in which he admitted that they did profess the Islamic credo [they performed *salat*, and observed the feast of *Ramadan*], but in his opinion, this was not enough to make them Muslim. Taymiyya, regarding the Mongols as *takfir* [excommunicated], stated; 'it has been established from the Book [Quran], from the *Sunna,* and from the general unanimity of the [Muslim] nation that he who forsakes the law of Islam should be fought, though he may have once pronounced the two formulas of faith'.[13] Taymiyya and his followers, the so-called neo-Hanbalites, presented a theory of resistance against illegitimate power, although Taymiyya did not specify how substantial a part of *Sharia'h* had to be transgressed in order for a ruler to become a *kafir*.

In promulgating such a theory 'Ibn Taymiyya has been the model for revivalists and vigilantes, for fundamentalist reformers, and other apostles of moral rearmament'.[14] Basing their views on certain Quranic texts, particularly the so-called sword verse, *Surah* 9:5, which commands Muslims to 'fight them [unbelievers] and slay the idolaters wherever you find them, and take them captive, and beleaguer them, and lie in wait for them at every place of ambush', radicals within

---

11　E. Sivan, *Radical Islam: Medieval Theology and Modern Politics,* op. cit., p. 96.

12　See Al-Mawardi, *Al-Ahkam al-Sultaniyya,* The Ordinances of Government and Ibn Taymiyya, *Al-Siyasa al-Shar'iyya* , Political Jurisprudence, see Sivan, *Radical Islam: Medieval Theology and Modern Politics,* ibid., pp. 90f.

13　Taymiyya, *Treatise on Public Policy in Islamic Jurisprudence,* see Sivan, op. cit., p. 92.

14　Sivan, ibid., p. 96.

Islam proclaim that violent *Jihad* is the 'neglected obligation',[15] a duty incumbent on all Muslims to struggle until the whole world is brought under Muslim rule. Islamists make great use of various traditions found in *Al Bukhari*, where we are told 'God answers him who goes forth [as a warrior] in his cause', and the proclamation that '*al-jannah* [Paradise] is to be found under the shadow of swords'.[16] Similar support for aggressive war is found in other *hadith* where it is asserted: 'The man who fights that the word of God may be exalted, that is the way of Allah', or in the tradition which claims that *Jihad* will be valid till the day of resurrection.[17] In other *hadith Qudsi* [sacred *hadith* where God is the speaker] Martyrdom is seen as the road to eternal reward, and the 'gate of *Jihad*' is presented as one of the entrances to Paradise.

Sayyid Abu al-Ala Mawdudi [1903-1979], regarded as 'one of the ablest theoreticians of the Islamic state in the Muslim world',[18] taught that the sole purpose of *Jihad* is world revolution, as Islam knows no boundaries and accepts no other systems but its own. 'The objective of the Islamic *Jihad*', he reasoned, 'is to eliminate the rule of an un-Islamic system and establish in its place an Islamic system of state rule'. Therefore, he opined, 'the aim of Islam is to bring about a universal revolution'.[19] He argued for the re-establishment of the *Khalifate*, believing that its abolition was brought about by westernised Turkish nationalists and by the betrayal of Islam by Arab nationalists. Adopting Taymiyyan ideology, he justified violent action against Muslim states that did not apply *Sharia'h* law. 'All such governments', he declared, 'should be wiped out'. According to Mawdudi 'the objective of Islamic *Jihad* is to put an end to the dominance of the un-Islamic systems of government [Western gov-

15   Title of a tract written by Muhammad al-Farag, see J. J. C. Janson, *The Neglected Duty*, NY: Macmillan, 1986.

16   *Al-Bukhari*, 56:22.

17   *Al-Bukhari* 56:15; *Abu-Dawud*, 14/2526.

18   K. R. Pruthi, (eds), *Encyclopeadia of Jihad*, New Delhi: Ammal Publications, 2002, vol. 3, p. 85.

19   See Mawdudi, '*Jihad fi'sabil Allah, War in the Cause of Islam*', lecture given on Iqbal day, 13 April 1939, trans. By K. Ahmad, (ed.) *H. Khatteb*, Birmingham: UKIM Dawah Centre, 1995.

ernments] and replace them with Islamic rule'.[20] Muslims are under a duty to 'rise to bring their king's land under His [Allah's] law, to destroy the power of those rebels among His subjects who have set themselves up as sovereigns, and to free His subjects from the burden of slavery to others'.[21] 'So I say to you', declares Mawdudi, 'if you really want to root out corruption, now so widespread on God's earth, stand up and fight against corrupt rule; take power and use it on God's behalf'.[22] As Mawdudi remarks: 'The name of this striving is *Jihad*'. The aim is 'to establish the *caliphate* [sic] of God on earth', asserts Mawdudi, 'so go forward and fight; dislodge the rebels of God from the government and take over the powers of the *caliphate*'. 'If you are a true follower of Islam', concludes Mawdudi, 'you can neither submit to any other *Din* [faith or judgement], nor can you make Islam a partner of it. If you believe Islam to be true, you have no alternative but to exert your utmost strength to make it prevail on earth: you either establish it or give your lives in this struggle'.[23]

Other significant figures influencing the *Jihadi* doctrine within contemporary Islam include Sayyid Qutb [1906-66] and Abdullah Yusuf Azzam [1941-89]. Qutb, an Egyptian writer, ideologue and early member of the Muslim brotherhood, in his famous book *Milestones* [1964], taught that Muslims and Muslim rulers who fail to implement God's laws live in a state of *jahiliyya* [ignorance] and must be opposed. In regarding such rulers as *takfiri* [excommunicated] Qutb revived and popularised Taymiyyan teaching, and influenced the rise of contemporary *takfiri* militants who use this doctrine to legitimise the killing of Muslim by Muslim for alleged apostasy.[24] Qutb was executed by the Egyptian government as a terrorist in 1966. Azzam,

20   Mawdudi, *Come Let us Change the World*, trans. Kaukab Siddique, Washington: The Islamic Party of North America, 1972, p 143.

21   S. A. Mawdudi, *Let us be Muslims*, ed. K. Murad, Leicester: Islamic Foundation, 1982, p. 289.

22   Mawdudi, *Let us be Muslims*, op. cit., p. 288.

23   Ibid., p. 300, 302.

24   *Milestones*, Damascus, Syria: n.p., 1962. For a concise evaluation of Qutb's political views see C. Tripp, 'Sayyid Qutb: the political vision', chapter seven in A. Rahnema, *Pioneers in Islamic Revival, Studies in Islamic society*, London: Zed Books, 2005, pp. 154- 83.

widely acknowledged not only as 'the reviver of *Jihad* ideals in the modern world', but also the mentor of Osama bin Laden,[25] argued for aggressive *Jihad* against every instance of *kafir* [unbeliever] infringement on Muslim land. By the early 1970's Azzam concluded that the Arab-Israeli problem would be won only by *'Jihad* and the rifle alone: no negotiations, no conferences and no dialogues.'[26] *Jihad*, in this sense, was seen by Azzam as obligatory on every Muslim. The reward for *Jihad*, he argued, is *firdaus*, the attainment of the highest place in *al-jannah*. At the King Abdul Aziz University, Jeddah, in 1978 he stated in a speech: 'the *Jihad*, the fighting, is obligatory on you wherever you can perform it. And just as when you are in America you must fast—unless you are ill or on a voyage—so, too, must you wage *Jihad*. The word *Jihad* means fighting only, fighting with the sword'.[27] He stressed how this 'call' is universal, 'nobody can abandon it, just like *salah* and fasting...'.[28] To ignore this duty, and to regard it as *Fard Kifayah*[29] was, in Azzam's opinion, the greatest sin'. 'The sin is not lifted off the necks of the Muslims', cries Azzam, 'as long as any area of land [which was once Muslim] remains in the hands of the *kufr*, and none are saved from the sin except those who perform *Jihad*'.[30] In reference to the call of *mujahideen* to fight in Afghanistan Azzam declares:

Oh you Muslims! *Jihad* is your life, your dignity and your existence, depend upon it. Oh you preachers! You have no value under the sun unless you bear arms and uproot the tyrants, infidels and wrongdoers. Those who believe that Islam can flourish, be victorious, without *Jihad* fighting, and blood in-

---

25   K. R. Pruthi, (eds), *Encyclopeadia of Jihad*, vol. 3, op. cit., p. 85.

26   Quoted by P. Bergen, *Holy War: Inside the Secret World of Osama bin Laden*, London: Phoenix, 2003, p. 56.

27   Speech of bin Laden recorded on videotape, see Richard Miniter, *Losing Bin Laden: How Bill Clinton's Failures Unleashed Global Terror*, Regnery Publishing, 2004, p. 8.

28   A. Azzam, *Join the Caravan*, Damascus: Azzam Publications, n.d., part 1, p. 6.

29   A communal obligation, which must be discharged by a sufficient number of people, else all will be sinful. Only those performing the duty are rewarded, although if they fulfil the duty, the sin is lifted off everybody, see Glossary, Azzam, *Join the Caravan*, op. cit.

30   *Caravan*, ibid., 1, p. 6.

deed are disillusioned and do not understand the nature of this religion. The prestige preachers, the influence of Islam, the dignity of Muslims, cannot be obtained without *Jihad*.[31]

The above discussion is not meant to be a full and concise presentation of the Islamic doctrine of *Jihad;* such is beyond the scope of this book. This brief appraisal is given so as to provide a context in which the reader can make a comparison between the different strands of teaching on *Jihad* to be found within Islam generally and the teaching on war and violence as taught by the *Ahmadiyya Jama'at.* Mirza Ghulam Ahmad's aim, as well as undermining the claims of Christianity and 'establishing the truth of Islam', was 'to convince the world that Islam, as its name showed, was the religion of peace, and that it could bring about a revolution in the world without the use of physical force'.[32] 'Everyone hearing this name [*Ahmadiyya* sect]', declared Ahmad, 'should realize that this sect has come into being for the spread of peace and security and that it would have nothing to do with war and fighting'.[33] 'The other task that I have been entrusted with', stated Ahmad, 'concerns rectification of the fallacious interpretation of "*Jihad*" which is current amongst some naïve Muslims'.[34] 'The doctrine of *Jihad* as understood by the Muslim divines of this age, who are called *maulvis*', wrote Ahmad, 'is utterly incorrect [and] totally contrary to the Quranic injunctions'. As such, the *Ahmadi* teach that mainstream Islam, in various ways, presents a false image of 'the beauties of Islam'. Vehemently advocating the Quranic principle: 'there is no compulsion in religion',[35] the *Ahmadi* 'strongly reject violence and terrorism in any form and for any rea-

---

31   Ibid., part 1, p. 6.

32   M. Ali, *The Ahmadiyyah Movement*, trans. S. M. Tufail, Lahore: *Ahmadiyyah Anjuman Isha'at Islam*, 1973, p. 12.

33   M. G. Ahmad, *Tohfa Qaisariyya*, pp. 9-10 cited by A. A. Chaudhry, *The Promised Messiah and Mahdi*, Islamabad: Islam International Publications, 1996, p. 5. See T. S. Ahmed, *A Study of Hadhrat Mirza Ghulam Ahmad's Exposition of Jihad*, Islam International Publications Ltd, Islamabad, Surrey: 1993.

34   A. A. Chaudhry, *The Promised Messiah and Mahdi*, op. cit., p. 5.

35   Quran 2:257.

son'.[36] In particular they reject the belief held by some Muslims 'that it is virtuous to kill all the non-Muslims in the world', for 'by holding this crooked belief ... instead of bringing people closer to Islam, they become the very cause of pushing people away from it'.[37] Ahmad, in his book *Government-I angrezi awr Jihad*, [*The British Government and Jihad*], presented *Jihad* mainly as a defensive doctrine. The *Ahmadi* recognize three legitimate types of war in Islam: war 'undertaken in self defence'; as 'chastisement for aggression' and 'those undertaken for the establishment of freedom of conscience, that is to say for breaking up the strength of those who inflicted death upon such as accepted Islam'.[38] Basing their teaching on the *hadith* of *Bukhari* the *Ahmadi* argue that the promised Messiah, [believed to be Mirza Ghulam Ahmad himself] would put an end to fighting for the faith. Ahmad told his followers that there would be occasions in the future when *Jihad* by the sword would be necessary. But there was need for postponement. 'No true Muslim', opined Ahmad, 'has ever believed that Islam should be spread by the sword'. In fact, he continued, 'those calling themselves Muslims, who seek to spread Islam by means of the sword are not aware of [the] inherent qualities' of the Quran, 'and their conduct resembles the conduct of wild beasts'.[39] Aggressive *Jihad*, according to the *Ahmadi*, is nothing less than 'murder in the name of Allah'.[40] Ahmad, in a publication dated 22 May 1900, declared how:

with the advent of the Promised Messiah [referring to himself] it is incumbent on every Muslim to give up *Jihad*. If I had not come, there could not have been some excuse for this misconception. But with my advent you have

36 M. Ali, *The Ahmadiyyah Movement*, op. cit., p. 13.
37 *Hadhrat* Ch. Zafrulla Khan, *Ahmadiyya Bulletin*, (September/October 2001), p. 35.
38 M. G. Ahmad, *Sitārah Qaisariyyah, Ruhani Khaza'in*, vol. 15, pp. 120-1, cited by A. A. Chaudhry, *The Promised Messiah and Mahdi* op. cit., p. 7.
39 M. G. Ahmad, *Sitārah Qaisariyyah, Ruhani Khaza'in*, vol. 15, pp. 120-1, op. cit.
40 Title of a book on *Jihad* by Mirza Tahir Ahmad, Cambridge: Lutterworth Press, 1998.

become witnesses at the appointed hour. Now you have no excuse for using swords for religious battles before God.[41]

Many mainstream Muslims believe in the doctrine of *Ghazi Mahdi*, that in the last age a divinely guided warrior will arrive spreading Islam by means of the sword. The *Ahmadi* repudiate this doctrine and see it as 'a slur on the holy religion of Islam'.[42] As Ahmad wrote, 'the commonly held doctrine professed by some of the divines that the promised Messiah will descend from Heaven and will fight the disbelievers and will ... offer only the choice of death or Islam, is utterly false'. Scathing in his criticism, Ahmad declared such teachings to be a 'brimful of all types of error and mischief', 'an invention of the impostors ... utterly opposed to the Holy Quran'.[43] Elsewhere in his numerous publications Ahmad asserted how 'the popular concept of *Jihad* prevalent among Muslims, such as the expectation of a bloodthirsty *Imam* and cultivation of malice for others, are no more than false notions harboured by short-sighted clerics'.[44] According to the *Ahmadi* the *Mahdi*, instead of being a bloodthirsty eschatological avenger, 'is no other than the promised *Messiah* who was to come to spread Islam, not with the sword, but by heavenly signs and arguments'. As Ahmad declared 'it is written that when the Promised *Messiah* appears, *Jihad* by the sword and all fighting for religion will come to an end as he will not take up the sword or any other earthly weapon'.[45] 'His only instrument will be his supplications', wrote Ahmad, 'and his only weapon will be his firm determination'.[46] As such Ahmad concluded: 'From now on, anyone who lifts a sword against the unbelievers and calls himself a *Ghazi* will be considered to oppose the prophet, the prophet who had informed 1300 years ago that

---

41   See www.alislam.org/library/articles.

42   Sher Ali, article entitled 'The differences Between *Ahmadi* and Non-*Ahmadis*', in *Review of Religions*, (April 1991), p. 29.

43   *Nur-ul-Haq, Ruhani Khaza'in*, 1894, vol. 8, p. 67 cited by A. A. Chaudhry, *The Promised Messiah and Mahdi*, op. cit., p. 7.

44   *Masih Hindustan Mein, Ruhani Khaza'in*, 1908, vol. 15, pp. 4-5, cited by Chaudhry, op. cit.

45   *Government Angrezi Aur Jihad, Ruhani Khaza'in*, 1900, vol. 17, pp. 7-8, cited by Chaudhry, ibid.

46   *Government*, op.cit, p. 8.

Jihad with the sword will be abrogated in the time of the Promised Messiah. Thus now after my arrival, there is no *Jihad*.[47]

Ahmadi emphasize how 'the holy Quran teaches respect for the sanctity of life and adherence to peace'.[48] In defence of this view the *Ahmadi* refer to *Surah* 41 of the Quran, verse 35, where Muslims are told: 'And good and evil are not alike. Repel evil with that which is best [goodness]. And lo, he, between whom and thyself was enmity, will become as though he were a warm friend'. Similarly the *Ahmadi* refer to the fourth *Surah*, verse 129, where Allah declares 'reconciliation is best', and *Surah* 23:97 where the prophet commands the followers of Islam to 'repel evil with that which is best'. The *Ahmadi* find further support for the use of non-violence in the Quranic statement: 'and whoso saved a life, it shall be as if he had saved the life of all mankind'[49], and in *Surah* 42:41 which contains the words: 'the recompense of an injury is an injury the like thereof; but whoso forgives and thereby brings about an improvement, his reward is with Allah. Surely, He loves not the wrongdoer'. As well as the Quran, 'the second source of the non-violence tradition in Islam' is seen in 'the model set by the Holy Prophet Muhammad himself'. It is argued that Muhammad 'was equipped superbly with the essential qualities for non-violence'.[50] It is claimed that he 'had a great deal of patience; love was the foundation of his existence; submission to the divine Will was his pride; and truth was his salvation'. Not only did he act 'as a mediator and arbitrator between the Jews, Christians and Muslims', and that he 'always believed in a fair justice for all', but it is suggested that, 'above all he prayed to Allah for the good welfare of his enemies'. The *Ahmadi*, as with Muslims generally, accept the Quranic description of Muhammad as 'an excellent model',[51] and how

47 *Khutba-Illhamia, Roohany Khazaen*, vol., 16, p. 28-9, cited in Government, ibid.

48 Yahya Yunis, address given at the Multi-faith Group of the International Fellowship of reconciliation held at Kufa gallery, London, 20 June 1993, reprinted in *Al-Baseerat*, (December 1993), pp. 4-6.

49 Quran 5:33.

50 Yahya Yunis, op. cit., p. 5.

51 Quran 33:22.

he is 'a mercy for *all* peoples'.[52] The *Ahmadi* accept the belief that 'up to the end of the Meccan period, the Holy Prophet's world outlook was one of a pacifist'.[53] Reference is made to the period in Mecca, during the early part of his ministry, when Muhammad, when faced by the request of his followers to respond to the opposition shown against them replied: 'I am not ordered to fight', and instead told his followers to migrate to Medina for refuge. While in Medina the Meccans continued to send their military expeditions against Muhammad. The *Ahmadi* believe it was during these times of hostility 'that the Holy Prophet received a new revelation granting him permission to fight for self-defence only under well defined limits'. Zafrullah Khan expresses the *Ahmadi* position well when he writes: the first Muslims faced the enmity and hostility of Christians and Jews who, motivated by 'rancour and jealousy' of the new movement, 'began to devise projects to harm the new faith' and 'consider means of wiping out Islam from the face of the earth'.[54] Despite the continued persecution against Muslims, 'they raised no cry'. Muhammad was 'repeatedly made the target of stoners that drew his blood; yet that mountain of truth and steadfastness bore all these torments with a cheerful and loving heart'. However, as Khan suggests, 'then God, who does not permit that cruelty and mercilessness should exceed all bounds, turned with compassion towards his persecuted servants. His wrath was kindled against the wicked. He informed his servants through the Holy Quran ... that he now gave permission to oppose their opponents and that He was Mighty and would not leave the wrongdoers unpunished'. This, argues Khan, 'was the commandment which was designated *Jihad*'. Referring to Surah 22:40-41 Khan explains that *Jihad* is allowed 'to those against whom war is made, because they have been wronged and Allah indeed has the power to help them. They are those who have been driven out of their homes unjustly'. 'It should also be remembered', explains Khan, 'that Is-

---

52   Quran 21:108.

53   Yahya Yunis, op. cit., p. 5.

54   *Jihad* ... from the writings of the Promised Messiah, extracts from *Essence of Islam* by *Hadhrat* Ch. Zafrulla Khan, *Ahmadiyya Bulletin*, (September/October 2001), op. cit., pp. 33-5.

lam permits the taking up of the sword only in opposition to people who themselves take it up first, and it permits the slaughter only of those who embark upon slaughter first'. Muhammad's desire to end conflict by negotiation rather than by war is stressed by reference to the 'twenty-three treaties and agreements with individual tribes and regions,' particularly the treaty of Hudaybiya, concluded with the Meccans in 628 AD. Much is seen in Muhammad's 'reconciliation of hearts', his policy of appeasement on his return to Mecca, in which he issued a general amnesty to all people.[55]

Qadiani and Lahori *Ahmadi*, although deeply divided over the issues of *Khalifate* and the prophetic nature of Mirza Ghulam Ahmad, are agreed on the interpretation of *Jihad* given by the founder of their movement. 'Look!', declared Ahmad, 'I have come to you with the message that from now on all armed *Jihad* has come to an end, and only the *Jihad* to purify your souls remains'.[56] Elsewhere he wrote: 'the present day onslaught against Islam is an intellectual challenge, which must, of sheer necessity, be answered in the same coin. Hence', he argued, '"*Jihad-bil-qalam*" [*Jihad* of the pen] must take the place of "*Jihad bi-saif*" [*Jihad* of the sword], in the present age'.[57] As the fourth *Khalifa* put it: 'swords can win territories but not hearts, force can bend heads, but not minds'.[58] *Jihad* is therefore defined as 'to struggle/strive to establish the will of Allah'.[59] The promotional literature of the movement explains how 'the definition of *Jihad* is akin to the Christian term "crusade" which is also understood to mean "the struggle or strife against evil"'.[60] By defeating 'evil', *'Ji-*

---

55 Yunis, op. cit., 5f.

56 M. G. Ahmad, *The British Government and Jihad*, Qadian: Diaul Islam Press, 1900, p. 43.

57 K. S. Bakhsh, *The Debt Forgotten*, Lahore, Columbus, Ohio, USA : *Ahmadiyya Anjuman Isha'at Islam*, 1993, p. 36.

58 The words of the fourth *Khalifa* cited by Waseem Ahmad, article entitled 'Problems faced by young Muslims growing up in a Western Society', *Al-Baseerat*, (March 1993), p. 4.

59 *Jihad* ... from the writings of the Promised messiah, extracts from *Essence of Islam* by *Hadhrat* Ch. Zafrulla Khan, *Ahmadiyya Bulletin*, (September/ October 2001), op. cit., pp. 33-5.

60 '10 Things You Wanted to Know About JIHAD ... But Were Too Afraid to Ask', *Tabligh* Department, *Majlis Ansarullah* UK, nd.

had is therefore the mode by which all that is good is established and preserved for the benefit of the wider society'. Emphasis is placed on *Jihadi Akbar*, 'the greatest *Jihad* which relates to the discipline of the self and spiritual inner purification',[61] and *Jihad al-shaifan*, the 'struggle against the lower self'. As such, the *Ahmadi* acknowledge how 'for a Muslim, *Jihad* is a duty and obligation. Men, women, and children all have a role to play in preaching the message of Islam and the Holy Quran [*Jihad-e-kabir*]'. This duty involves 'making efforts to bring about a spiritual awakening within themselves [*Jihadi Akbar*]'. There is also great emphasis on *Jihad al-tarbiyyat*, 'educational *Jihad*, a *Jihad* characterised by learning, argument and demonstration. 'It is an age of reason and rational thinking', wrote Ahmad, 'and the best way to present Islam to the modern world was through propagation by utilizing the modern means of platform and press'.[62] He adamantly believed that 'it is through missionary propagation [*tabligh* and *Isha'at*] that the revival of Islam is destined'.[63] The conclusion he reached was that 'propagation of Islam, response to criticism by opponents, spreading the magnificence and merits of the Islamic faith, demonstrating the truth of the Holy Prophet [PBUH] in the world, is *Jihad* in this era'.[64] Islam, he argued, 'will capture the hearts of people by the sheer beauty of its teaching'.[65] Therefore by the methods of peaceful *tabligh*, the *Ahmadi* 'strive hard to spread the message of Islam peacefully and not by force'.[66]

Although the *Ahmadi* renounce violence in the present age it must be remembered that the movement is not totally pacifist. The *Ahmadiyya Jama'at*, accepting the 'the principle of self defence',[67] teaches

---

61 '10 Things You Wanted to Know About JIHAD ... But Were Too Afraid to Ask', op. cit.

62 Bakhsh, op. cit., pp. 37-8.

63 Bakhsh, ibid., p. 35.

64 Letter by Ahmad to Meer Nasir Nawab, quoted by B. A. Rafiq, *Truth about Ahmadiyyat*, nd., p. 154.

65 M. Ali, *The Ahmadiyyah Movement*, op. cit., p. 13.

66 Ali, ibid., p. 14.

67 '10 things you wanted to know about JIHAD ... but were too afraid to ask', op. cit.

that the application of *Jihadi Asghar*, or Holy War, 'will depend on the situation'. As one of the *Ahmadi* promotional leaflets states:

During the time of the Holy Prophet [sa] ', there was the battle of Badr when Muslim men, women and children participated in the defence of their small and meagre community. In the Holy Quran God explains to the believers that whilst they may find fighting abhorrent they must do so in order to preserve their community from the evil of their enemies. The principle of self defence is a universally accepted one which has been practiced by nations and religions alike throughout the ages. The early Muslims under the Holy Prophet [sa] suffered persecution and martyrdom during thirteen years before emigrating to Medina. Therefore the example of the Holy Prophet [sa] shows a great desire and will to avoid any form of bloody confrontation.[68]

As explained above, Ahmad taught that one should fight in the cause of God in a defensive war, that conflict should be waged against wrong-doers, against those who treated Muslims unjustly, but that they should not, in their turn, become transgressors. *Jihad* was considered to be wrong if it was an attempt to force other people to give up their own faith and convert to Islam. Ahmad taught 'Islam does not allow the use of the sword for the faith; except in the case of defensive wars, or in the case of wars waged to punish a tyrant or to uphold freedom'.[69] On this basis the *Ahmadiyya Jama'at* has got involved in various conflicts. During the 1930s Muhammad Ahmed, the second *Ahmadi Khalifa*, verbally supported the Kashmiri Muslims against the Hindu Maharaja, expressing his views in *Al-Fazl*, the official newspaper of the movement.[70] In 1948, after the creation of Pakistan, when the Dogra Regime and the Indian forces were invading Kashmir, the *Ahmadi* community raised a volunteer force, the Furqan Force which actively fought against Indian troops. During the violence that accompanied the partition of India and Pakistan in 1947 the *Ahmadiyya Jama'at*, for its own safety, formed its own militia. The second *Khalifa* gave his full support for the British dur-

---

68   '10 Things You Wanted to Know About JIHAD ...', ibid.

69   M. G. Ahmad, *Jesus in India, Being an Account of Jesus' Escape From Death on the Cross and His Journey to India*, 1899, later translated, London: Islam International Publications Ltd, 1989, p. 12.

70   See S. Lavan, *The Ahmadiyya Movement: A History and Perspective*, Delhi: Manohar Book Service, 1974, pp. 145-82.

ing the Second World War, urging his followers to receive military training and join either the Police Force or the Army. Consequently a significant number of young *Ahmadi* formed their own company in the Punjab Regiment. J. D. Shams, the Qadiani missionary in London, in a presentation to the King on New Year's Day [1946] stated:

H.M. the King will be pleased to know that our *Jama'at* has provided all possible help in securing the victory for Britain. There were fifteen thousand *Ahmadi* soldiers, two to three hundred of Commissioned and Non-Commissioned Officers served in the Second War. It is quite a large figure as compared to the total population of our *Jama'at*.[71]

Some Muslims, believing that Ahmad fashioned his beliefs so as to gain British support, have branded him 'a stooge of the late British government, who banned *Jihad* and inculcated loyalty to the British government'.[72] The *Ahmadiyya Jama'at* has accordingly been seen as 'a handmaid of Imperialism', its missionaries acting as spies serving 'British and Zionist political interests', particularly in Russia and Afghanistan.[73] Others, particularly Christian writers, have viewed Ahmad's teaching on *Jihad* as an apologetic device casting Islam in a more acceptable, peaceful light. As seen in chapter two, Islam, during Ahmad's life, was threatened by aggressive Christian missionary activity. During the second half of the nineteenth century the number of Christian converts in the Punjab rose from 3,912 in 1881 to 37,980 by 1901. Such figures frightened Muslim and other faith leaders. As one writer put it: 'the Christian missionaries were seen as part of a government machine that first defeated the Punjabi, next sought to govern him, and then to convert him'.[74] With Christian missionaries successfully proselytising throughout the Indian sub-continent, and the *Arya Samaj*, a Hindu sect, spreading its anti-

71 *Al Fazal*, Qadian, (9 March 1946).

72 Criticisms raised against Ahmad, summarised by K. S. Bakhsh, *The Debt Forgotten*, op. cit., p. 9.

73 B. Ahmad, *Ahmadiyya Movement: British Jewish Connection Internet*, Anti-Ahmadiyya Movement in Islam, pp. 1, 4.

74 K. W. Jones, *The New Cambridge History of India: Socio-Religious Reform Movements in British India*, Cambridge: Cambridge University Press, 1989, p. 87.

Islamic teaching, Ahmad believed that the time had come to defend Islam. 'Seeing the ground slipping from under the feet of Islam and the Muslims', Ahmad's aim, as one of his biographers states, was 'to counteract the Christian onslaught against Islam'.[75] One way to do this was by refuting the image of Muslims as aggressive and warlike, and presenting Islam as a way of peace. As one writer remarks, due to the constant attacks against Islam by Christian missionaries criticising Islam's apparently warlike stance, Ahmad's teaching on *Jihad* bears 'a conspicuous apologetic tinge'.[76]

Is *Ahmadi* teaching on war merely to be seen as white-washing; a sugar-coated doctrine to win favour with the occupying power? If we are to understand Ahmad and his message it is important to place him in his historical context. In Ahmad's time the British ruled the Indian sub-continent and many Muslims, although resenting being conquered by a European power, looked with gratitude to the religious tolerance of British rule in contrast to previous regimes of oppression. With this in mind Ahmad wrote:

To every persuasion the [British] government has granted full freedom to preach one's beliefs. Hence an opportunity has been afforded for followers of all faiths to scrutinise and assess the principles on which various faiths are based ... for this reason again and again in my writings and my speeches I have been making a mention of the favours of the British Government.[77]

Ahmad argued that Islam 'does not lay down that the Muslims, while they are the subjects of a non-Muslim sovereign who deals with them with justice and equity, should take up arms against him as rebels'. In his opinion, 'according to the Holy Quran this is the way of the wicked and not of the righteous'.[78] As such, Ahmad reasoned, 'when one lives under the canopy of a just government, like the realm

---

75 N. A. Faruqui, *Ahmadiyyat in the service of Islam*, Lahore: *Ahmadiyya Anjuman Isha'at Islam*, 1983, p. 8, 6.

76 Y. Friedmann, *Prophecy Continuous: Aspects of Ahmadi Religious Thought and its Medieval Background*, Berkeley: University of California Press, 1989, p. 180.

77 M. G. Ahmad, *Rooyedad-e-jalsa Doa*, Qadian: Ahmadiyyah Publications, nd.

78 M. G. Ahmad, *Anjam-e-Atham, Ruhani Khaza'in*, 1897, vol., 11, p. 37 cited by K. S. Bakhsh, *The Debt Forgotten*, op. cit., p. 19.

of our Empress [Queen Victoria,] contemplating a revolt is certainly not *"Jihad"*. Instead, it is a barbaric and an unenlightened act'. In fact, argued Ahmad, 'where one can live with freedom, there is rule of law and one is permitted to satisfactorily carry out one's religious responsibilities, any act against the government, with an ill intent, is a crime and certainly not *Jihad*. Accordingly, remarked Ahmad, 'one must remain entirely obedient to a benevolent government like our British Government'.[79]

In assessing Ahmad's motives for assuming a defensive doctrine of *Jihad* it must be kept in mind that he was not the only supporter of British rule to be found in the Muslim community of India at that time. At the end of the nineteenth century many leading Muslim scholars in India made similar pronouncements on *Jihad*. The *Anjuman-i-Himayat-i-Islam* [The Society for the Defence of Islam] founded in 1866 in Lahore by Muhammad Shafi and Shah Din, emphasised loyalty to the British-Indian government. Sayyid Ahmad Khan [1817-1898], realizing the value of Western ideas, organised ceremonies of loyalty to the British, and, in 1866 created the British-Indian Association of the NW Provinces as an expression of his desire for closer relations with Britain.[80] *Moulvi* Muhammad Husain Batalvi, a prominent leader of *Ehle Hadith*, stated:

where there is complete peace and there is freedom to practice one's faith, Muslim subjects are not permitted either to fight themselves or in any way assist those who fight their own government even if the government be Jewish or Christian. On this basis, for Muslims in India, opposition to and revolt against the British government is totally prohibited.[81]

Similarly *Maulana* Mohammad Ismaeel Shaheed, while delivering a sermon at Calcutta, was asked if it was permissible to engage in *Jihad* against the British. In reply he said 'on no account is *Jihad* permitted against a government which is benevolent and is free from prejudice'.[82]

---

79 M. G. Ahmad, *Tohfa Qaisariyya*, Qadian: Ahmadiyyah Publiucations, nd., pp. 9-10.

80 See K. W. Jones, *The New Cambridge History of India*, op. cit., p. 65.

81 M. G. Ahmad, *Ishaautul-Sunna*, vol. 6, no. 12.

82 M. G. Ahmad, *Sawaneh-Ahmadi*, p. 57.

In the light of the events of 9/11, and other terrorist attacks in London, Madrid, Bali and many other places around the world, it is pertinent to finish this section by considering the *Ahmadi* view of terrorism and suicide bombing. The *Ahmadi*, vigorously opposing the claims made by militant Islamic groups justifying terrorist activity, argue that those 'who claim to be participating in a Holy War are misusing and abusing this institution', and are merely using violence 'to further their own political aspirations and objectives'.[83] Agreeing with the Just War doctrine outlined above, the *Ahmadi* maintain that any war must be fought according to certain rules of engagement. For example it is argued that 'a response against the aggressor must be targeted and proportionate: no civilians are to be targeted; no acts of mutilation or torture undertaken; places of worship not attacked or destroyed;' and 'even trees may not be damaged'.[84] The *Ahmadi* also stress that true *Jihad* 'can only be declared by a prophet of God or by the *Khalifa* [*Ameer-ul-Momineen*] of the Islamic State'. In reference to Osama bin Ladin, or any other 'self proclaimed leader of the Islamic world', the *Ahmadi* maintain that 'the call to *Jihad* by an ignorant *Mullah* holds no value, nor should it be entertained by a true believer'.[85]

Just as with *Jihad*, there is much debate within contemporary Islam as to the legitimacy or otherwise of suicide bombings. For some Muslims suicide killings are regarded as *istishad* [martyrdom], and those who undertake such killings are *shahids*, [martyrs], those who bear witness to Allah. Some regard the Palestinian suicide bomber, not as a terrorist, but as a warrior of God, adopting desperate measures in a desperate situation. Another extreme example of committing suicide for Allah was seen in the case of the *baseeji* in the Iran-Iraq war of the 1980s: young boys, who willingly faced death, as they ran across minefields preparing the way for the main ground assault force.[86] *Shia* Muslims, remembering the martrydom of Husayn [the

---

83   Leaflet, '10 Things . . .', op. cit.

84   Leaflet, ibid.

85   Ibid.

86   Robin Wright, *Sacred Rage: The Wrath of Militant Islam*, London/New York: Touchstone Book, Simon & Schuster, 1985, p. 37.

third *Imam*] at Karbala in 680 AD, have developed a cult of martyrdom and a willingness to sacrifice life to fulfil the divine purpose.
Such martyrs find support for their actions in the teaching of the
Prophet. 'There are those who would give away their lives in order to
find favour with God' declares Muhammad.[87] The Quran infers that
anyone who dies in *Jihad* is guaranteed a place in Paradise.[88] Texts
such as these have given rise to a breed of Muslim men, women and
children who, fuelled by decades of anger and frustration against the
West generally, and America particularly, are prepared to give their
lives for what they believe is the will of Allah.

The *Ahmadi*, sharing the view held by the majority of *Sunni*
Muslims, regard suicide as a sin and 'an Islamic heresy'.[89] Suicide
bombing is seen as 'a double crime because firstly the person kills
themselves and secondly because he kills others. Both are violations
of the principles of Islam'.[90] As one *Ahmadi* stated in the *Ahmadiyya
Bulletin*, suicide bombing is seen as 'a clear breach of the simple, un-
ambiguous, Quranic injunction: "And kill not yourselves, for Allah
has been merciful to you".'[91] 'The Arabic word *"shahadat"*', he continued, 'also means witness [and] does not necessarily mean dying
for a cause; it also denotes living for it'.[92] Suicide bombing is seen as
one of many instances of how non-*Ahmadi* Muslims have misinterpreted the Islamic faith. With vehemence the *Ahmadi* declare that
'the concept of suicide in Islam does not exist and anyone practicing
this is in violation of the doctrine of preservation of life'.[93] Life is seen
as a gift of God and should not be wasted or abused. The Prophet
declared: 'how can you disbelieve in Allah? You were without life and
He gave you life, and then will He cause you to die, then restore you

---

87   Quran 2:207.
88   Quran 3:140f.
89   Waqar Ahmad Ahmedi, Letter, *Ahmadiyya Bulletin*, (April 2002), p. 19.
90   Ataul Mujeeb Rashed, *Ahmadiyya Bulletin*, (March 2003), p. 7.
91   Quran 4:30.
92   Waqar Ahmad Ahmedi, *Ahmadiyya Bulletin*, Letter, op. cit.
93   Leaflet, 10 Things You Wanted to Know About JIHAD ... But Were Too
      Afraid To Ask', op. cit.

to life, and then to Him shall you be made to return'.[94] Similar support for an anti-suicide stance, although of a more tenuous nature, is
found in *Surah* 2:206 where it states that 'Allah loves not disorder'.
In *Bukhari*, there is a tradition in which it is said that 'he who kills
himself with an instrument will be punished with the same instrument for all eternity'. Similarly reference is made to another tradition
found in *Bukhari* which tells of a man with a terrible wound who cut
his own wrist so as to end the pain. It is recorded that the prophet
declared: 'my servant has hurried his own death. I will not allow him
to enter paradise'.[95] Confirmation of this belief is seen in Muhammad's farewell address in which, inter alia, he remarked how, even as
the month is holy, the day is holy, so Allah has made each individual
life holy.[96] On one occasion it is believed that Muhammad refused
to officiate at the burial of a man who had committed suicide. 'The
modern day suicide bombers who in their ignorance give up their
own lives and that of numerous innocent civilians for the presumed
cause of Allah', proclaim the *Ahmadi*, 'are fooled into this action by
the unholy Muslim clerics motivated by political agendas and objectives. The actions of suicide bombers', it is argued, 'are prompted by
feelings of frustration, desperation, and pessimism, all traits which
are declared by the Holy Prophet [sa] to be outside the hallmarks of a
true believer'.[97]

---

94   Quran 2:29, 30.
95   Farewell sermon, *Bukhari* and *Muslim*.
96   Farewell sermon, op. cit.
97   Waqar Ahmad Ahmedi, Letter, *Ahmadiyya Bulletin*, (April 2002), op.
     cit.

10
TABLIGH AND DA'WA:
RECRUITING FOR ISLAM

Believing itself to be the true way, the religion to unite all religions, the *Ahmadiyya Jama'at* is a strongly proselytising faith. Reference has already been made to the fact that, like most other sects, the *Ahmadi* have a distinct eschatological teaching which declares how, despite fierce opposition and persecution, they will be triumphant and their message vindicated in the last age.[1] As stated previously, the *Ahmadi* believe in an Islamic revival in the last days when Christians would reject their faith, and 'billions of people will enter *Ahmadiyyat*—the true Islam'.[2] With this eschatological framework in mind, *tabligh* and *da'wa*, [preaching and propagation of the faith], are the life-blood and *raison d'être* of the movement. Similar to the views held by members of any sect, the *Ahmadi* believe that non-members are 'spiritually blind', ignorant of 'their illness', and unaware or not caring 'how ill they are'.[3] As one *Ahmadi* remarked: 'We have to take the medicine to those who are spiritually ill'.[4] Recognising that 'only Allah changes the hearts and minds of people', *Ahmadi* believe themselves to be 'vehicles for transmitting the message of true Islam', people given the moral responsibility to 'take the cup of spiritual medicine to other

---

1   See the end of chapter six.

2   Khuddam News, *Al-Bareesat*, (February 1997), p. 8.

3   The undated transcripts of talks given by Dr Hameed Khan at the London Mosque.

4   Khan, op. cit.

211

people'.[5] Only by fulfilling this obligation will the movement grow and prosper. Aftab Ahmad Khan, addressing the *Khuddam Ijtema* at Islamabad, UK, in September 1996, reminded the assembled men that the individual *Ahmadi*, as well as 'show[ing] obedience to the *Khalifa*', 'his main task is to do *tabligh*'.[6]

To become *Ahmadi* the convert, motivated by *taqwa* [fear of God,] and characterised by *tauba* [repentance], turning away from sin, and adopting *roju*, [piety],[7] will take *bai'at*, the pledge of obedience to the *Jama'at*. As part of the *bai'at*, the convert has to agree to ten conditions. These are as follows:

1. to abstain from *shirk* [the association of any partner with God) right up to the day of his death.
2. to keep away from falsehood, fornication, adultery, trespasses of the eye [looking at women other than near relatives], cruelty, dishonesty, mischief and rebellion; and not permit himself to be carried away by passions, however strong they may be.
3. to regularly offer the five daily prayers and to try his best to be regular in offering the *Tahajjud* [pre-dawn supererogatory prayers] and invoking *Darood* [blessings] on the holy prophet.
4. to cause no harm to the creatures of Allah in general, and Muslims in particular, neither by his tongue, his hands nor by any other means.
5. remain faithful to God in all circumstances of life, in sorrow and happiness, adversity and prosperity, in all misfortunes that may arise in life.
6. refrain from following un-Islamic customs and lustful inclinations and completely submit himself to the authority of the Holy Quran and the sayings of the prophet Muhammad, making them the guiding principles of life.

---

5 Ibid.

6 The words of Salim Ahmad Malik, secretary of *tabligh* UK, *Al-Baseerat*, (September 1996), p. 12.

7 *Ahmadiyya Bulletin*, (December 2002/January 2003), p. 29.

7. entirely give up pride and vanity and adopt humility, cheerfulness, forbearance and meekness.

8. that the cause of Islam and his faith will be dearer to him than his own life, wealth, honour, children and all other dear ones.

9. keep himself occupied in the service of God's creatures and shall endeavour to benefit mankind to the best of his abilities.

10. enter into a bond of brotherhood with the founder of the movement, keeping this up till the day of his death, obeying him in all good things, exerting such a high devotion in observing this bond in such a way that has not been seen in any other worldly relationships.[8]

Membership into the *Jama'at* can be by birth or by conversion. As part of their recruitment litany the *Ahmadi* present examples of notable conversions to the movement. Many *Ahmadi* told me with pride the story of Bashir Orchard, a white British soldier who, while serving in the Army in India during the Second World War[9], having visited an *Ahmadi* holy man in Qadian, and eventually meeting with the *Khalifa*[10], accepted the *Ahmadi* faith. The *Ahmadi* emphasize how, in the case of Bashir Orchard, the most significant factor in his conversion was the example set by individual members of the sect rather than doctrine. As Bashir stated: 'generally I was much impressed by everyone I met. This is what attracted me towards Islam more than anything else'.[11] The promotional literature of the movement stresses how *Ahmadiyyat* provided Bashir with 'moral guidance in a Godless secular society'. As he remarked: 'I had no goals or ambition before I accepted *Ahmadiyyat*' spending [my] pre-conversion days 'drifting

---

8 This is a paraphrase of a much lengthier *bai'at* Statement, see K. Zirvi, *Welcome to Ahmadiyyat: The True Islam*, Silver Spring, USA: Ahmadiyyah Movement in Islam, 2002, pp. 272-73.

9 'Life Sketch of Bashir Orchard', originally printed in the *Muslim Herald*, April 1982, reproduced in *Review of Religions*, (July 2002), pp. 46-58.

10 *Mufti* Muhammad Sadiq, a companion of Mirza Ghulam Ahmad and the first *Ahmadi* missionary to the United States of America. The *Khalifa* was Mirza Bashiruddin Mahmud Ahmad.

11 Life Sketch, *Review of Religions*, op. cit., p. 52.

through life like a capsized boat in the open sea'.[12] Following his conversion to *Ahmadiyyat*, Bashir worked as an *Ahmadi* missionary in the Caribbean, Scotland and England. As with conversion accounts in any religious movement converts to *Ahmadiyyat* contrast the filial bond and community spirit of their adopted faith with the apparent indifference and lack of love of other faiths and groups. Bilal Atkinson, presently serving as the *Amir* in North East England, claims that he joined *Ahmadiyyat* because the *Ahmadi* 'practiced what they preached without enmity or rancour, but in peace'.[13] As he states, during a visit to Rabwah and Qadian, 'it was so refreshing to meet so many people, rich and poor alike, who lived life with such humility, a quality that initially attracted me to *Ahmadiyyat*'. Other converts have made similar professions of faith. In a scathing criticism of Christianity another convert confessed: 'I live in a so-called Christian community, so it is strange to me that the "Christian spirit" I found more abundantly in the *Ahmadiyya* community instead of a Christian congregation'.[14]

For some converts their acceptance of the *Ahmadi* faith is the culmination of an intellectual odyssey. Euan, a Scot in his early 40's, a technology consultant whom I met at the *Jalsa Salana* in June 2003, shared the details of his conversion experience with me. Having had difficulties in understanding various teachings of Christianity, particularly the Trinity, original sin and the resurrection, he found the Islamic faith to be more rational and logical. In his opinion he saw Islam as the only system to bring about justice in the third world. Having tried the *Shia* faith, he was finally converted to *Ahmadiyyat*, not only by what he perceived to be the truth and rationality of the claims made by Mirza Ghulam Ahmad, but by 'the interest *Ahmadi* showed in him as a person'.

With *tabligh* or preaching perceived as being 'the true *Jihad*',[15] and every *Ahmadi* regarded as 'an embodiment of *'ebaad ur Rahman'*

---

12   Life Sketch, ibid., p. 56.

13   '100ᵗʰ Qadian Jalsa Salana', in *Al Baseerat*, (February 1992), p. 10.

14   Daood Summers, 'What the Holy Quran Means to me', in *The Muslim Herald*, (December 1982), p. 11.

15   The fourth *Khalifa*, *khutba* notes, *Al-Baseerat*, (September 1997), p. 3.

[servants of the gracious God],[16] each member of the *Jama'at* is encouraged to evangelise. As mentioned previously, in an attempt to share the teachings of the Prophet with all man-kind, *Ahmadiyyat* has its own global satellite television station, *Muslim TV Ahmadiyya International*, which transmits programmes twenty-four hours a day in several major languages.[17] On the individual level new converts are told of the importance of becoming *dai'ilallahs*, a 'caller to God',[18] someone who invites others to Islam. As the fourth *Khalifa* stated to the *Jama'at* at the 1995 *Jalsa Salana*, 'it is a must for every *Ahmadi* to become *dai'ilallah* and embark on the task of preaching Islam with full determination, trust in Allah and earnest prayers'. 'Everyday you must do your utmost to do *tabligh*', extolled one missionary while addressing the Bradford *Jama'at*, 'and everyday you must pray hard for Allah to help you and give you the incentive and opportunities to do *tabligh*'.[19] The convert is encouraged to say 'two extra *nuwaffil* [voluntary, optional prayers]' during *Tahajjud*, 'to pray that Allah' will make him '*dai'ilallah*'. The state of *dai'ilallah* can be achieved by the performance of *tabligh;* 'Anyone who on a regular basis devotes some time to *tabligh* could be classified as *dai'ilallah*'.[20]

Tabligh can take various forms as well as direct preaching. For example '… individual efforts, individual actions and individual personal examples are' classed as 'the most important ingredients of *tabligh*'.[21] As the UK *Amir* remarked while addressing the men at the Bradford mosque in April 1994, every *Ahmadi* 'should be a model of blessings, giving kindness and love, as our slogan says, "Love for all, hatred for none" '.[22] 'We must make *tabligh* our foremost duty',

---

16   Words of the fifth *Khalifa*, inaugural sermon preached at the *Baitul Futuh* Mosque, 3 October 2003, cited in *Ahmadiyya Bulletin*, (January 2004), p. 8.

17   Muslim TV Ahmadiyya International, can be found on Sky Channel 675.

18   *Al-Baseerat*, (October 1996), p. 5.

19   Tahir Selby, '*Tabligh* Message', in *Al-Baseerat*, (November 1994), p. 4.

20   The words of Naseem Bajwa in his opening address at the North Region *tabligh* Seminar, Manchester, 12 November 1995, see *Al Baseerat*, (November 1995), p. 8.

21   *Al-Baseerat*, (October 1994), p. 5.

22   Cited in *Al-Baseerat*, (April 1994), p. 3.

he continued, 'and ensure that our own personal example is good enough to impress people and make them want to be like us'. 'Perhaps it is well to be reminded now and then', stated the President of *Lajna Immaillah* to the *Tabligh* Seminar at Bradford in 1994, 'that our personal actions and examples are vital ingredients of *tabligh*'.[23] Another example of *tabligh* is *waqfi-arzi*, 'temporary dedication', where different individuals within the community, either male or female, dedicate their private time, usually from two to six weeks, to work for the *Jama'at*.[24] Those doing this work, usually working in pairs, undertake various tasks such as visiting the homes of members of the *Jama'at*, 'encouraging' them to pray more, read the Quran, and attend the mosque. *Imam* Bajwa, in explaining this term to me, described how he first undertook *waqfi-arzi* when he was seventeen in Pakistan in 1968. He was paired with an elderly man from whom, as he remarked, 'I learned much'. Naseem stated with some pride how, due to the witness of himself and his mentor, fourteen people were converted to the movement, one of them a local robber who was 'gloriously changed in character'. The earnestness of *Ahmadi* to share their faith, to live in such a way so as to attract people to the movement, and something of their sense of moral responsibility, is seen in the 'rallying call' made by the Head of the *Ahmadi*yya Muslim Community in America, in the concluding speech at the *Jalsa Salana* in 2006, when he stated:

It is a duty of every *Ahmadi*. . . that after coming into the fold of *Ahmadiyyat* there should be a visible positive change in you. This is addressed to those who have accepted *Ahmadiyyat* recently. [The] majority of those who have been *Ahmadis* for a long time have great faith. They should train the new-comers and teach them by setting good examples. I also exhort the newcomers that they should bring about such a change in themselves that will make them stand out among their peers. An *Ahmadi* should be the hardest worker, should be the most truthful, should be the most mindful of others rights, should be the most forgiving, should be the least interested in worldly pleasures. And when this spirit is developed in you, these are the good deeds that will cause you to tread the path of righteousness. This will enable you to cause a revolution in your lives and your surroundings. I want to convey this

---

23   *Al-Baseerat*, (October 1994), p. 5.

24   The scheme was introduced by the *Ahmadi* in 1967.

message to all office-bearers in the *Jama'at* and the missionaries: ... give up
your egos and instead of finding faults in others pay attention to doing good
deeds yourselves. When you have set good examples, the other members of
the *Jama'at* will, automatically, be transformed into the moulds created by
you. Always remember that you have a great responsibility. You have been
entrusted with certain duties. Discharge them well.[25]

Every year the *Jama'at* in every region draws up a *tabligh* plan based
on the requests of the *Khalifa*. A target is given to each district to
meet in the coming year, based on its adult membership.[26] Registers
are kept of 'inactive *Ahmadis*' and 'active *daeen ilallah*'. The *Khalifa*
regularly emphasizes the need for 'people who are charged with the
spirit of *Dawat illallah*'.[27] Active *dai'ilallah* teams were established in
the mid 1990's 'in each region, to discuss on a regular basis how to
improve *tabligh* activities'. Such *tabligh* teams consist of two members from each *Qaidat* [district]. The national UK *Jama'at* was given
a target for 1993 of 1,000 *bai'ats* for the year. However, the *Ahmadi*
authorities in the UK soon became concerned at the relative failure
to gain converts and to meet annual targets. In October 1993 the
Khalifa, Khalifatul Masih IV, pointed out that 'the UK *Jama'at* is lag-
ging and slow in this field and is being left behind by small *Jama'ats*
like Holland and Belgium'.[28] Waleed Ahmad, talking to the *Tabligh*
Seminar at Manchester, in October 1992, spoke on the 'current state
of *tabligh* in the UK'. Using 'graphs, based on reports received, to
project to the audience the poor performances of all the *Jama'ats* in
the UK', he lamented how *tabligh* had 'resulted in only 106 *bai'ats*
over the year'. As such, those in a position of leadership were 'rightly
worried and concerned about the casual attitude of most of the
members of the UK *Jama'ats*'.[29] The Secretary of *Tabligh UK*, Salim
Ahmad Malik, called to his fellow *Ahmadi*: 'we must wake up [and]

25   *Jalsa Salana*, Ahmadiyya Muslim Association, September 2007, cited by
     http://www.jalsasalana.org/usa/2006/JSUSA20060903-EN.html, accessed
     February 2007.

26   Report of the *tabligh* seminary, North and Scottish Regions, held at
     Bradford, 11 September 1994, in *Al-Baseerat*, (October 1994), p. 4.

27   *Al-Baseerat*, (September 1996), p. 3.

28   The words of the UK *Amir, Al-Baseerat*, (April 1994), p.3.

29   'Message from the Centre', in *Al-Baseerat*, (November 1993), p. 4.

discard any lethargy and put all our efforts into *tabligh* now'.[30] Concern was expressed by Tahir Selby to 'the Regional *Jama'ats* with the low number of *bai'ats* and *bai'at* promises and that *tabligh* committees were not being set up or utilised properly'.[31] Bary Malik, the President of the Bradford *Jama'at* informed the members that Bradford 'has got more than 500,000 residents from different parts of the world speaking more than seventy-five different languages'. Therefore, he remonstrated, 'we have to get *bai'ats* in large numbers: therefore, I humbly request you to get rid of your laziness and start tabligh'.[32] With this constant failure to meet the convert targets set, some within the *Jama'at* criticise the community for its 'lethargic attitude' brought about, as some believe, 'through materialism as the members have become more worldly and laid more importance to winning the pleasures of the world rather than the blessings of Allah'.[33] Such has been the rhetoric of most messianic sects throughout history.

Tabligh can take many different forms. Stress is placed on the development of friendships by each *Ahmadi* with non-*Ahmadi*. 'What is most important', declared the speaker at the Bradford *Tabligh* Seminar in October 1994, 'is one-to-one contact that can blossom into deep understanding and trust which ultimately gives you success'. With evangelical earnestness he implored his listeners: 'you should not be content with inviting a friend to a meeting once or twice a year. *Tabligh* must be done on a regular basis'.[34] Believing totally in the truth of *Ahmadi* claims, and how converts can be won by the lifestyle and example of others, he gave the following advice:

Building friendships allows a person to be in your company and be affected by your example. Your friend needs to discuss and question the message of Islam. Think about it and then return to discuss more, until they are totally convinced that this is the truth.

One *Ahmadi*, an elderly man who spoke excellent English, noticing me sitting on the floor at the back of the hall at the main mosque

---

30   *Al-Baseerat*, (November 1993), p. 4.

31   *Al-Baseerat*, (November, 1994), op. cit.

32   *Al- Baseerat*, (October 1992), p. 3.

33   'Message', *Al-Baseerat*, (October 1995), p. 3.

34   Editorial, *Al-Baseerat*, (June 1997). *Al-Baseerat*, (October 1994), p. 5.

at Qadian in India during Friday *Juma* prayers, came to shake my hand. Having *salaamed* he asked me if I was *Ahmadi*; I told him 'no'. With a sincere, avuncular smile, gripping my hand tightly, he told me how having now 'heard the message' at the mosque:

all we can do is tell you the truth. We cannot force you to believe. On the day of judgement we will not be responsible for you. We have done our duty. It is up to you. *Khuda hafiz* [God protect you].

An *Ahmadi* at the Bradford mosque, in England, a kind old gentleman whose name I never knew yet his face would always light up with sincere friendship every time he saw me, manifesting the unshakable belief held by all members of the *Jama'at* in the veracity of their faith, inquired of me: 'You have heard the true message of Islam. You have read *Huzur's* works. Why are you not *Ahmadi?*'

Throughout the year each district within the wordwide *Jama'at* organizes training days for *tabligh*. Taking Bradford as an example, and 1993 as a year chosen at random for analysis, a special training day occurred in June at the mosque and a similar one in October, when talks were given in both Urdu and English on different methods of *tabligh*. On Sunday 10 June 2002 I attended a *tabligh* training day held at the Bradford mosque. More than 100 people attended, representatives from eight different *Jama'ats*. After the usual *tilawat*, [translation,] and welcoming speech by the regional *Amir*, Naseem Bajwa spoke on the importance of preaching. Different people were then allowed to speak for twenty minutes on their chosen topics followed by a forty-minute question and answer session. Subjects included 'the biblical prophecies of the advent of the Holy Prophet and those relating to the Advent of the promised Messiah'; 'Objections against Islam' and 'Common Objections of non-*Ahmadis* against *Ahmadiyyat* and their Answers'. Proceedings ended with 'a lively quiz', the questions based on the talks given. Closing remarks were made by the National *Tabligh* secretary and prizes given to various members for their effort in *tabligh*.[35] At such meetings *Ahmadi* discuss 'how to make friends with people'; 'how to improve our character',

---

35   Report on the *tabligh* Training Class, *Ahmadiyya Muslim Association*, NE 2001-2002 Annual Report, pp.18-9.

and 'the importance of *tabligh*'.[36] Teams appointed for *tabligh* are told to 'listen to different cassettes, videos etc., in which 'the *Khalifa* has 'spoken on this subject'. Individual *Ahmadi* are told to 'make [their] own individual *tabligh* plan'.[37] *Tabligh* discussion groups are occasionally organised for a specific ethnic minority group 'in which they may attend and discuss religious topics in their native language, with *Ahmadi* Muslims from the same ethnic background'.[38] As well as the *tabligh* training meeting, in 1993 an exhibition of *Ahmadiyyat* literature was held at Bradford Central Library. Throughout that year several visits to the mosque were arranged for groups of police officers or for school parties such as that of 'Fulneck Boys' School'.

The *Eid Milan* Party is seen as an opportunity to build bridges with the local community and get *Ahmadi* views and beliefs more widely known. In 1993 over 200 guests attended including the Lord Mayor of Bradford; Gary Waller, local Labour MP; the Chief Constable of West Yorkshire and the Chief Executive of Bradford Council. An Advance Group meets regularly to devise ways of improving the *Eid Milan* Party. In 1993, it met in August 'and worked on designing pamphlets'.

Daeen ilallah are told to hold house meetings in their own homes where the invited guest can watch 'appropriate videos or parts of it to create interest'.[39] The UK *Amir*, writing in the *Ahmadiyya Bulletin*, asks the readers: 'Are you holding a house-based *tablighi*, sitting in your home? If not then start planning now!!!'[40] The editor of the same periodical informed its readers: '*Ameer Sahib* has instructed that every single *Ahmadi* household MUST [sic] try and hold a one-to-one *tablighi* sitting in their home as soon as possible'. As the *Khalifa* suggested 'it is important that *daeen ilallah* should first see the video he/she proposes to show to his/her friends and select what he/she

---

36 Topics discussed at the Northern Region *Tabligh* Seminar, Manchester, 4 October, reported in *Al-Baseerat*, (October 1992), p. 3.

37 *Al-Baseerat*, (September 1996), p. 4.

38 A Tabligh Guide, Commemorating Twenty Years of Al-Baseerat, (July 1996), p. 19.

39 *Ahmadiyya Bulletin*, (December 2002/January 2003), p. 29.

40 *Al-Baseerat*, (September 1996), p. 4.

considers the most appropriate portion for the invitee'. He further remarked: 'this will save you embarrassment and at the same time improve your knowledge'. If such meetings are held, each *Ahmadi* is told to 'keep your own record of those who were invited, what was discussed and what was your reaction and future plan'. In order to assist debate, and hopefully win others to the movement, the *Ahmadi* is told to 'prepare your own notebook of references and arguments which are required in day-to-day discussions'. In an attempt to educate me about the *Khalifa* and the movement [and of course to convert me] whenever I visited the Umar[41] family at their home in the Leeds Road area of Bradford, Tariq, friendly but strained in manner, would hold what were obviously carefully orchestrated conversations with me while we shared a meal. Then, usually preceded by a brief discussion in Urdu between him and his wife, Tariq would turn the television on, flicking the channel over to MTA, the *Ahmadiyya* satellite channel. I would then be subjected to long sessions of *sawala-jawab*, in which the *Khalifa*, or some other leading figure within the movement, sat at carefully stage-managed question and answer sessions, often in Urdu. Tariq's wife, Fatima, and their daughters, would often perform *namaz* in the same room as us, as we conversed, in full accord with the *Khalifa's* exhortation: 'you should pray whilst the guest is in your home and also get your children to pray for those people'.[42] I was flattered that I was considered worthy of their prayers.

Atfal and *Nasirat*, boys and girls under the age of sixteen, do not escape the responsibility and challenge of *tabligh*. In delivering a prize essay to a UK meeting of the *Atfal*, one *Ahmadi* youngster, referring to the number of *Ahmadi* in the world declared: 'we youngsters can double this number by preaching to non-*Ahmadi* people'. He then continued by describing different ways that such preaching can take place. He reminded his peers that giving out leaflets and books to non-Muslims, informs people about 'the lives of the Holy prophet (s.a.w.) and his successors'. 'Tell them about the life of the

---

41 As in chapter eight, for reasons of confidentiality the surname and first names are pseudonyms.

42 *Ahmadiyya Bulletin*, (December 2002/January 2003),op. cit., p. 29.

promised Messiah and his successors' he continued. As well as this the young man encouraged his colleagues to:

bring your class from school to the mosque where *maulvi sahib* [resident Imam] will give them a lecture on Islam and *Ahmadiyyat*. Tell them about the *Eid* festival and other events organised at the mosque. Bring your friends to your house and have a religious discussion while playing. Show them video tapes of *Huzur's* live Friday *Khutbas*; introduce them to MTA as this is a world-wide production and is also broadcast in many different languages.

'If your friends are interested', he continued, 'you can explain to them what the five pillars of Islam and the five articles of faith are'. Writing with maturity and insight beyond his years, the youth reminded his readers that 'you should be a good Muslim yourself before preaching to anyone else [i.e. you should keep yourself away from bad company and refrain from bad deeds].' He then encouraged others to take their friends to 'the weekly *Atfal* classes and the *Atfal Ijtema* that goes on at London and Manchester' where 'they can meet and talk to other *Ahmadi* children'.[43] Another youth, presenting the content of his prize-winning essay at the same event, added the comment that *maulvi Sahib* could be invited to the school or, if that was not possible, the *Ahmadi* youth could give a talk to his class about his faith. This was, in fact, how I first heard of the *Ahmadiyya Jama'at* : as Head of Religious Studies at Bradford Grammar School in the late eighties and nineties, I invited pupils in the fifth form, [whom I later discovered to be *Ahmadi*], to give talks on a topic of their choice.

As an important part of *tabligh* and *da'wa*, members of the *Jama'at* are requested to 'distribute literature in abundance but with discretion and *hiqmat* [wisdom]'.[44] A considerable amount of literature has been produced by the *Ahmadi* for the purpose of evangelism. As already indicated, the movement has produced its own translation of the Quran, with commentary. Known as the Farid version, it has

---

43 Essay written by an Atfal member as part of their syllabus entitled 'How we as Youngsters can be More Effective in Preaching', see *Al-Baseerat*, (February 1995), pp. 4-5.

44 This is a paraphrase of a much lengthier *bai'at* statement, see K. Zirvi, *Ahmadiyyat, the true Islam*, Silver Spring, USA: Ahmadiyya Movement in Islam, 2002, pp. 272-3.

been translated into more than fifty different languages. However, as one missionary stated, due to the fact that the Quran 'doesn't flow like a novel ... in the way that the Holy Bible does', if a non-Muslim shows interest in Islam 'then give a Quran with commentary and advise them to use it for references whilst they read other Islamic books'.[45] 'Instead of giving them the Holy Quran', suggests the Missionary, 'give them the Introduction to the Study of the Holy Quran by the second *Khalifa*', a useful summary of many aspects of Islam and the life and teaching of Mirza Ghulam Ahmad. As well as books and other literature which can be purchased or borrowed, the movement has produced many high quality leaflets to give free of charge to interested parties. A series of small booklets has been printed, including titles such as *Some Distinctive Features of Islam* and *Revival of Religions*. Another series of leaflets has been produced on *Selected Sayings of the Holy Prophet*, *Selected Verses of the Holy Quran*, and *Selected Writings of the Promised Messiah*. The movement has special books targeted at children such as *Islam my religion* by B. A. Rafiq. A bi-monthly periodical, *Review of Religions*, is published as an educative magazine for members of the movement but also for those non-*Ahmadi* who have an interest in religion. If a person's interest in Islam grows then members are advised to give them a biography of the life of the prophet. The usual recommended text is *Muhammad, The Excellent Exemplar* by Muhammad Zafarulla Khan or *The Life of the Prophet* by the second *Khalifa*. Iain Adamson's book on *Mirza Ghulam Ahmad* is highly regarded, but particularly his *A Man of God*, is acknowledged as 'a very good book to give to your friend as it captures the true character of our current beloved *Huzur* perfectly'.[46] If a potential convert is ready for 'some deeper reading' the works of the founder of the movement are recommended such as *The Philosophy and Teaching of Islam* which 'explains the Islamic teachings beautifully and is responsible for bringing more people to *Ahmadiyyat* than any other book'. Other books used by the *Ahmadi* for evangelistic purposes include *Welcome to Ahmadiyyat*, *The True Islam* by Karimul-

45   *Maulana* Tahir Selby, in an article entitled 'Introducing the *Jama'at* Books', *Al-Baseerat*, (December 1993), p. 3.

46   Tahir Selby, 'tabligh message', in *Al-Baseerat*, (November 1994), p. 3.

lah Zirvi, and *Invitation to Ahmadiyyat* by M. B. Ahmad. In order to make an enquirer 'more aware of God and develop their love for God' *Ahmadi* are advised to provide copies of *Life Supreme* by B. A. Orchard; and other titles such as *Remembrance of Allah* by Kalamazad Mohammed; *Wisdom of the Holy Prophet* by Rashid Ahmad Chaudri and *The Gardens of the Righteous*, a collection of sayings of the prophet Muhammad by Muhammad Zafrulla Khan. If a person is convinced by such literature, and wanting 'to know how to do the prayers, [and] read the Holy Quran etc.,', *Ahmadi* are told to give such new converts copies of *The Muslim Prayer Book* ... along with an audio tape' which 'will help them with the prayers'. Similarly 'The *Yassarnal Quran* [a book which shows a Muslim how to read, and correctly pronounce, the Arabic text] along with the video tapes, will help them read the Holy Quran'.[47] Considerable literature is published by the movement to show 'the errors of Christianity'. For the purpose of refuting the Christian belief in the crucifixion of Christ, *Ahmadi* are advised to give their Christian friends *Death on the Cross* by Abul Atta Jalandhri, 'a small book that contains ten arguments'; *Jesus in India* by Mirza Ghulam Ahmad and 'as a follow up, *Truth About the Crucifixion*, [which] brings in more present day arguments'. 'One of the best books', states Tahir Selby, 'is *Deliverance From the Cross* by Muhammad Zafarulla Khan, who tackles the arguments beautifully'.[48] Further books suggested as being useful in convincing Christians of the truth of *Ahmadiyyat* include *An Eyewitness Account of the Crucifixion; Where Did Jesus Die?* and *Jesus Among the Lost Sheep* which 'tackles some of [Jesus'] early ministry and links the old Jewish tribes with the Kashmiri tribes'.[49]

As well as printing books which attempt to refute the arguments of Christians, the *Ahmadiyyat* has produced numerous apologetic publications to use against other faiths. When arguing with mainstream Muslims, *Ahmadi* are advised to refer to *Khataman Nabiyeen*, a booklet that explains the meaning of the phrase 'the seal of the

---

47 *Maulana* Tahir Selby, in an article entitled 'Introducing the *Jama'at* Books', *Al-Baseerat*, (December 1993), p. 3.

48 'Introducing the *Jama'at* Books', op. cit., p. 3.

49 Ibid., p. 4.

prophet'. *The Truth About Ahmadiyyat* by B. A. Rafiq, as one missionary stated, 'covers many of the arguments put against us as does *Ahmadiyyat or Qadianism* by Naseem Osman Memon'.[50] Books are donated to the libraries of local prisons. Although the importance of giving out suitable literature as a method of evangelism is stressed, the *Ahmadi* is reminded how 'the books are only a part of bringing your friend to *Ahmadiyyat*, the true Islam, but without prayer to open up your friend's heart to the truth, no matter how good the arguments are, your friend will be lost'.

In assessing the proselytising techniques practised by the *Ahmadi* I saw distinct parallels with the evangelistic activities adopted by different fundamentalist and conservative groups within the Christian Church, and those practiced by various cults such as the Moonies and Jehovah's Witnesses. I thought of my own upbringing in the Open Brethren Assemblies in Liverpool, and later in various Baptist and Evangelical Churches belonging to the FIEC.[51] I was reminded of the methods used for conversion: the learning of biblical texts, 'spiritual bullets' [such as John 3:16, a biblical verse explaining the necessity of spiritual new birth, or Revelation 3:20 which reminds the hearer that God is constantly inviting the sinner to repent and enjoy fellowship with him]; entering relationships with others solely to lead them to Christ; going out into the streets [usually in twos] armed with leaflets, and the study of Scripture so as to convince others of the veracity of their message. Just as those in these Christian movements desire to be good and faithful witnesses for Jesus, leading others into a conversion crisis and faith in Christ, the *Ahmadi* have a strong desire to lead others into, what they believe, is a relationship with Allah, and adopt similar methods in achieving this goal. Although, as yet, they do not undertake door-to-door visitation [this may come if their numbers increase] they do, wherever possible, participate in outdoor witness. In Bradford the *Ahmadi* have used surveys whereby passers-by would be approached and 'questions were directed to the state the modern society is presently in, to whether Jesus would be returning to help mankind and if so, how would he be

---

50   Ibid., p. 4.
51   Fellowship of Independent Evangelical Churches.

coming?'[52] As the editor of *Al Baseerat* opined: such surveys 'proved to be a very good way to approach [people] and get them to talk about religion'.[53] Before the events of 11 September 2001 *Imam* Naseem Bajwa would regularly take groups of *Ahmadi* men to Bradford City centre, often with bookstalls giving away literature, talking to any passers-by who may be interested. After a halt in activities following 9/11, these *tabligh* stalls were resumed in January 2002. Over 8,000 millennium leaflets were distributed throughout the North East region from January 2002 to the end of that year.[54] People spoken to in this way were offered copies of *Review of Religions*, the *Jama'at's* own monthly periodical. It is interesting to note that in all of these activities the *Ahmadi* psychology accepts, even welcomes, persecution. 'If we are true to our faith', remarked one of the leaders of the main mosque in Rabwah, 'we will be persecuted. When we are lax we are not a challenge to others, and they will leave us alone'. As such, opposition is seen as the opposition of *Shaitan* [Satan], while converts are seen as reward for faithfulness.

52 Ibid., p. 5.
53 'Message from the Centre', in *Al-Baseerat*, (November 1993), p. 4.
54 *Ahmadiyya Bulletin*, (December 2002/January 2003), p. 29.

11
THE AHMADI: A PERSECUTED PEOPLE

In November 2002 Dr Rashid Ahmad, an *Ahmadi* Orthopaedic surgeon, was caring for patients at his clinic at Rahim Yar Khan, in the Pakistani Punjab. According to independent witnesses two men entered the ward brandishing rifles, shouting 'where is the heretic?' On identifying the doctor they pointed their weapons and began to fire. One bullet hit him in the neck, others in the chest, causing him to fall to the floor, blood flowing freely from the wounds. Riddled with bullets, he remained in a coma for six days before dying. The culprits were caught by the police. On being questioned they claimed they had been paid to do the job, and encouraged by the local *Mullahs*.

Abdul Waheed, an *Ahmadi*, had lived in Karim Nagar, Faisalabad, Pakistan, for most of his life. On the morning of 14 November 2002, similar to most other weekday mornings, he went to the market to buy items of food. As he waited to purchase his goods he chatted with other men in the queue. On hearing a disturbance further down the street, the shoppers turned round and saw a man, a known opponent of the *Ahmadi*, walk hurriedly towards them shouting *Allah Akbar*. The *Ahmadi* claim that the man advanced towards Abdul, and with hatred in his eyes, pushed a knife into his victim's chest before running away. Abdul fell to the ground. The crowd, apparently indifferent to the man's plight, began to walk away, leaving him lying in a pool of blood. His family, on hearing of the incident, hastened to the scene of the crime. They called for an ambulance but, despite the care of medics, Abdul died before he reached the hospital. Although the Police apprehended the man who had carried out the attack, and despite the fact that there were numerous witnesses to the crime, he was not charged.

In August 2002 an international seminar was organised at Jakarta, Indonesia, by *The Islamic Institution of Research and Investigation* on 'The Danger of the *Ahmadiyya* Community'. It called for the Indonesian Government, particularly the Ministry of Religious Affairs and the Attorney General, to ban the *Ahmadiyya* Community in Indonesia. Fired by the anti-*Ahmadi* views expressed at the seminar, and views aired on national Indonesian radio and television stations, 'an unruly mob attacked the *Ahmadiyya* Muslim Mission house in Maluku, East Indonesia, burning it to the ground. The homes of local *Ahmadi* Muslims were broken into and looted as the owners could merely stand by and watch'.[1]

As a consequence of alleged doctrinal deviancy, the *Ahmadi* have become a persecuted people, the persecution being perpetrated by other Muslims. In Pakistan for example, early in 1953, militant Muslims, led by the *Anjuman-I ahrar-I Islam* [Society of Free Muslims, a puritanical political group], called for a banning of the *Ahmadi* sect and the removal of Chaudry Zafrulla Khan, a prominent *Ahmadi*, from his position as Foreign Minister. Rioting, and arson attacks against *Ahmadi* property, took place in various places, particularly in Lahore and other Punjabi towns. As one Muslim writer argued, there was a need 'to uproot from the abode of Islam *Shi'ite* extremists and other heretics, such as the *Baha'is* and *Ahmadis* ... in order to cleanse our abode from all apostates and render it pure unto the Muslims'.[2] In an attempt to put down such disturbances Martial Law was imposed in March of that year, and several leading members of the *ulema*, including Mawdudi, founder of the *Jamaat-i- Islami*, were arrested. Mawdudi had inflamed the passions of many Muslims against the Ahmadi by publishing his pamphlet *The Qadiani Question* and his book *The Finality of Prophethood*. Both works contained a scathing

---

1 These three incidents are recorded in *Ahmadiyya Bulletin*, (December 2002/January 2003), pp. 14, 15.

2 Hawwa, *Jund Allah*, pp. 446-7 cited by E. Sivan, *Radical Islam: Medieval Theology and Modern Politics*, New Haven/London: Yale University Press, 1985, p. 115.

attack on *Ahmadi* teaching, especially the idea that there can be prophecy after the Prophet. Despite the imprisonment of leading protagonists, and the crack-down on anti-*Ahmadi* protesters, the persecution of the *Ahmadi* continued unabated. In March 1954 the second *Khalifa*, whilst preaching, was attacked by a would-be assassin with a knife. Although the tip of the knife broke off becoming embedded in the *Khalifa's* jugular vein, the wound was not fatal.[3]

Mainly due to the fierce opposition of the majority of *ulema*, particularly the *Khatme Nabuwwat* [Committee to secure the Finality of Prophet-hood], persecution of the *Ahmadiyya Jama'at*, has continued in Pakistan to the present day. On 7 September 1974, President Bhutto and the National Assembly of Pakistan passed a resolution which declared that all *Ahmadi* in that country were to be regarded as a non-Muslim minority. Under this legislation *Ahmadi* have the freedom to practice their religion amongst themselves providing they do not represent themselves as Muslims. Article 260 of the Constitution states that 'a person who does not believe in the absolute and unqualified finality of the prophet-hood of Muhammad is not a Muslim for the purposes of the Constitution or Law'. In response to this new legislation the *Ahmadi* presented the *Mahzarnama* [a memorandum] to the Special Committee of the National Assembly of Pakistan, 'to establish that the members of the *Ahmadiyya Muslim Jama'at* are Muslims and to explain its basic tenets, as well as refute the baseless allegations levelled against it'.[4] Following the submission of this document members of the *Ahmadiyya Jama'at* were subjected to a grilling inquisition for eleven days by the Attorney General of Pakistan and leading clerics. The third *Ahmadi Khalifa* appeared before the inquiry to answer specific questions. The *Ahmadi* regard it as vindication of their message that the Committee failed to define what a true Muslim was, and that the Report written up by the Committee is not available to the public.

---

3   K. Zirvi, *Welcome to Ahmadiyyat: The True Islam*, Silver Spring, USA: Ahmadiyya movement in Islam, 2002, op. cit., p. 309.

4   *The Memorandum*, Tilford, Surrey: Islam International Publications Ltd, 2003, p.iii.

In 1977 General Zia ul-Haq, having removed the Bhutto regime by force, became President of Pakistan. In an attempt to curry the favour of the main religious leaders he allowed a further period of fierce persecution against the *Ahmadi* to take place. Consequently *Ahmadi* shops were burnt, mosques desecrated, cemeteries violated, individual *Ahmadi* beaten up or even murdered. The police did little to prevent such activity or to find the culprits. On 26 April 1984 Zia, influenced by those who wanted to destroy the *Ahmadi* sect, introduced Ordinance XX which added sections 298(b) and 298(c) to the Pakistani Penal Code. The aim of these sections, as the Ordinance states, is to prevent the 'anti-Islamic activities of the Qadiani Group, Lahori Group and *Ahmadis*'.[5] Under this legislation it was an offence, punishable by a prison sentence of up to three years, the imposition of a fine, or both, for an *Ahmadi* who:

directly, or indirectly, poses himself as a Muslim, or calls, or refers to, his faith as Islam, or preaches or propagates his faith, or invites others to accept his faith, by words, either spoken or written, or by visible representations, or in any manner whatsoever outrages the religious feelings of Muslims.[6]

This legislation prohibited the *Ahmadi* from using the *Azan* [the call to prayer]; calling 'his place of worship as *Masjid* [mosque]'; praying according to Islamic custom; using the *kalima* [declaration of faith] and inscribing Quranic verses on their mosques. Under 298(b) *Ahmadi* are forbidden to refer to, or address, 'any other person, other than a caliph [sic] or companion of the Holy Prophet Muhammad as *Ameerul Mumineen* [commander of the faithful]; *Khalifa-tul-Mumineen* [*Khalifa* or leader of the faithful]; *Khalifa-tul-Musilmeen*' [*Khalifa* of Muslim believers]; *sahaabi*' [companion of the Prophet] or *Razi Allah Anho* [may God be pleased with them]'. Likewise they could not 'refer to, or address, any person, other than a wife of the Holy Prophet Muhammad as *Ummul-Mumineen* [mother of the faithful]'.

---

5   Ordinance XX, and a full report of the persecution of *Ahmadi* in Pakistan can be seen in Jonathan Ensor (ed.) *Rabwah: A Place for Martyrs*, London: Report of the Parliamentary Human Rights Group, 2007.

6   *Persecution of Ahmadi Muslims in Pakistan*, Lahore: Ahmadiyya Muslim Association, n.d., p.6.

In May 1984, due to continued fears for his life, the *Khalifa* was removed from Rabwah to new headquarters in London. The *Ahmadiyya Jama'at*, facing the enforced exile of their spiritual leader, was subject to further repressive legislation in 1986 when the Pakistani government inserted 295 (c) into the Penal code. This stated that the penalties for blaspheming the prophet Muhammad were death or life imprisonment with fines. This was later amended in 1991 to make the death penalty the only punishment for blasphemy.[7] It is recorded that nobody has been executed by the state under these provisions although religious extremists have killed some people accused under them. Under the Conduct of General Elections Order, 2002, the 'status of *Ahmadis* etc.,' was 'to remain unchanged'. Under this regulation 'the status of the Qadiani Group or the Lahori group or a person who does not believe in the absolute and unqualified finality of the Prophet-hood of Muhammad, the last of the prophets, or claimed or claims to be a prophet, in any sense of the word or of any description whatsoever, after Muhammad, or recognises such a claimant as a Prophet or a religious reformer shall remain the same as provided in the Constitution of the Islamic Republic of Pakistan 1973'. Under Article 7(c) a person is denied the right to vote as a Muslim unless they subscribe to the article described above. *Ahmadi* are effectively barred from Higher Education, as Muslim students must declare in writing that they believe in the unqualified finality of the prophet-hood of Muhammad. Their right to citizenship, and the right to travel outside the country, is also restricted by virtue of the fact that the pro forma for obtaining a Pakistani passport asks applicants to sign a declaration that they 'consider Mirza Ghulam Ahmad *Qadiani* to be an imposter *nabi* and also consider his followers whether belonging to the Lahori or Qadiani group to be Non-Muslim'. Dr Saeed, the *Amir* of the Lahori *Ahmadi*, expressed the feelings of many *Ahmadi* in his poem 'Precious Stones', when he wrote:

The *Kalima* is trodden, *azan* banned,
The idol breakers' now mosques break.

---

7   J. Ensor, (ed.) Rabwah: A Place for Martyrs, London: report of the Parliamentary Human Rights Group, op.cit.

Before the people recognise the Truth,
Oh Allah, what sacrifices it will take.

Writing to President Benazir Bhutto in January 1990 John Porter, co-chairman of the Congressional Human Rights Caucus, and Gus Yatron, Chairman of the Subcommittee on Human Rights and International Organisations, Congress of the United States, highlighted the overt persecution of *Ahmadi* in Pakistan in the early 1990s. 'As we understand it', they stated:

under Ordinance 20 of Pakistan's Constitution, *Ahmadis* ... are prevented from practicing their faith: they cannot call prayers, name their places of worship '*masjid*' or mosque, wear their insignia in public or private, or call themselves Muslims. All these daily practices, which are otherwise regarded as laudable, are made criminal under Ordinance 20 when performed by *Ahmadis* and punishable by three years imprisonment and an unlimited fine. *Ahmadi* have been imprisoned for as long as two years for exchanging the simple greeting, 'peace and blessings be upon you'.[8]

Porter and Yatron referred to the 'killing of 19 prominent *Ahmadi* and three *Ahmadi* residents of Chak Sikandar' in July 1989 'without one indictment'. Similarly the writers mentioned how 'nine *Ahmadi* mosques have been destroyed and 21 have been damaged without any action taken against the perpetrators. Twelve *Ahmadi* mosques have been sealed by the government and hundreds have been desecrated, again, without intervention by the police'. Further reference was made to 'incidents in Chak Sikandar and in Nankana' in April 1989 leaving '70 *Ahmadi* homes burnt and looted'. The letter described how:

freedom of expression is another basic right that may be available to other Pakistanis but is not a right enjoyed by *Ahmadis*. The only *Ahmadiyya* daily newspaper was banned for four years and its editor, publisher, and printer have been indicted for exercising freedom of expression. *Ahmadiyya* books and publications have been banned and confiscated and 200 criminal cases have been registered against *Ahmadis* for distributing their religious litera-

---

8   In an attempt to justify this action, the government of Pakistan published a White Paper under the title *Qadiyaniyyat Islam kay liya' Sangin Khatrah': Qadiyaniyyat - A Grave Threat to Islam*. Information gained from *Persecution of Ahmadis in Pakistan during the year 2003: A summary*, http://www.thepersecution.org/nr/2003/y2003/html.

ture. In total approximately 185 *Ahmadi* books and magazines that were in circulation for 80 years have been banned'.[9]

The official statistics put forward by the *Ahmadi* showing a 'summary of the cases instituted against *Ahmadis* in Pakistan from April 1984 to April, 2004' makes horrendous reading. According to these sources the number of *Ahmadis* charged for displaying the *Kalima* was 756; 37 for calling *Azan*; 404 'for posing as Muslims'; 131 for using Islamic epitaphs; 590 for preaching; 213 charged under the Blasphemy Laws and 845 'for various other cases against *Ahmadis* under anti-*Ahmadi* Ordinance 298 B/C'.[10] A charge sheet was made by the authorities against the entire *Ahmadi* population of Rabwah in December 1989 accusing them of inscribing '*kalmia Tayyaba* and other Quranic verses on their graves, buildings, offices of *Ahmadiyya* community, places of worship and business centres in spite of the legal prohibitions of 1984'.[11] 'Moreover', declared the charge sheet, 'they persistently preach their religion to Muslims in different ways' such as 'deliberately saying *Asslamo Alaikum* [peace be on you] to Muslims, reciting *Kalima Tayyaba* in loud voice in groups in the town at the time of call to morning prayers and by repeatedly indulging in similar Islamic activities'. The list goes on.[12]

The Commission on Human Rights, in August 1985, expressed 'its grave concern at the promulgation by Pakistan of Ordinance XX of 26th April, 1984, which, prima facie, violates the right to liberty and security of the persons, the right to freedom from arbitrary arrest or detention, the right to freedom of thought, expression, conscience and religion, the right of religious minorities to profess and practice their own religion, and the right to an effective legal remedy'.[13] Concern was also expressed at the way 'persons charged with and

9   See the report published by the Human Rights Commission of Pakistan, www.thepersecution.org/hrcp04/html.

10   Human Rights Commission of Pakistan, op.cit. See also J. Ensor (ed.) *Rabwah: A Place for Martyrs*, London: Report of the Parliamentary Human Rights Group, annex II: summary of cases instituted against *Ahmadi* in Pakistan from April 1984 to December 2005, op.cit.

11   HRCP, ibid.

12   Ibid.

13   Ibid.

arrested' under the 1984 Laws 'have been reportedly subjected to various punishments and confiscation of personal property, and that the affected groups as a whole have been subjected to discrimination in employment and education and to the defacement of their religious property'.[14] Such conclusions have been substantiated by later Reports.

While visiting Faisalabad, Pakistan in 2004, I met with Muzaffir Ahmad Zafir, a lecturer in English jurisprudence and *Amir* of the *Ahmadiyya Jama'at* in that area. I met with him, and other men, in a side room of the mosque where we spoke at length on life as an *Ahmadi* in that region. They told me of their fears, the constant persecution, the imprisonment of members for simply practicing their faith. Zafir shared with me the problems he faced as a legal advocate, how certain judges prevent him from practicing because he is *Ahmadi*. Others in the group told me how various traders in the district refuse to have anything to do with *Ahmadi*. When I visited both the Lahori *Ahmadi* and their co-religionists at Qadian I heard similar accounts of victimization and harassment. At Rabwah I was given a considerable amount of material describing the persecution they were facing in Pakistan, persecution mainly brought by *Mullahs* stirring up hatred of *Ahmadi* in their sermons, and carried out apparently with the tacit support of the police. Of particular interest was the *Ahmadiyya* Report for 2003. I was moved with sympathy, if not compassion, as I read of 'Mian Iqbal Ahmad, District President of the *Ahmadiyya* Community, Rajanpur' who was 'murdered at his home office by unknown gunmen'; 'Brigidir Iftikhar Ahmad', a retired army officer, 'shot dead at home' at Rawalpindi; the attempt of 'two bearded men to murder Mr Munawwar Ahmad Khan, an *Ahmadi*, at his home in the early hours of the morning'. I read how the prevalent legislature could be used 'to impose a wide range of penalties on *Ahmadi*, from death [for blasphemy] to three years in prison or a hefty fine [for posing to be a Muslim]'. I read of mosques being destroyed, *Ahmadi* shops being closed and a *fatwa* issued against the *Ahmadi* by a newspaper in Lahore forbidding any Muslim to 'be polite to them, to address them, to invite them to your functions or to attend their

---

14   Ibid.

THE AHMADI: A PERSECUTED PEOPLE

functions'.[15] This literature is politically sensitive and controversial in both India and Pakistan. Reference has already been made to the problems I encountered while attempting to cross the Wagah border into Pakistan with *Ahmadi* literature in my possession.

In Bradford, West Yorkshire, I came across several *Ahmadi* who had sought asylum in Britain due to the persecution they faced in the country of their birth. The particular life-story of one *Ahmadi*, whom I shall name Rashid, clearly illustrates the nature of the persecution taking place in Pakistan against *Ahmadiyyat*, and the reasons why they seek asylum in Britain and elsewhere. I have met Rashid and his family on many occasions, enjoying conversation with him [although through an interpreter as his English is limited], and hospitality in his home. Rashid, a happy, cheerful man in his mid-fifties came to the UK with his wife and son from Rawalpindi in Pakistan in 1998. Following the passing of certain *Ahmadi* laws in that country in 1974, Rashid and his family tried to keep their religious faith secret. However when he did make his faith known he and his family were subjected to 'abuse and harassment' and, after further anti-*Ahmadi* legislation in 1984, to 'violence and persecution'. In May 1998 a new *Maulvi* [religious leader at the mosque] arrived in his town and aroused much hatred amongst local people against the *Ahmadi*. Rashid and his relatives became 'targets of hatred and attacks in a way which they had not experienced before'.[16] At the same time as the arrival of the new *Maulvi* an anti-*Ahmadi* group called *Khatme Nabuvat* became active in the area. Being regarded as *Kafirs*, [unbelievers], Rashid and his family lived in constant fear for their lives. On one occasion a mob assaulted the family home using sticks and stones to smash a satellite dish due to the *Ahmadi* programs received on it. At another time Rashid's son was knocked off his bicycle by the

---

15   Report dated 15/12/89, report No 5. According to a complaint lodged, prepared and sent by Mohammad Ashiq Marath, Station House Officer, Rabwah PPC 298C, *Ahmadiyya* Report, *Ahmadiyya* Muslim Association, Rabwah, 2003.

16   Statement made by the United Nations Sub-Commission on Prevention of Discrimination and Protection of Minorities on 'the situation in Pakistan', Thirty-eighth Session, agenda item 6, E/CN.4/Sub.2/1985/L.42, 27 August 1985.

Maulvi, resulting in hospital treatment. Although complaints were made to the local police, nothing was done. On another occasion Rashid was attacked by the *Maulvi* and two of his assistants. Soon after this the police tried to arrest Rashid for preaching the *Ahmadi* faith. He and his family, realising they needed to escape, hid for a few days in their house. Having gained a visa to visit England for the purpose of visiting relatives Rashid and his family made their way to the United Kingdom, arriving on 23 August 1998, and claimed asylum. In January 2001 the Home Office rejected this claim and so an appeal was made against that decision. Further documentation was produced and oral evidence from himself, his wife and son. Claiming that, due to 'a well-founded fear of persecution for reasons of race, religion, nationality or membership of a particular social group or political opinion', a return to his home in Pakistan would be dangerous and therefore the British government would be in breach of the relevant immigration and asylum law.[17] In September 2002 the appeal was successful mainly on the basis of the failure of the country of origin [in this case Pakistan] to provide protection for Rashid and his family from the persecution and threats of the local community.

Persecution of *Ahmadi* in the UK by other Muslims does take place. It is a point of interest, if not grave concern, that mainstream Muslims in Britain rightly claim equality for themselves and their faith under British law yet they are not willing to grant such equality to minority groups such as the *Ahmadi*. One Leicester *Imam* expressed the views of many within mainstream Islam when he said of the *Ahmadi*: 'they appear righteous, holy, but inside they are *kafir,* hypocrites, inwardly plotting to undermine the faith'.[18] Naseer, an *Ahmadi* living in Manchester stated, 'many local Muslims hate us. Many will not even receive our *assalam*'. 'Non-*Ahmadi* Muslims are concerned about trying to stop us from delivering our message', declared Tahir Selby. 'Huge campaigns are launched telling lies about

---

17 Reference is made to the 'refugee convention' under s69(1) of the Immigration and Asylum Act 1999, and s3 of the European Convention for the protection of human Rights and fundamental Freedoms. Information gained from the official Home Office papers.

18 The names of *Imams* etc are changed for reasons of confidentiality.

us, what we believe, what *Hadhrat* Mirza Ghulam Ahmad did or said'.

Incidents of anti-*Ahmadi* activity occur sporadically in Bradford. As part of their *tabligh* campaign the *Ahmadiyya* Student's Association in September 1986 organised a 'Religious Founders' Day', with a large meeting held at the Central Library, Bradford. People from all faiths had been invited to discuss the theme 'religious under-standing'. Local Muslims were angered, not only by the fact that the *Ahmadi* were advertising themselves as 'Muslim', but also because the *Ahmadi* used 'peace be upon him' after the names of Ram and Guru Nanak, a blessing usually reserved for Islamic prophets. The Bradford Council for mosques led a large demonstration against the meeting and actually entered the library in protest, causing it to be cancelled. The police led the *Ahmadi* out of the library by a back exit and arrested seventeen protesters.[19]

Further anti-*Ahmadi* feeling was seen in 1996 when Bradford Council and a Voluntary Service Group working on behalf of the Council, published *The Global Village Guide to Bradford,* a directory of ethnic minority groups in the Bradford Metropolitan District. Due to fears of protest by mainstream Muslims within the city the *Ahmadiyya* Muslim Association was omitted from the Muslim section of the book and placed in the section for 'other' religious groups.[20] After complaints were made by the *Ahmadi Jama'at,* rather than place *Ahmadi* in the Muslim section of the book, all the copies that had been distributed were recalled. Other cases of mainstream Muslims persecuting *Ahmadi* take on a more sinister nature. A chemical attack was made on the Leamington Spa Mission House, Warwickshire, in September 2003. Members opening the building for a Sunday Class, to their consternation, found white powder everywhere. On inspec-tion it was discovered that someone had put the powder through

19   *Telegraph & Argus,* (6.10.86 and 7.10.86). Also see History of the Bradford Jama'at, 20th anniversary edition, *Al-Baseerat,* (September 1997), p. 44.

20   David Fitch, person in charge of the Lister Hills inter-faith centre at that time and main consultant for the *Global Village Guide,* informed me that due to the animosity of mainstream Muslims against *Ahmadi* the decision had been taken to prevent any protests taking place by refusing to acknowledge the *Ahmadi* as 'Muslim'.

the letter-box sending the substance, and fumes, all over the house. Fortunately the powder was later identified as chemicals used in fire extinguishers causing coughing but nothing more serious.[21]

How is the hostility of mainstream Muslims towards *Ahmadi* to be explained? As discussed in some detail in Chapter Six, *Ahmadi* are regarded as *kafir* [unbelievers] by the majority of Muslims because they deny 'the finality of prophet-hood of the Prophet Muhammad'; they accept the teaching of Ahmad 'who claimed to be a prophet and/or the Messiah and/or one who had received revelation from God'; they reject 'the virgin birth and immaculate conception of Jesus Christ' and '*Jihad* or religious war against unbelievers in Islam'.[22] Mainstream Muslims regard *Ahmadiyyat* as a new religion, a sect which 'hypocritically claims to be Muslim and damaging the faiths of simple-minded Muslims who lack deep knowledge of Islamic sciences'.[23] As stated earlier, mainstream Islam adamantly affirms that 'a person who does not regard Muhammad as the last Prophet of God is not a Muslim, for the finality of Muhammad's prophet-hood is one of those fundamental articles of faith which a Muslim must understand and believe'.[24] On this basis alone the *Ahmadi*, or anyone else rejecting this doctrine, 'will be declared an infidel', and regarded as being 'outside the pale of Islam'.[25] Muhammad Iqbal, the Indo-Pakistani political and religious writer and leader, and the greatest Urdu poet of the twentieth century,[26] summed up the view of the majority of mainstream Muslims about the *Qadiani Ahmadiyyat* when he stated: 'any religious society, historically arising from the

21 *Al-Barakat*, the Magazine for the Midlands *Ahmadiyyat Jama'at*, (September 2003), p. 3.

22 Nur Hosain Majidi, *The New Nation*, Bangladesh's Independent News Source, editorial, (10 May 2006).

23 Ibn Nujaim, *Canons of Fiqh*, cited by Mawdudi, *Finality of Prophethood*, Lahore: Islamic Publications, 1975, p. 36.

24 Shaikh Ismail Haqqi, *Commentary Ruh-ul-Bayan*, Mawdudi, *Finality of prophethood*, op. cit., p. 37.

25 Z. Aziz, 'The Ahmadiyya Movement of Lahore, A survey of the Origins, History, Beliefs, Aims of the Ahmadiyya Anjuman Isha'at Islam Lahore', *The Light and Islamic Review*, (September-October 1977), p. 11.

26 J. L. Esposito, *The Oxford Dictionary of Islam*, op. cit., sv.

bosom of Islam, which claims a new prophet-hood for its basis and declares all Muslims who do not recognise the truth of its alleged revelation, as *kafirs*, must therefore be regarded by every Muslim as a serious danger to the solidarity of Islam'.[27]

On talking with mainstream Muslims in various parts of Britain it became apparent that much of the opposition to the *Ahmadi* is due to envy of the success of the *Ahmadiyya Jama'at*, particularly their considerable rate of conversions, and also MTA, the satellite television station. Many Muslims that I spoke to poured out their scorn against the *Ahmadi* but, when asked, failed to give reasons for their hatred. On deeper enquiry it became clear to me that most Muslims are ignorant of the beliefs of the *Ahmadi* and sadly their opposition merely reflects the hatred they perceive in the *khutba* delivered by the *Imam* at *Juma* prayers at the local mosque. Many *Mulla*hs and *Imams* in Bradford for example have come from rural Pakistan. As such they bring the views and opinions of the *ulema* from that country with its dislike of *Ahmadiyyat*. Muslims in Bradford go to such men for advice and guidance and are told that *Ahmadi* are *kafir* and must be opposed.

How do *Ahmadi* react to such persecution? Tertullian, speaking of how the persecution of Christians by the Romans in the second century AD encouraged rather than eradicated the earliest followers of Christ, remarked that 'the blood of the martyrs is the seed of the Church'. *Ahmadi* often view persecution in the same light as the early Christian believers. In many ways they regard persecution as a necessary evil. As the Bradford *Tabligh* Seminar concluded in 1994: 'opposition should be used as a catalyst and not as an obstacle in our way'.[28] The *Ahmadi* of Lahore, Faisalabad, and Rabwah whom I met, manifested a stoical, benign resignation to the daily persecution they faced. There is a clear 'wisdom-through-suffering' theme in *Ahmadi* literature and conversation. Mirza Ghulam Ahmad remarked:

---

27   Dr Sir Muhammad Iqbal, Statement re the *Qadianis*, 1936, cited by M. Ali, *The Ahmadiyya Movement*, trans. S. M. Tufail, Lahore: *Ahmadiyyah Anjuman Isha'at Islam*, 1973, p. 349.

28   *Tabligh* seminar Meeting, Bradford mosque, reported in *Al-Baseerat*, (October 2004), p. 5.

'Now just as I do not pay any attention to their abuse I advise my community also that they should listen to abuse and tolerate it and they should never retort with abuse for, by doing so the blessing will be lost'.[29] Believing that such opposition had been foretold, if not welcomed, by Mirza Ghulam Ahmad, and believing in the ultimate triumph of their faith, the *Ahmadi* have refused to react violently to such persecution. Throughout the times of fierce persecution experienced by the movement, to their credit, the *Ahmadi* have adopted a policy of restraint. Mubarak, a cheerful and amiable middle aged member of the *Jama'at* in Rabwah remarked to me: 'Local Muslims spit at us, but we do not react. We must react with love. Like *Isa* [Jesus], he taught to turn the other cheek, that is the best way'.

---

29   The words of Mirza Ghulam Ahmad, *Malfoozat,* vol. III, p. 181, cited in *Al-Baseerat,* (September 1990), front page.

12

'IN ALLAH DO WE TRUST'
CONCLUSIONS AND COMMENT

The Prophet Muhammad had predicted there would be seventy-three sects within Islam, seventy-two would go to hell. As one recent writer remarked; 'every Muslim group claims to be the one saved sect, and implicitly or directly argues that the other groups are, by definition, aberrant, not really Muslim, and hence destined to doom in hell'.[1] *Ahmadiyyat* believes it alone is the fulfilment of Muhammad's prediction, the movement to restore the pristine splendour of Islam. However, as indicated throughout this book the *Ahmadiyya Jama'at* is not accepted by mainstream Islam as being a 'Muslim' group, instead *Ahmadi* are regarded as *kafir* [unbelievers] and *murtad* [apostate]. Similar to the *Alawites*, a Syrian *Shia* group teaching that God has appeared seven times on earth in human form, the last time as Ali; the *Druze, Shia* believing in reincarnation and the divinity of *al-Hakim*, the sixth *Khalifa*; the *Ismaili*, another *Shia* sect, accepting Ismail bin Jafar as the seventh *Imam* who, presently hidden, will return in the last days; the *Khojas*, Hindu Indian converts to *Shia* Islam led by Agha Khan; the *Bahais* in Iran and other minority groups in Islam, the *Ahmadi* have been classed as heterodox and non-Muslim. Persecuted, despised and rejected by other Muslims, the *Ahmadi*, despite their laudatory efforts to be accepted by non-Muslims, remain marginalised and ignored. 'Despite all its services to Islam', declares

---

1   Y. Sikand, *Muslims in India Since 1947: Islamic Perspectives on inter-faith relations*, London: Routledge, 2004.

241

one writer, 'the *Ahmadiyya* now stands alone against the rest of the Muslim world'.[2]

Is *Ahmadiyyat* a Muslim movement? Are mainstream Muslims justified in arguing that *Ahmadi*, despite strong claims of orthodoxy, are non-Muslims? As indicated throughout this book the *Ahmadi* differ from other Muslims in their interpretation of certain teachings within the faith, particularly the teaching relating to *Khataman Nabiyeen*, the seal of the Prophet. This raises the question; can a person be rejected as a Muslim by the *Ummah* worldwide, although that person may be devout and sincere with regard to all the usual duties incumbent on a Muslim believer, solely on the basis that he holds an allegedly deviant view of prophet-hood within Islam? Many members of the *ulema* have declared belief in Muhammad as the last of the Prophets as the main criterion for acceptance as a Muslim believer. Shaikh Ismai'il Haqqi, representative of mainstream Islam generally, remarked: 'anyone who casts doubt about the finality of Muhammad's prophet-hood, will be declared an infidel, because any claim to prophet-hood after Muhammad is absolutely false'.[3] As such, *Ahmadiyyat*, and other groups such as the *Bahai*, is regarded by some as a religious sect forming a new faith.[4] As Nur Hosain Majidi said of the *Ahmadi* within the context of Bangladesh, the *Ahmadi* 'must declare their religion as a separate religion other than Islam and choose a new name for that, ... they must declare themselves as non-Muslims, select a name for their religion [*Qadiani* or any other new name], refrain from using Islamic terms such as 'Islam', 'Muslim', '*mu'min*', '*Iman*', '*salat*', '*masjid*' etc. and correct their literature [dropping such Islamic terms] and enjoy full freedom of a religious

2   Y. Friedmann, *Prophecy Continuous: Aspects of Ahmadi Religious Thought and its Medieval Background*, Berkeley: University of California Press, 1989, p. 183.

3   Commentary, Ruh-ul-Bayan, cited by M. A. Mawdudi, *Finality of Prophethood*, Islamic Publications, Lahore: Shaalom Market, 1975.

4   The faith of the followers of Bahai U'llah who argued that God has revealed himself in a chain of prophets by progressive revelation including Judaism and Christianity. All religions with a prophet are accepted by the *Bahai* as having intrinsic truth. Certain Muslims, such as the *Ithna' Ashariyyah Shi'a*, regard the *Bahai* as heretics: See G. D. Newby, *A Concise Encyclopedia of Islam*, Oxford: One world, 2004, sv.

minority group like Hindus, Buddhists, Christians etc'.[5] Therefore 'to avoid law and order situations arising out of the confusion created by *Qadianis* and protect the religious right of the Muslim majority, the government should take the necessary steps to persuade them to do so'. Others suggest that the continued existence of the *Ahmadi*, a new religious sect outside the pale of Islam, requires the establishment of an Independent *Ahmadi* State.

Is it justified to judge the sincerity of a Muslim's faith merely by reference to one particular doctrinal belief? Various judicial bodies have made legal decisions concerning the nature of belief in Islam. The Munir Court of Enquiry in 1953-4 investigated the anti-*Ahmadiyya* disturbances that occurred in the Punjab at that time and considered the question: *what is a Muslim?* Having examined the evidence put forward by leading members of the *ulema*, the court decided that 'no two learned divines are agreed on this fundamental' question, consequently 'the *ulema* of various sects within Islam condemn each others sect as *kafir*'.[6]

In 1982-5 a Court in South Africa deliberated over the similar question of whether *Ahmadi* were Muslim or not.[7] The case is interesting for various reasons. Not only does it clearly reveal that internecine squabbling, and proverbial mud-slinging, takes place within Islam just as in other faiths including Christianity, but it also presents to the non-Muslim world what Muslims think a true believer in Islam should be like. Certain Muslim groups, mainly the Muslim Judicial Council [MJC] of Cape Town, published defamatory literature which classed *Ahmadi* as *kafir*. It was alleged that *Ahmadi* 'were outside the fold of Islam' and therefore 'called upon the Muslim community to ostracise members' of the movement.[8] *Ahmadi* were also forbidden access to a certain mosque and Muslim cemetery, meant to be open to all Muslims. The *Ahmadi*, obviously aggrieved by this, took the

---

5   Nur Hosain Majidi, *The New Nation*, Bangladesh's Independent News Source, editorial, 10 May 2006.

6   Z. Aziz, trans.*The Ahmadiyya Case: Case history, judgement and evidence*, Newark, CA: Ahmadiyya Anjuman Isha'at Islam Lahore Inc., 1987, pp. 24f.

7   Aziz, *The Ahmadiyya Case*, op. cit.

8   Saeed Ahmad Khan, Foreword, in Aziz, op. cit., p.i.

matter to Court to gain an injunction preventing further publication of the offending literature. The defendants [the MJC] argued that a true Muslim, not only believes in and practices the five pillars, but also acknowledges that 'the Prophet Muhammad is the last and final prophet'. The final verdict, given by a non-Muslim Court after three years of litigation, was pronounced in favour of the *Ahmadi* concluding that the sect was Muslim.

In the *Mahzarnama*, 'The Memorandum' of 1974, the *Ahmadi* presented an outline of their doctrinal beliefs to the Special Committee of the National Assembly of Pakistan. As Vakil Tasneef states in the preface, 'the purpose of this document was to establish that the members of the *Ahmadiyyat* Muslim *Jama'at* are Muslims and to explain its basic tenets, as well as refute the baseless allegations levelled against it'.[9] The *Ahmadi* asked the Committee can it be legitimate 'to declare someone to be outside the pale of Islam notwithstanding someone's belief in the five pillars of Islam, just because one's interpretation of a few verses of the Holy Quran is unacceptable to some Muslim divines of certain sects; or if one is declared to be outside the pale of Islam for entertaining a belief which runs counter to Islam in the view of certain sects...'.[10] After the submission of the *Memorandum* the Head of the *Ahmadiyya Jama'at, Hadhrat Khalifatul Masih III*, with four assistants, was questioned for eleven days by the Attorney General of Pakistan and leading religious clerics. Although still condemned as non-Muslim, as stated previously, the Commission produced no report accessible to the public.

The *Ahmadi* vehemently assert their orthodoxy as Muslims. In a torrent of pious prose Ahmad, adamant that he and his followers were not only Muslim, but were the only *true* Muslims, declared:

As for us, we certainly have the faith of Muslims. We are, by our very nature, the servants of the Ultimate of all Prophets [*Khatm-ul-Mursaleem*], peace and blessings of Allah be upon him. We consider associating partners with God [*shirk*], and innovating in religion, to be repulsive, ... We faithfully accept all the injunctions [of Islam], our body and soul are sacrificed in

9   *The Memorandum*, Islam International Publications Ltd, Tilford, Surrey: 2003, p.iii.

10   *Memorandum*, op. cit., p. 12.

this blessed course, we have already given our heart away, leaving this mortal body with us. But our only wish is now to even sacrifice this body.[11]

In their claim to be Muslim the *Ahmadi* put forward various arguments from both the Quran and *hadith*. Much is made of the Quranic passage which states: 'this messenger of ours [Muhammad] believes in that which has been revealed to him from his Lord, and so do the believers'.[12] The passage then gives a list of the things which have been revealed, the things which the Prophet and his followers believe. It describes how 'all of them believe in Allah, and in His angels, and in His Books, and in His Messengers, saying, "We make no distinction between any of His Messengers", and they say "we have heard and we are obedient. Our Lord we implore Thy forgiveness and to Thee is the returning".' This passage summarises in a few words the basic beliefs of a Muslim, beliefs readily accepted by the *Ahmadi*. Like Muslims generally the *Ahmadi* firmly believe in Allah, that He is the one God without partner, the supreme being who created the universe and everything that exists in it. The *Ahmadi* also believe in His Angels and His messenger Muhammad. Based on this interpretation of this Quranic passage the *Ahmadi* maintain that they come within this definition of 'believers'.

According to the letter of Islamic law—the *Sharia'h*—the mere performance of *shahadatayn* [the double formula of faith] was sufficient to confirm a person as a Muslim. Generally speaking within mainstream Islam, [with the exception of Pakistan, where a person must declare Mirza Ghulam Ahmad to be an apostate before he is considered a Muslim,] anyone professing *shahada* is considered to be a believer. As discussed throughout this book the *Ahmadi* observe all the duties required of Muslims including *shahada*, the declaration of faith. The *Ahmadi*, desirous to be accepted as Muslims, rely on the words of Muhammad who, according to one reliable *hadith* said: 'whoever offers his prayers as we do, and turns his face to the *Qibla* to which we turn our faces and partakes of our *dhabiha* [animals slaughtered for food according to Islamic tenets] is surely a Muslim

11   *Memorandum*, ibid., p.iii
12   Quran 2:286.

who is under the protection of Allah and his messenger'.[13] In Abu Dawud, one of the six main collections of *hadith,* Muhammad is recorded as saying: 'one who says "There is no god but Allah" do not call him *Kafir* for any sin, nor expel him from Islam for any misconduct'. The *Ahmadi* find further support for their claim of orthodoxy in the words of Imam Abu Hanifa who remarked: 'whoever intends to enter the fold of Islam, let him solemnly declare and believe that there is none worthy of worship but Allah and Muhammad is His messenger. If he does this, he is surely a Muslim even if he is unaware of the fundamental injunctions of Islam'.[14] Reference is made to the Quranic text which forbids Muslims to say to anyone who greets you with *Assalamo Alaikum* 'you are not a believer'.[15] Similarly *Ahmadi* apologetic literature refers to the *hadith* in which Muhammad rebukes one of his followers for killing a stranger although he recited the *shahada.* The implication is that it is God alone who knows the heart, and judges who is a believer or not. However, although placing much reliance on this claim that the pronouncement of *shahada* is sufficient to confirm a person as Muslim, and the belief that no one but Allah can judge a person's faith commitment, the *Ahmadi* show some inconsistency in asserting that anyone refusing to accept the claims of their founder, even a person pronouncing *shahada,* cannot be regarded as a true Muslim.

Having spent much time with many *Ahmadi* I know the majority of them to be men and women who submit totally to pleasing their God. It is a great irony that some Muslims, despite ignoring the basic requirements of their faith are accepted as being believers because they pronounce *shahada,* while the *Ahmadi,* the vast majority meticulous in their observance of religious duties, are rejected because of alleged doctrinal deviancy. Mahmood, a young, energetic *Ahmadi* based in Manchester, proud of his faith and disciplined in his spiritual life declared to me; 'we are condemned by Muslims who

---

13   *An-Nihaya,* cited by K. Zirvi, *Welcome to Ahmadiyyat: The True Islam,* Silver Springs, USA: Ahmadiyya Movement in Islam, 2002, p. 43.

14   Commentary of the *Fiqh-i-Akbar* by Imam Abu Mansur Muhammad Bin Muhammad Hanifa, p. 34, cited by K. Zirvi, *Welcome to Ahmadiyyat: the true Islam,* op. cit., p. 43.

15   Quran 4:95.

drink alcohol, smoke, go clubbing, and do not live as they should. They are regarded as Muslim merely because they occasionally go to prayers and say *kalmia*. I try my best to live the way of the prophet [pbuh] but yet I am persecuted because I accept the claims of *Hadhrat Ahmad*'. According to the Quran 'surely Allah lets go astray whom He wills and guides whom He wills'.[16] This has generally been interpreted by the *ulema* as meaning that only God can judge a person's soul and therefore, if a person professes to be a Muslim the believing community must accept this.[17] If God alone is to be the final arbiter regarding the sincerity or otherwise of a person's faith, and the performance of religious duties is indicative of *niyyat* [intention of the heart] and commitment to the Islamic faith, then the *Ahmadi* must be seen as true Muslim believers. Zahid Aziz, having lectured to the Lahori *Ahmadi* on the subject 'What is a Muslim?', in London, in August 2004, concluded; 'our prayer is as stated in the Quran; 'In Allah do we trust. Our Lord, judge between us and our people with truth, and Thou art the Best of Judges'.

16   Quran 35:9.

17   T. Sonn, *A Brief History of Islam*, Oxford: Blackwell Publishing, 2004, p. 131.

BIBLIOGRAPHY

Abercrombie, N, S. Hill & B. S. Turner, *Penguin Dictionary of Sociology*, London: Penguin Dictionary of Sociology, 2000.

Adamson, Iain. *Mirza Ghulam Ahmad of Qadian*, Islamabad, Surrey: Elite International Publications, 1989.

Adamson, Iain. *Ahmad the Guided One: A life of the holy founder of the movement to unite all religions*, Islamabad, Surrey: Islam international Publications, nd.

Adamson, Iain. *A Man of God: The astonishing story of his holiness Khalifatul Masih IV*, Bristol: George Shepherd Publishers, 1991.

Addison, J. T. 'The Ahmadiyya Movement and its Western Propaganda', *Harvard Theological Review*, vol. 22, (1929).

Ahmad, K. N. *Jesus in Heaven on Earth*, Woking: Woking Muslim Mission & Literary Trust, 1952.

Ahmad, M. B. M. *Invitation to Ahmadiyyat*, Islamabad, Surrey: Islam International Publications, 1997.

Ahmad, M. G. *Jesus in India*, Islamabad, Surrey: Islam International Publications, 1989.

——, *A Misunderstanding Removed*, Rabwah, Pakistan: The Oriental and Religious Publishing Co., 1901.

——, *A brief sketch of my life*, Lahore, Pakistan: Ahmadiyya Anjuman Isha'at Islam, 1996.

Ahmad, M. T. *Revelation, Rationality, Knowledge and Truth*, Islamabad, Surrey: Islam International Publications, 1998.

Ahmad, W. *A Book of Religious Knowledge for Ahmadi Muslims*, Athens, Ohio: Fazl-I-umar Press, 1988.

Ahmadiyya Muslim Association North East, 2001-2002 Annual Report, Bradford: Ahmadiyya Muslim Association, 2003.

Ahmed, Akbar S. *Discovering Islam, Making sense of Muslim History and Society*, London: Routledge, 1988.

———, *From Samarkand to Stornoway: Living Islam*, London: BBC Books, 1993.

Al-Baseerat: Centenary Thanksgiving Number, Bradford: n.p., August, 1989.

Ali, Muhammad. *The Ahmadiyya Movement*, trans. S. M. Tufail, Lahore: Ahmadiyyah Anjuman Isha'at Islam, 1973.

———, *The Founder of the Ahmadiyya Movement*, Lahore: Ahmadiyya Anjuman Isha'at, Islam, 1984.

———, *True Conception of the Ahmadiyya Movement*, Lahore: Ahmadiyya Anjuman Isha'at, Islam, 1996.

Ali-Nadwi, S. A. H. *Qadianism: A Critical Study*, Lucknow, India: Academy of Islamic research and publications, 2nd., 1967.

Anthias,F. & N. Yuval-Davis, *Racialized Boundaries*, London & New York: Routledge, 1992.

Ata-ur-Rahim, *Jesus: A Prophet of Islam*, Karachi: Begin Aisha Bawany Waqf, 1981

Aziz, Zahid. 'The Ahmadiyya Movement of Lahore, A survey of the Origins, History, Beliefs, Aims of the Ahmadiyya Anjuman Isha'at Islam Lahore', *The Light and Islamic Review*, (September-October, 1977).

Bakhsh, K. S. *The debt forgotten*, Columbus, Ohio, USA: Ahmadiyya Anjuman Isha'at Islam, Lahore, 1993.

Baljon, J. M. S. *Religion and the Thought of Shah Wali Allah Dihlawi 1703- 1762*, Leiden: n.p.,1986.

Balzani, M. 'Traditional marriage among Ahmadi Muslims in the UK', *Global Networks*, vol. 6, 4, (October 2006), pp. 345-55.

Barker, Eileen. *The Making of a Moonie: Choice or brainwashing?*, London: Blackwell Publishing, 1984.

Brown, Claude. *Manchild in the promised Land*, New York: New American Library, 1966.

Chaudhary, A. A., *The Promised Messiah and Mahdi*, Islamabad: Islam International Publications, 1989.

———, *Jesus Among the Lost Sheep*, Islamabad, Surrey: Islam International Publications, 1992.

Dard, A. R. *Life of Ahmad: Founder of the Ahmadiyya Movement*, Lahore: A Tabshir Publication, 1948.

Ensor, J. (ed.) *Rabwah: a place for martyrs*, London: Report of the Parliamentary Human Rights Group, 2007.

Esposito, John L. (ed.) *The Oxford Dictionary of Islam*, London: Oxford University Press, 2003.

Esposito, John L. *The Islamic Threat: Myth or Reality*, London: Oxford University Press, 2002.

Fadil Khan, M. *Hadrat Pir Meher Ali Shah of Golra Sharif*, Lahore, 3rd ed., n.p., 1989.

Farid, M. G. (ed.) *The Holy Quran: Arabic Text with English Translation and Short Commentary*, Islamabad, Surrey: Islam International Publications, 1994.

Faruqi, A. M. A. *Truth Triumphs*, Lahore: *Ahmadiyya Anjuman Isha'at Islam*, 1966.

Faruqui, N.A. *Ahmadiyyat: in the service of Islam*, Lahore: *Ahmadiyya Anjuman* Isha'at Islam, 1983.

Festinger, L. Riecken H. W. & S. Schachter, *When prophecy Fails*, NY: Harper Torchbooks, 1955.

Fisher, H. J. *Ahmadiyyah: A study in contemporary Islam on the West African Coast*, London: Oxford University Press, 1963.

Friedmann, Yohanan. *Prophecy Continuous: Aspects of Ahmadi Religious Thought and its Medieval Background*, Berkeley: University of California Press, 1989.

Gibb, Hamilton, A. R. *Modern Trends in Islam*, Illinois: University of Chicago Press, 1947.

Glasse, C. *The Concise Encyclopaedia of Islam*, San Francisco: Harper Row, 1989.

Gualtieri, A. R. *Conscience and Coercion: Ahmadi Muslims and Orthodoxy in Pakistan*, Guernica: Montreal, 1989.

Gualtieri, A. R. *The Ahmadi: community, gender and politics in a Muslim society*, Montreal: McGill-Queens University Press, 2004.

Haddad, Yvonne. (et.al), 'Mission to America: Five Islamic Sectarian Communities in North America', *International Journal of Middle East Studies*, vol., 27, (February 1995), pp. 93-7.

Hammann, L. J. *Ahmadiyyat: An Introduction*, Washington: Ahmadiyyat Movement in Islam, 1985.

Hinnells John R., (ed), *Dictionary of Religion*, London: Penguin, 1995.

Hornsby, J. *Persecution of the Ahmadis in Pakistan*, London: Parliamentary Human Rights Group, 1996.

Iqbal, Muhammad. *Qadianism: return to the dark age*, London: Council on the Preservation of the Finality of Prophethood, 1989.

Jalandhri, A. A. *Death on the Cross? Ten Arguments from the Bible*, London: The London Mosque, nd.

'Jihad: The True Islamic Concept', Leaflet produced by the Ahmadiyya Muslim Association UK.

Jones, K. W. *Socio-religious reform movements in British India*, Cambridge: Cambridge University Press, 1989.

Kaiser, A. *Jesus died in Kashmir*, New York: Gordon and Cremonesi, 1977.

Kersten, H. *Jesus lived in India*, London: Penguin, 1981.

Khan, M. Zafrulla, *Deliverance from the Cross*, London: The London Mosque, 1978.

——, (trans.) *The Essence of Islam*, by Mirza Ghulam Ahmad, Rabwah: Tabshir Publications, n.d.

——, *Ahmadiyyat: The Renaissance of Islam*, Rabwah: Tabshir Publications, 1978.

Khatamun Nabiyeen: interpretations by eminent learned scholars of Islam, London: The London Mosque, 1982.

Lavan, Spencer, *The Ahmadiyya Movement: A History and Perspective*, Delhi: Manohar Bookservice, 1974.

Liebow, Elliot. *Tally's Corner: A Study of Negro Street Corner Men*, Chicago: Little Brown, 1967.

Mahzarnama: the Memorandum, Submission by the Ahmadiyya Muslim Jama'at to the National Assemby of Pakistan regarding its basic tenets, trans. by Saleem-ur-rehman, Ghana: 1999, reprinted Islamabad, Surrey: Islam International Publications, 2003.

Mawdudi, Sayyid A. *The Finality of Prophethood*, Lahore: Islamic Publications, 1975,

——, *The Qadiani Problem*, Lahore: Markazi shoe-ba-e-Nashr –o–Ishaat, Jama'at-i-Islami, 1953.

——, *Come let us change the world*, trans. Kaukab Siddique, Washington: The Islamic party of North America, 1972.

——, *Let us be Muslims*, ed. K. Murad, Markfield, Leicester: Islamic Foundation, 1982.

Mirza, Bashir-Ud-Din Mahmud Ahmad, Khalifatul Masih II, *Invitation to Ahmadiyyat*, Islamabad, Surrey: Islam International Publications, 1997.

Mosques around the world: A pictorial Presentation, Silver Springs, USA: Ahmadiyya Muslim Association, 1994.

Muhammad, H. S. *True facts about the Ahmadiyya Movement*, Lahore: Ahmadiyya Anjuman Ishaat-i-Islam, nd.

Munir, Muhammad. *From Jinnah to Zia*, Lahore: Vanguard, 1979.

Nazir, Q. M. *Truth Prevails*, Rabwah: Nazarat Isha'at Literature-wa- Tasnif, 1966.

Newby, G. D. *A concise encyclopaedia of Islam*, Oxford: Oneworld, 2004.

Notovitch, Nicholas. *The Unknown Life of Jesus Christ*, 1894, reprinted, Joshua Tree, California: Tree of life Publications, 1990.

Pappas, P. C. *Jesus' tomb in India; the debate on his death and resurrection*, Fremont, California: Jain publishing Co, 1991.

Pruthi, K. R. (ed.), *Encyclopaedia of Jihad*, New Delhi: Ammal Publications, 2002.

Rafiq, Bashir A. Truth about Ahmadiyyat, Al Islam, official website of the Ahmadiyya Community, n.d.

——, *The African Martyrs: The tragic tale of the first Martyrs of Ahmadiyyat in Kabul, Afghanistan*, Islamabad, Surrey: Raqeem Press, 1995.

Rainwater, L. (ed.) *Soul: Black Experience*, New Brunswick, NJ: Transaction Books, 1970.

Rememebrance of Allah, a lecture delivered by Hadhrat Mirza Bashiruddin Mahmud Ahmad, Islamabad, Surrey: Islam International Publications, 1993.

Sarwar, Ghulam. Islam: Beliefs and teachings, London: The Muslim Educational Trust, 2003.

Shams, J. D. *Where did Jesus die?* Islamabad, Surrey: Islam International Publications, 1996.

Siddique, M. *Moral Spotlight on Bradford*, Bradford: M.S. Press, 1993.

Sikand, Y. *Muslims in India since 1947: Islamic Perspectives on interfaith relations*, London: Routledge, 2004.

Sivan, Emmanuel. *Radical Islam: Medieval Theology and Modern Politics*, New Haven/London: Yale University Press, 1985.

Tayo, S. P. *Facts About the Ahmadiyya Movement*, Trinidad: n.p., 1979.The London Mosque: The Rising of the Sun from the West (Regarding the *Jama'at in England)*, Centenary Souvenir, London: Jama'at Ahmadiyya, UK, 1989.

The truth About the Crucifixion, transcripts from the International Conference on the deliverance of Jesus from the Cross, held at The Commonwealth Institute, London, on 3rd, 4th, and the 5thJune 1978, published by the London Mosque, 1978.

Titus, M. T. Indian Islam: A religious history of Islam in India, New Delhi: Oriental Books Reprint Corporation, 1979.

Valentine, Simon R. *Love for All, Hatred for None*, Bradford: Ahmadiyya Muslim Association, 2002.

——, 'Muslims in Bradford, background paper for COMPAS, Oxford: University of Oxford, 2006.

——, '*A Guide to Islam*, Sheffield: S. Yorkshire Police Authority, 2007.

Wright, Robin. *Sacred Rage, the wrath of militant Islam*, London: Touchstone, Simon & Schuster, 1985.

Zirvi, Karimullah *Welcome to Ahmadiyyat: The true Islam*, Silver Springs, USA: Ahmadiyya Movement in Islam, 2002.

INDEX

Aamala, 80
Abrogation, vii
Abu Bakr, Khalifa, 57, 82
Abu Bakr, mosque, Bradford, 101, 105
Addingham, Yorkshire, 164
adhan, [azzan], vii, 105, 230, 233
Afghanistan, 51, 68, 69-70, 196, 205
Ahmad, Chaudhry Mansoor, 72
Ahmad, Mirzaan, 42
Ahmad, Mirza Ghulam, vii, xi, xii, xiii, xvi, 8, 19, 20, 22, 23, 24, 32, 33, 37, 38-53, 57, 59, 67, 69, 70, 77, 81, 84, 98, 112, 117, 121, 128, 132, 144, 146, 147, 148, 149, 159, 190, 197-200, 202, 203, 205-7, 214, 223, 224, 231, 237, 238, 239, 240, 244, 245; homeopathy 118, The Philosophy & Teaching of Islam, 223; views on women 173-4, 180
Ahmad, Mirza Basheer-ud-Din Mahmood, second Ahmadi Khalifa, 19 fn4, 36, 56, 58, 70, 71, 90, 94, 95, 167, 181, 204, 213, 223, 229; homeopathy 118; 'New Scheme' 121
Ahmad, Mirza Masroor, fifth Khalifa, 56, 75, 79,
Ahmad, Mirza Nasr, third Khalifa, 19fn4, 33, 56, 73, 77, 90, 121,

146, 157, 175, 176, 229, 231, 244
Ahmad, Mirza Tahir, the fourth Khalifa, 34, 56, 71, 94, 95, 124, 144, 142-3, 143 fn77, 145, 146, 148-9, 158, 160, 167, 184, 215, 217; homeopathy 118, 120-1
Ahmad, Waheed, 49, 217
Ahmad, Waseem, 153-4
Ahmadiyya Anjuman Ishaat-i-Islam, 57, 58
Ahmadiyya Majlis-i- Aamah, 60
Ahsan, Sayyed Muhammad, 52
Aisha, wife of Muhammad, 135
'ajûza, 139
Akhirah, judgment, 127
Al Aqsa mosque, Qadian, 87-8, 102
Al Aqsa mosque, Rabwah, 87, 102
Al-Badr, newspaper, 52, 68
Al-Baseerat, vii, 72, 81, 110, 114, 116, 124, 153, 163, 164, 226
Al-Fadl International Weekly, 68
Al-Fadl, newspaper, 68, 175, 204
Al-Fatihah, 107
Al Faz, newspaper, 90
Al Ghazali, 130
Al-Hakam, newspaper, 52, 68
Ali, Abdullah Yusuf, 130
Ali, Muhammad, 19 fn4, 33, 57, 58
Ali, Muhammad's cousin son-in-law, 82, 83
Al-jannah, 173, 194, 196, 209, 210

255

Al-Muhajiroun, 84, 84 fn23
Al-wassiya, "the Will", vii, 56
al-Zawāhirī, Ayman 163, 190
'amal, 127
Aman see *jihad*
Amela, vii
America, see United States.
Amini Textiles, Bradford, 166
Amir, vii, 59, 62, 64, 65, 93, 95, 96, 97, 123, 169, 215, 220
Amoora 'Amma, 94
Amoora Kharijiyyah, 95
Amritsar, 12, 40, 68
Angels, see *Mala'ikah*
Anjuman-i-ahrar-I Islam, 228
Anjumn-i-Himayat-i-Islam, 207
Ansar, 111,
Ansarullah, vii, 94, 96, 163
Arkan, see five pillars of Islam
Argentina, 69
Arya Samaj movement, 44, 45, 47, 48, 205
Atfal, vii, 111, 112, 221
Atfal chanda, 99
Atham, Abdullah, 50, 146
Atkinson, Bilal, 95, 113, 214
Atonement, Christian doctrine of, 17, 18
Atta, Muhammad, 163
Att'awwuz, 107
Aziz, Zahid Dr, 61, 62, 151, 247
Azzam, Abdullah, 190, 195-7

Badr, battle of, 40, 204
Badshahi mosque, Lahore, 63
Bady, Anwar, Sheik, 117
Bahishti Maqbara, 'heavenly grave-yard', Qadian, vii, 40
Baghdad, 69
Bai'at, viii, 52, 80, 82, 140, 160, 212, 217, 218
Baitul Fikr, 41

Baitul Futuh mosque, London, 74, 102, 125,
Baitul Hamd, mosque, Bradford, 72-3, 81, 101, 109, 178, 219
Bajwa, Naseem Ahmad, 74, 75, 92, 95, 105, 106, 109-11, 112, 114, 115, 139 n63, 140, 141, 157, 162, 178, 180, 184, 189-90, 216, 219, 226
Bangladesh, 7fn9, 8fn11, 89, 120, 140, 242
Barahin-i- Ahmadiyyah, 45, 46, 47, 137
Baraka, viii, 104, 140, 141
Barelwi, 1, 9, 36, 139
Barker, E. 4, 4fn5
Batala, near Qadian, 41
Batalvi, Muhammad Husain, 207
Batley, 164
Battle, John, MP, 112, 113
Belguim, 217
Berlin, 61
Bhutto, Benazir 232
Bhutto, President of Pakistan, 144, 145, 229, 230
Bid'at, viii, 140, 173
Biradri, viii, 178, 184
Birmingham, 140, 178
bismillah' viii, 141
Bosnia, 164, 165
Bradford, xiii, xvi, 1, 2-8, 21, 35-36, 62, 72-4, 81, 95, 96, 97, 101-2, 105, 119, 124, 156, 161- 2, 164, 166, 168, 215, 218, 221, 235, 237, 239
Bradford Council of Mosques, 73, 237
Brahmo Samaj, 45
Brown, Claude, 4, 4fn7
Buddha, 147
Buddhism, 26-7, 147
Bukhari, collection of *hadith,* viii, 104, 130, 190, 194, 198, 210

Burma, 61, 69
Burqa, 171, 175
Byrom Street mosque, Bradford, 109

Canada, 69
Chachasti, 139
Chador, see *burqa*
Calcutta, 207
Chak Sikandar, Pakistan, 232
Chanda, viii, 37, 94, 95, 97-100
Chanda Aam, 99
Chanda Jalsa Salana, 99
Chanda, Tariq, 99
Chanda Tehrik-i-Jadid, 99
Chanda waqf-i-jadid, 167
Chaudhry, A. A., xv fn2,
Chenab Naghar, see Rabwah.
Chilla, 51, 114
Christian Catholic Apostolic Church, 49
Christianity, 10, 17-8, 21, 23-4, 26, 28, 29, 31, 32, 33, 34, 38, 44, 45, 46, 55, 108, 111, 147, 148, 149, 197, 214, 224, 225; Salvation Army in Rabwah, 89-90; Unitarian Church, 143
Colonel Gaddafi, 84
Copenhagen, Denmark, 69

Dad, Fazal, Imam, 105
Dai'ilallah, viii, 215, 217, 220
Dajjal, 58
Dars ul Hadith, 116
Darul harb see *jihad*
Darul Islam see jihad
Darul Qada, internal courts, 123
Dar-ul-Quran, 115
Darul sulh see *jihad*
Darus Salaam, New Garden Town, Lahore 61, 62
Darveshan-i-Qadian, viii, 39
Da'wa, viii, 190, 211, chapter ten,
Dayananda, Swami, 47-8

Denmark, 69, 75
Deobandi, 1, 9, 101, 139
Dhikr, viii,
Dhu al-hijja, viii
Din, Shah, 207
Divorce, see marriage
Dowie, John Alexander, 49-50
Dreams, 143-4
Dua-iyya, gathering for prayers, 60
Dubai, 61, 62
Dunya, 191

Eaton, Margaret, former Leader of Bradford Council, 112, 165
Egypt, xvi, 9, 69
Eid fund, 99
Eid Milan, 3
Eid Milan Party, 112-3, 165, 179, 220
Electoral College, 81
Esposito, John, L., 32, 32 fn1, 32 fn2
"Evil eye", 139, 141

Faisalabad, 75, 190, 234
Fard, viii
Fard kifayah, 196
Farid, translation of the Quran, 142 fn69
Faruqi, Al-Hajj Mumtaz Ahmad, 59
Fatwa, viii, 51, 123, 193, 234
Fazal Mosque, London, 71
Fazl-e-Umar hospital, Rabwah, 86
Festinger, Leon, 2, 2fn2, 3
Fidiya, 99
Fiji, 69
Finality of Prophethood, [see *Khataman Nabiyeen*]
Fisabi'l illah, 190
Fitna, 192
Fitrana, 99
Five pillars of Islam, vii, 31, 127, 222, 244
Foote-Whyte, William, 4, 4 fn6

Formosa, 61
France 69, 71
Friedmann, Yohanan, xv fn1, xvi, 58n11, 69
Furqan Force, 204

Germany, 69, 71, 75
Ghana, 61
Gandhi, Mrs, 144
Ghazi Mahdi, 199
Gibb, H. A. R., 76
Glasgow, Scotland, 71, 72
'Global village Guide to Bradford', 73
Gospel of Barnabas, 24
Great Ormond St. Hospital, London, 164
Guyana, 61, 69

Hadith, 134-5, 174, 183, 190, 245
Hadith qudsi, 194
Haifa, 69
Hajj, vii, ix, 31, 70,
Hakim, 119,
Hakimiyyah, 103, 138
Halifax, Yorkshire, 110
Hamburg, Germany, 69
Hamza, Abu, 190
Hanbal, Ibn, 192
Hanfia mosque, Bradford, 101
Haq mehr, see marriage
Haq, Mirza Abdul, 92
Haqqi, Ismaiʾil, 242
Haque, Abdul, 72
Haram, ix, 109
Harbi, see *jihad*
Hartlepool, 95, 110,
hawia, 'death or utter disgrace', 145
Hazratbal mosque, Srinigar, 11
Headley, Lord, 71
Herzegovina, 164
Hijab, 171, 175, 178,
Hijri Shmasi, calendar, 127
Hiqmat, 191, 222

Hizbut Tahrir, 84, 84 fn23
Holland, 61, 71, 217
Homeopathy, 118-21
Hong Kong, 69
Hoshiarpur, 51,
Hudaybiya, battle of, 202
Huddersfield, England, 8, 71, 95, 110, 118, 119,
Hungary, 69
Hurmat Bibi, Ahmad's first wife, 42
Husayn, 209
Hussein, Saddam, 84

Ibrahim, Muhammad's son, 135
iftari, meal, 116
Ijtema, viii, 99,
Ijtema chanda, 99
Ilham, 136
Ilm, 191
Imam, 80, 108-111
Imam-Mahdi, 136
Iman, 127
India, xvi, 2, 8, 12, 13, 14, 43-4, 53, 68, 70, 78, 140, 167, 207, 213
Indonesia, 61
Iqamat, 107, 108
Iqbal, Muhammad, 238
Iran, 19,
Iraq, 208
Ireland, 71
Isa, see Jesus.
Isha'at-i-Islam Lahore, 59
Ishaat secretary, 94
Islahi committee, ix, 123,
Islamabad, Surrey, ix, 8, 77-80, 111, 178, 212
Istikharah, prayers, 141, 182
Istishad, [martyrdom], 194, 208
Itikaf, 114-6

Jaidad, secretary, 94
Jahiliyya, 195

Jalsa Salana, ix, 8, 77-80, 95, 99, 124, 144, 178, 214, 215, 216

Jama'at-i-Islami, 104, 228

Jamia Masjid, Srinigar, 11

Japan, 69

Jazia'h, [*jizyah*] ix, 48, 192

Jesus, 8, 17-29, 44, 47, 50, 85, 136, 148, 149, 224, 238

Jihad, ix, xiii, xiv, xv, 48, 107, 238 aman, 192; chapter nine; *darul harb*, 192; *darul sulh* 192; harbi, 192; *jihada*, 190-1; *jihadi akbar*, 191, 203; *jihad al-shaifan*, 203; *jihad al- tarbiyyat*, 203; *jihad-bil-qalam*, 202; *jihad bi saif*, 202; *jihad-e-kabir*, 203: *jihadi asghar*, 191, 204; *qital*, 191; *siyar*, 191

Jinn, ix, 51, 103, 139, 142-3

Jordan, 69

Juma prayers, 3

Karbala, battle of, 209

Kabul, Afghanistan, 70

kalmia shahada, ix, 58, 232

Kangra earthquake, 51

Karygiannis, Jim, MP, 75

Kashf, 43

Kashmir, xvi, 8, 9, 11-17, 20, 21, 27, 28, 50, 148, 204

Kashyap Rishi, 13

Kathir, Ibn, 131

Keech, Marion, 2

Keighley, 95, 110, 111

Kenya, 69

Khalifa, ix, 56, 68, 78, 81, 82, 84, 92, 96, 97, 110, 116, 124, 125, 130, 181, 202, 208, 212, 217

Khalifate, ix, 56, 59, 81, 83-4, 93, 112, 194, 195, 202

Khalifat-i-Rashida, 82, 83

Khaliq, Ghazanfer, Lord Mayor of Bradford, 112

Khan, Abdul Sami, 91

Khan, Aftab Ahmad 212

Khan, Chaudrey Muhammad Za-frulla, Sir, 75

Khan, Chaudhry Rehmat, Imam, 72

Khan, Sayyid Ahmad, 207

Khan, Zafrulla, 228

Khataman nabiyeen, x, xv, 129-138, 225, 129- 138, 238, 242

Khatme Nabuwwat, x, 229, 235

Khidmat-e-khalq, 163

Khilafat Day, 112

Khost, Afghanistan, 70

Khuddam, x, 96, 97, 99, 111, 112

Khuddam chanda, 99

Khuddam ul-Ahmadiyya, x, 97

Khutba, 62, 107

Khutbah Thaniyya, 108

Krishna, 47, 147

Kufir, [or *kufr*], ix, xv, 35, 36, 39, 51, 58, 117, 148, 196, 235, 236, 239, 241, 243, 246

Kushoof, 144

Ladin, Osama bin, 163, 190, 196, 208

Lady Diana, Princess of Wales, 164

Lahore, Pakistan, 9, 52, 57, 59, 60, 61, 62, 63-5, 190, 207, 228, 234

Lahori Ahmadi, 19 fn4, 33, 55-67, 68, 71, 76, 128-9, 151-3, 171, 202, 230, 234, 247

Lailatul-Qadr, see 'Night of power'.

Lajna, x, 96, 111

Lateef, Yusef, 76

Latif, Syed Abdul, 70

Lavan, Spencer, xvi,

lawa-e- Ahmadiyyat, the *Ahmadi* flag, 80

Leamington Spa, 237

Leeds, 95, 110, 164

Lebanon, 69

Leicester, 178, 236

Liebow, Elliot, 4, 4 fn4,

London, 8, 17, 21, 61, 67, 68, 71, 74, 77, 78, 85, 111, 124, 125, 146, 151-3, 164, 178, 208, 222, 231, 247
London Central mosque, 117
Ludhiana, x, 44, 52

Madrasah, x, 91
Mahdi, 45, 47, 57, 84, 136, 199, 229, 244
Mahzarnama [the Memorandum], 229, 244
Majidi, Nur Hosain, 242
Majlis Aamah, x, 60
Majlis-i-Aamalah, 93
Majlis-i-Moatemideen, 60,
Majlis-i-Muntazimma, 60,
Majlis-il-Mushawarat, see Majlis-i-Shura
Majlisi-i-Shura, 93
Mala'ikah, angels, 127, 141-2, 144
Malik, Bari Abdul, 112, 164, 165, 166, 168, 175, 177, 184, 218
Malik, Salim Ahmad, 218
Mal secretary, 94
Malta, 69
Manchester, 178, 217, 222
Marabout, 140
Marham-i-Isa, 25
ma'rifat, 139
marriage, 179-84; arranged, 181; divorce, 183 haq mehr, 181; nikah, 181; polygamy, 182, 183
Martyrdom, see istishad
mas'ala, 123
mâ'shâ'allah', 141
Masih Maud Day, 112
Ma'siya, 192
Mauritius, 68
Mawdudi, Sayyid A., 36, 104, 104 fn7, 106, 106 fn13, 108 fn16, 129, 129fn10, 194, 195, 228; Finality of Prophethood, 131, 228; The Qadiani Question, 228

Mecca, 124, 201, 202
Medina, 201, 204
Mehndi, 122
Messiah, 19, 23, 40, 46, 47, 49, 57, 84, 112, 136, 137, 198, 200, 219, 238
Minaratul Masih minaret, Aqsa mosque, Qadian, 40, 102
minbar, 106
Mir, N. U., 166
Mir, Rafi, 166
Mirza Ghulam Murtaza, father of Ahmad, 41, 42
Morocco, xvi, 9, 17, 140
Moti Masjid, the 'pearl Mosque', Lahore, 65
MTA, Ahmadi Satellite TV station, 76, 78, 80, 116, 168, 215, 221, 239
Muakhat, brotherhood, 97
Mubahalah, x, 47, 49, 145,
Mubarak Mosque, Rabwah, 87
Muezzin, 8
Muhaddath, 47, 57
muhaddathun, 136
Muhammad, the prophet, ix, x, xv, 11, 19, 22, 31, 35, 36, 40, 43, 44, 47-8, 57-8, 67, 82, 83, 109, 112, 114, 116, 128-37, 141, 143, 149, 162, 163, 166, 172, 173, 174, 175, 181, 183, 184, 192, 199, 200, 203, 204, 209, 212, 229, 231, 238, 241, 242, 244, 245, 246
Mujaddid, x, 39, 45, 46, 57, 128
Mujahideen, 196
Munir Court of Enquiry, 243
Murtad, x, 241
Muscat, 69
Mushrik, 148
Musi, testator, 94, 100
Musleh Maud day, xi, 112,
Muslim Brotherhood, 19
Mu'takifins, 114, 115, 116

Nabi, 136, 137
nafaqa, 173
nafs, 191
Naib Amir, 93
Namaz, [see also *salat*], xi, 103, 115, 184
Nankana, Pakistam, 232
Nasibus,
Nasirat, xi, 111, 221,
National Media Cell, 169
Nepal, 28
New Scheme, 121
Nietzsche, 22
Nigeria, 37, 61, 69
'Night of power', x, 114
Nikah, see marriage
Niyaz, Ghulam Nabi, Imam,
Nizam-e-Jama'at, 97, 121-125,
Noor-ud-Din, first Ahmadi *Khalifa*, 40, 41, 56, 68
Noor-ul-Haq, [light of truth] 51
Notovitch, Nicholas, 20, 20fn9, 21

Orchard, Bashir, 213-14, 224
Ordinance XX, Pakistan Penal Code, see Pakistan, Constitution
Otley, Yorkshire, 164

Pakistan, xv, xvi, 2, 8, 9, 10, 12, 14, 21, 26, 35, 37, 39, 49, 57, 58. 60, 64, 70, 75, 140, 147, 167, 175, 176, 177, 182, 204, 216, 245
Pakistan, Constitution, Article 260 229; Ordinance XX, article 298 (b) & (c) 230, 230 fn5; s295(c) 231-4; Article 7 (c) 231
Paradise see *al-jannah*
Persecution, 211, 226, chapter eleven,
Pir, xi, 139, 140
Pir Marouf Hussain Shah, 36
Purdah, 151, 156, 174, 175, 176, 178

Qada, court, 96

Qa'dah, 107
Qadi, 123
Qadian, India, xi, xvi, 8, 12, 34, 39, 40, 41, 42, 52, 55, 57, 59, 66, 68, 69, 70, 77, 85, 157, 179, 190, 213, 214, 219, 234
Qibla wall, 106, 115, 245
Qital, see *jihad*
Qiyam, 107
Quran, xi, 18, 19, 22, 42, 45, 69, 82, 83, 91, 103, 104, 107, 113, 115, 124, 127, 129, 134-5, 141, 148, 149, 157, 162, 163, 172, 173, 174, 175, 176, 184, 189, 191, 193-4, 200, 206, 209, 212, 223, 245, 246, 247; Farid translation, 223; inerrancy 116-8
Qutb, Sayyid, 195; Milestones, 195

Rabwah, Pakistan, xi, xvi, 8, 21, 39, 49, 64, 66, 68, 70, 78, 81, 85-92, 95, 175, 177, 179, 185, 214, 226, 231, 233, 234,
Rahman, Abdur 70
Rainwater, Lee, 5, 5fn8
raka'ats, 106, 108, 115
Raku, 107
Rama Chandra, 147
Ramadan, 31, 47, 113-4, 116
Ram Lekh, 48,
Ram, Malik, 76
Rasul, 136, 137
Religious Founders Day, xi, 73, 112
Resurrection, Christian doctrine of,
Review of Religions, periodical, 52, 68, 83, 223, 226
Rishta Naata, 94, 182
Rizvi, Mohsin, xvfn4
Rooney, Terry, MP, 112
Roza bal, 27
Russia, 69, 205
Rwanda, 164

Saeed, Professor Abdul Karim, 62, 64, 231
sabat Qudmi, 88
sadaqa, 100
Sadr-Anjumen Ahmadiyya, 52, 55-6, 86,
Sadr Khuddamul Ahmadiyya, 95
sajdah, 107
Salam, Abdus Dr., 75, 90
Salafi, 1, 9,
Salat, vii, xi, 31, 103-4, 107, 157
Salik, Ameen ullah Khan, 72
Sami Basri secretary, 94
San'at-o-Tijarat, 95
Satr, 175
Sawab, 104, 114
Sawala-jawab, 221
Sawm, vii, xi, 31
Scunthorpe, 110, 111
Sehra, 122
sehri meal, 115
Selby, Tahir, 33, 97, 98, 103 fn3, 123, 124, 154-5, 218, 224, 236
Selby, Tahir, Mrs, 179 fn33,
Shafi, Muhammad, 207
Shah, Mansoor, Ahmad, 155
Shahada, vii, 31, 58, 245, 246
Shaheed, Mohammad Ismaeel, 207
Shahid College, Pakistan, 110
Shams, J. D., 205
Sharam, 174
Sharia'h xi, 82, 123, 132, 135, 136, 181, 190, 193, 194, 245
Sheffield, England, xvfn4, 2, 8, 95, 110
Shirk, xi, 33, 138, 148, 212, 244
Shura, 111
Sialkot, 42
Sierra Leone, 69
Singapore, 69
sirat-i-siddiqui, 137
Siratun Nabi, 112

Smith, David, Rt. Rev., former bishop of Bradford, 112
South Africa, 69, 243
Southfields mosque, London, 71
Spain, 69
Spen valley, Yorkshire, 95, 110, 111, 164
Sri Lanka, [Ceylon], 68
Srinigar, Kashmir, 8, 11-12, 16-17, 21, 26, 27, 66, 69, 179
Stewart, Ian, former Chief Executive, Bradford Council, 112
Suicide bombings, 208-10; *baseeji,* 208
Sunna, xii
Surinam, 61
Sweden, 71
Switzerland, 69
Syaal, Chaudhry Fateh Muhammad, 71
Syria 69

Tabari, Ibn-i-Jarir, 130
Tabligh, xii, 97, 203, 211, chapter ten; tabligh plan, 217, 220;
Tadhkirah, xii
Tahajjid prayers, xii, 79, 212, 215
Tahrik-Jadid Ahmadiyya, 86, 95
Tahrik-i-jadid, secretary, 94
Takfir, 193, 195
Taklif, 136
Taleem secretary, 94
taliif-i-isha'at,
talim-i-tarbiyyat, 90
Talim-ul-Islam College, Rabwah, 86
Taqdir, 128
Taqwa, xii, 108, 157, 191, 212
Tarbiyyat, xii, 111
Tarbiyyat secretary, 94
Tauba, 212
Taweez, xii, 139, 140
Tawhid, 127, 138
Tawrat, 127

Taymiyya, Ibn, 193, 194, 195
Telegraph & Argus, 165
Terrorism, 208-9
Thailand, 61
The Hague, 69
ti'awat and *nazm*, xii, 219
Tibet, 20, 28
Trinidad, 61
Truth Prevails, 59
Truth Triumphs, see Faruqi, 59
Tunisia, xvi, 9, 17, 140

Ul-Din, Khawaja Kamal, 57, 71
Ul-Haq, Zia, General and President of Pakistan, 35, 71, 145, 230
Ummah, xii, 2, 7, 34, 35, 43, 73, 103, 104, 108, 128, 131, 140, 242
*Umm*ati prophet, 135, 136
umur-i-kharija, 90
United Arab Emirates, xvi, 61
United States of America, xvi, 2, 3, 35, 49, 61, 68, 69, 71, 209, 216
Uthman, *Khalifa*, 116

Wagah border, Pakistan, 40, 59, 66, 235
Wahhabi, 1, 36
Wakilut-Tabshir, director of *Tahrik-i-Jadid*, 95

Waller, Gary, MP, 220
waly, 57
waqar-i-amal, 72, 78, 112
Waqfe, xii
Waqfe arzi, xii, 216
Waqfe Jadid, 94
Waqfe Nau, 184
Waqfe Nau secretary, 94, 184
waqfin, 184-5
Wassiyat, 100
Wassiyat secretary, 94
Wazir Khan mosque, Lahore, 63
Woking, Surrey, 71
wudu, 105

York Minster, 164
Yorkshire Post, 165
Yugoslavia, 69

Zabur, Psalms of David, 127
Zafir, Ahmad, 234
Zakat, vii, xii, 31, 100
Ziafaat secretary, 94
Zilli prophets, 133
Zirvi, Karimullah, xv fn3, 32fn3, 37
Zoroaster, 147